All You Care to Eat

A Novice Buys a Restaurant

Susan Church-Downer

I.G. FELS PUBLISHER

Dedicated to my dear friend and former business partner, Ari Camarota,
to my loving, patient husband, Richard Downer,
and to the crew members who gave their all, or at least their some

The unconditional support of Joel Neuberg's memoir class through Santa
Rosa Junior College has given me the encouragement and motivation to
actually complete this book. Thanks also to beta reader Kate Risling-Sholl
who kindly characterized what I thought was a nearly finished manuscript
as "a good first draft." She was absolutely right.

The back cover photo of me and Ari in a calm moment and my author
photo are reproduced courtesy of Roger Bolt Photography.

"If you want to make a small fortune in the restaurant business, start with
a large fortune."
Adapted from a quote by Leo Fuld

Advance praise for "All You Care to Eat"

"The author never planned to own a restaurant. She certainly didn't plan to buy one in her 60s with her ex-boyfriend-turned–best friend, Ari, as cook and manager. The restaurant was a vegetarian buffet in Santa Rosa, California, originally run by a devotee of Hare Krishna, where Church-Downer and Ari would often dine together. When the eatery went on the market in 2009, the friends—both in need of income following the economic downturn—decided to buy it, along with all the vegetarian recipes. They imagined their new endeavor as something more akin to a community center than a mere restaurant: a "vibrant venue with music, art, spoken word, and politics, supported by delicious, nourishing food." Thus, Gaia's Garden was born....

Church-Downer writes with refreshing sincerity and candor. The book is about running a restaurant, and the restaurant provides the narrative with its color, but the meat of the memoir is the reliably combustive friendship between the author and Ari.... With huge personalities in the kitchen, ungrateful customers in the dining room, and little money to be made, the narrative provides a demystifying look at restaurant ownership. At the same time, the book captures what it is that makes a restaurant such an inviting setting—the dynamism of a place that must be recreated every day from the same small number of ingredients. Church-Downer's time at the Garden has a lot to reveal about long-term friendships, second acts, and the imperfect nature of any community.

A lighthearted but unflinching look at running a restaurant."
— *Kirkus Reviews*

Library of Congress Control Number: 2024924092

Developmental Editor: Justin Brouckaert
Cover design: Adam Hay Studio, UK

No part of this book was generated by AI.

CONTENTS

INTRODUCTION

I wrote this book for anyone who has fantasized about owning a restaurant as well as those who are actually doing it. That seems to include most of the population. It is not a how-to-run-a-restaurant-successfully book, though—quite the opposite. At its heart are the stories of the crew that came and went—their tragedies and triumphs—and the struggles of two best friends to stay friends while dealing with them.

Some will buy it just for the recipes. Years after Gaia's Garden closed, I still get requests for the dahl or coconut tapioca or almond blend dressing or corn bread recipes, and I've kept saying, "Wait for the book."

We embarked on this adventure in the middle of 2009 and ended it at the beginning of 2020, two weeks before the COVID-19 pandemic led to lockdowns in California. Since then, much has changed in the restaurant world. Employees and owners are giving deeper consideration to how they want to spend their life energy. Food costs have skyrocketed while customers, as ever, are reluctant or unable to spend more. Successful owners have had to be nimble, creative, and patient. There have been significant technological advances. I am in awe of those who have persevered and prevailed. Some things will always remain the same, though, particularly the unpredictability of employees, customers, and the economy.

This book came from a need to make sense of my stint as a restaurateur. We had loyal customers, earned great scores on review sites, and won some awards, yet I lost buckets of money. It's been painful to see how many mistakes and errors in judgment I made and to see how often I was wrong when I felt sure I was right. I gave it my best, and it's not easy to admit my best was not better. I hope anyone considering becoming a restaurateur will learn from my experience and have a satisfying outcome. For that reason. I've touched on most of the moving parts of this type of business, although I've tried not to get too far into the weeds, as we say.

In my defense, while certain issues may be evident to the reader, as they now are to me, everything was happening at once. I have extracted most stories out of context. As these events were going on, we were cooking, prepping, shopping, marketing, bookkeeping, cleaning, dealing with customers, hiring and firing and mediating, organizing events, and doing everything else that happens in a restaurant day in and day out.

Most names have been changed. We were blessed with a diverse crew, but race and ethnicity have been mentioned only when they pertain to the story. Over a ten-year span, we had over eighty employees; some stayed a few days, others three years or more. Though I am inclined to mention them all, I have taken pity on the reader and limited their appearances here to those who made the greatest impressions on us. Don't worry if it's hard to keep track: each story should stand on its own. The experiences with my employees and some of my customers were the best part of the journey, and I hope no one feels unfairly portrayed. Everything is from my point of view, though, with some input from Ari. If you recognize yourself in this book, I hope you agree. If not, write your own book! I'll buy it.

PART 1

IF NOT NOW, WHEN?

HOW IT HAPPENED

Frequently asked questions:

"Did you always want to own a restaurant?"

No, not really.

"Have you always loved to cook?"

Not particularly.

"So why did you buy a restaurant?"

Here's how it happened:

In 1997, twelve years before I bought the restaurant, I was near the end of a troubled relationship. We had been together for fifteen years but in truth, I had been miserable for the last half of that time, which we had spent "working on it."

Eventually I learned that, as I had suspected, there was someone else. I had put so much energy into trying to stay together and not give in to suspicion and jealousy that I had blown past years of red flags. Confirmation of his string of infidelities was the end of it, although my character flaw of denial would just take new forms in the coming years.

The next months brought grief, anger, jealousy, fear, and finally some peace. The man was gone, my stepson was in college, I would be losing my dream house, my niece had opted out of living with me, and my fancy office had been given to a colleague with better numbers. I was nearly fifty years old, and I had suddenly lost much of my identity, but the emptiness was also a chance to make conscious decisions about what I wanted to do and whom I wanted to do it with. What I had left was a stressful job, a beat-up Mercedes, good friends, and—most importantly—seventeen consecutive years of recovery from alcoholism. That proved to be enough to start over.

I had drifted through most of my life and, other than the decision to get and stay sober, had rarely formed goals or made independent choices, instead accepting a succession of men, jobs, houses, and friends because they were available. Now I had a chance to chart my own path. It was time to consider: what makes me happy?

In my sad and confused state, I couldn't think of anything except Fred Astaire movies. That seemed odd but was what came up, so I went with it and rented some. Halfway through *Top Hat*, it hit me. I loved to dance and hadn't for years. So, I started my new life with dancing.

On my first solo venture to a club, I met Ari, sax player for soul singer Diana Swann. He was my age and a fabulous, energetic dancer as well as a consummate musician and entertainer. I found him attractive—tall, dark, and Italian. He was originally from the Bronx and, despite decades spent in California, still had an East Coast edge I found refreshing. I missed male company and needed a dance partner, so I was interested in getting to know him.

Ari was more focused on a vivacious blonde who shared my table, but the next week I came back, and she didn't. Ari and I started a friendship based on music and dancing, and after a year our sensual and intimate conversations moved from the dance floor to the bedroom. For me, the experience of being friends before becoming lovers was unique, and I felt a degree of trust and comfort that had been missing from most of my previous relationships. Each night held the childlike excitement of a sleepover with my best friend—and adult benefits.

The first two years were magical. We started a DJ business together and collaborated on political events that supported our shared liberal values. Then we tried to live together, and the next five years were progressively more painful as our differences—particularly around housekeeping (both physical and emotional)—created an insurmountable rift. We were unable to problem solve effectively, and resentments festered. Ari, who had been such a delightful companion and caring confidant, became depressed. It seemed only anger gave him enough traction to escape the pit, and that anger became focused on everything I said and did. As I saw it, his rage became so toxic I could no longer continue. We broke up in our therapist's office, both crying, both resolved.

I left for a week while he was moving out and dreaded coming back to my empty house, with big holes where his things had been. To my surprise, he had moved furniture to fit and left some of his, adding touches like tablecloths and ornaments to make the rooms inviting. He had even assembled and made up my new bed, which had arrived early.

Over the next years, we continued as friends. Not "just friends" but true friends. We spent time together, went places, shared our hopes and fears, and supported each other's efforts to find romance elsewhere. We had emerged stronger for having survived the painful breakup of our romantic relationship, and now I could again delight in Ari as the creative and empathetic person he could be. I came to believe I would never have another serious relationship and knew Ari would be the male friend I could count on in my dotage—to come fix something or lift something or accompany me somewhere. The agreement was unspoken, but it gave me great comfort. Our bond and loyalty seemed inseverable.

We often dined together and particularly enjoyed a vegetarian gem called Govinda's. The cuisine was billed as "international," and the offerings drew mainly on the traditions of Southern India and Italy. Located near the junior college in Santa Rosa, California, it was run by Gopal, a devotee of Hare Krishna who exuded wisdom and calm. His restaurant was an oasis of tranquility. For $7.95, we could stock up on salad, vegetables, rice, curry, dessert, and chai from the buffet—and we did so often. I was not a vegetarian but had been raised as one and didn't require meat at every meal. The delicious, healthy food and the comfortable ambiance nourished not only our bodies but our maturing friendship.

I had retired from being a stressed-out mortgage broker but still needed to work part time. I loved my job with our local newspaper, answering phones and compiling event calendars, obituaries, and anniversary announcements. My entire team was laid off on Halloween of 2008—a particularly bizarre event because many of my coworkers were in costume. Coincidentally, that same night saw the consummation of a thirty-year flirtation. Richard and I had met in an alcoholic recovery program and had been circling each other for years. A retired truck driver, he was a very handsome man who had survived years living on the streets and was now sober, gentle, and spiritual, as well as sexy. There had always been a spark, but usually at least one of us was involved with someone else when our paths crossed. Then, it was our time. As he recalls it, "You got laid off and laid on the same day."

Richard was not thrilled to learn Ari was among my most dear friends, and he certainly didn't understand my gratitude for theoretical future support I wouldn't need now that I had him. I struggled, with little success, to assure and reassure him that when Ari and I had given it our best shot, the romance between us had sickened and died in a most painful way. Yes, we were bonded by love, but not like that, and neither of us had any desire to go back. "Think of him like a brother," I said.

"Yeah, a brother you had sex with."

By the time I returned from a solo trip to Egypt, I knew Richard was special, my soft place to land. He was kind and loving and proud to be with me. I was proud to be with him too, confident in his integrity and impressed by his humble, fervent trust in God. He seemed more comfortable with the Ari situation and also adjusted to my need to maintain a separate residence. These were both big concessions, out of his experience and comfort zone. This arrangement afforded me several days a week of the solitude I craved as well as the space to maintain my other friendships, including, of course, with Ari.

It was now 2009, and I was sixty-two years old. I had worked for other people most of my life and had never acquired much in savings. Fortunately, I had inherited significant money a few years before but had lost a lot of it in the recession of 2008, which had also damaged Ari's private teaching practice, his main source of income. The DJ business we still had together was exhausting and not enough to sustain either of us. The main topic over our dinners at Govinda's now was where we would each go from there. I had not expected it would be together until he called me one morning. "I have news. It could be life changing!"

He had gone to Govinda's to ask the owner, Gopal, if there were some way he could be involved there when he saw a sign: "Govinda's needs new management." Gopal was not looking for a manager, it turned out, but a buyer. Ari was looking for an investor. I still had some money, and we started making plans. We would be business partners, but I would be sole owner. Ari would cook and manage the restaurant; I would do the paperwork. It seemed doable, given that Gopal ran the operation himself, with one employee from 8:30 a.m. to 2:30 p.m. and two kids who came in at night to prep and wash dishes during the dinner shift of 5 to 8.

Ari and I had worked together before, organizing community events and our somewhat successful mobile DJ business. I had worked in restaurants, in banking, and as a mortgage broker. Ari had seen the insides of clubs and restaurants for decades as a performing musician and had the experience and contacts to organize our cultural events. Between us, we believed we had the skills to carry this off. Unlike most new restaurateurs, we had sufficient capital—or so we thought. I prayed on it, asking for guidance. Barriers came up but soon dissolved. Was that a sign?

Gopal wanted $125,000 but accepted my counter of $105,000 with $60,000 down and a carryback of $40,000. An additional $5,000 would be paid to him when we received our beer and wine license. He had an investor who declined the carryback, but I was able to come up with the $100,000 in cash. It was a turnkey operation that included the recipes, and Gopal would train us for a month.

Things moved swiftly. I immediately began having mixed feelings and examining my motives. As we stood on the threshold of old age, I wanted my friend to have something concrete—a business that would sustain him financially and professional success that had eluded him as a talented but not-famous musician. When I looked at just that part, I saw codependency red flags lining the road. This had been an issue for me in the past—doing for others what they should do for themselves, meddling with other people's fates, and exhausting myself. I had been privileged in my upbringing and resources, and, on the positive side, I was something of a crusader, empathetic and pained by injustice, striving to level the playing field. But at times these noble motives had become entwined with toxicity—a self-centered drive to feel loved, important, and indispensable, a need to control. Usually both my "project" and I left with resentments. I thought I had worked through the dark side of my good side, but now I was questioning my motives. Was I once again drifting with someone else's tide? Had I learned nothing?

I looked at my side of this venture. Was it all about Ari? I managed to conclude it was not. I wanted a home run for myself. I had done well enough at jobs and small businesses but had never had a smashing success. I hungered to create something of value, to express myself, to test my creativity and leave a legacy. This seemed to be a great opportunity and, given my age, probably my last chance to do so professionally.

Creating an eclectic community center—a vibrant venue with music, art, spoken word, and politics, supported by delicious, nourishing food—excited me and seemed a practical application of fantasies both Ari and I had spun for years, separately and together. We would finally be in charge—no longer taking orders from bosses, club owners, brides and brides' mothers—free to realize our own vision, to succeed or fail on our own merits. Ari and I had successfully collaborated on events and performances; this would be like that, just bigger.

But how was I going to tell Richard? We had been a couple for six months, just getting the feel of it. My decision was made. I expected him to leave me over it. There was the Ari thing for one and the commitment of time to this venture—time that would not involve him. It was my same lifelong struggle. In one relationship after another, I had been willing to trade huge chunks of myself for the illusion of a man's love. The older and more sober I had gotten, the less willing I had become to cede any personal ground, anticipating the life older women in my family had—uncoupled and vital for their last decades. I could do worse than be alone—and I certainly had. But then Richard had come forward with true love in his heart.

I had a difficult choice to make. It wasn't between Richard and Ari. It wasn't even between Richard and the restaurant. It was between my hunger for a mate and my need to make my own decisions and follow my own dreams. This one time, I had to choose the latter. If not now, when?

I waited until the last minute to tell him. Struggling to breathe, I could barely get the words out: "I'm buying a restaurant—with Ari." I said I had prayed on it, that it felt like God's will. (I left out the part about possibly rushing headlong into a codependent disaster.) Waiting for him to tell me we were over, I was amazed when his reaction was mild. He expressed surprise and concern. Did I know how difficult this would be? I assured him I did. He told me very kindly that if I believed this was God's will for me, I should do it, and he would have my back.

PART 2

HIGH HOPES AND LEARNING THE ROPES

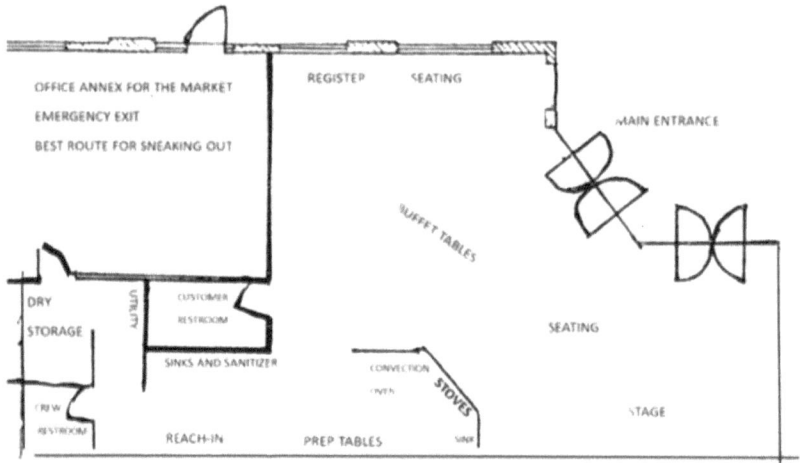

ON YOUR MARK...

It was on! I had bought a restaurant! We needed a month to acquire all the necessary permits and approvals and to put insurances in place before it would be official. Gopal's paperwork showed a profit of about $3,000 a month. My accountant reviewed it and reported that the numbers seemed legitimate. She optimistically recommended I set up a C corporation so profits could be retained in the corporation and not taxed until distributed to me, the sole shareholder.

Almost immediately after I signed the agreement to purchase, the old dynamics between Ari and me resurfaced. I had fond memories of the successful collaborations of the past but had conveniently forgotten how bad we were at problem-solving together. And this time, there was another major issue: I had all the money and was the sole owner. We never spoke about that. I wanted us to be full partners, so I tried to avoid any indication that I held a dominant role. Sometimes I would be too passive, trying to compensate for my innate advantage. The discrepancy would become evident, though, when there were checks to be written, since I was the one writing them. I had veto power, which I both overused and underused.

It had been a few years since Ari and I had been under stress together, but I was again experiencing his irritability. He had grand plans for new menu items and décor, and he resented my insistence that we delay making changes. Buffeted by the tempest of his creative genius, I clung fearfully to the mast of the turnkey concept, lacking confidence in our readiness to strike out on our own and alarmed by the deposits and unexpected expenses in the thousands that seemed to crop up daily. We had never really dealt with our deepest conflicts, only changed the situation to avoid them. "Omigod," I thought, "I've just married him."

Still, momentum and excitement over the new venture overrode what would be prescient fears. Santa Rosa, California, is a medium-size city about sixty miles north of San Francisco in the middle of wine country. In addition to wine grapes, it is an area rich in local produce and people who appreciate it. A good proportion of citizens there are health conscious, and many are either vegetarians or vegans. We were only a few blocks from Santa Rosa Junior College, with a concentration of students who prioritized healthy eating and compassion toward animals.

We were so confident we had a winning combination of food and community benefit that it was easy to imagine not only local success but that we would one day franchise the concept. We envisioned our salad dressings and other unique and delicious products gracing store shelves everywhere.

Our area was sublet from the Santa Rosa Community Market—a venerable health food store located behind the frontage spaces of the restaurant and our next-door neighbor, the Last Record Store. The Market's proximity was a huge convenience—their customer base and ours had significant overlap, and we could run back there for an extra loaf of bread or whatever else we might be missing. I referred to them as our "pantry." This easy access to their retail side often saved the day when our attempts at organization failed. They also let us combine bulk orders with them at cost plus ten percent.

Before we could take possession, there was a lot of paperwork to do—something I've always liked. I wrote an optimistic business plan, gathered up my financials, and created pro forma projections to submit to the Market. I applied to the Franchise Tax Board for a sales tax permit, to the City of Santa Rosa for a business license and a wastewater disposal permit, to the County Health Department for a food facility permit, and to the police for an alarm permit. We needed a million dollars in liability insurance and also workers' compensation insurance. I obtained a URL for the website I was creating and filed a DBA (doing business as) application to keep the rights to the Govinda's name as well as the name we had chosen: Gaia's Garden.

Gaia (Guy-a) was the Greek goddess of creation. Like most of those deities, she had a dark side—incest, murder, that sort of thing; one of her children was the Cyclops. We were more focused on the Gaia Principle, which states that the earth is not just a platform but a living entity. All things are connected, and what we do matters. At Gaia's Garden, it would be "Earth Day Every Day."

As the training began, Gopal educated us about the Indian cooking style known as *satvig*. His was a simplified version, but in keeping with the Hare Krishna tradition, no onion, garlic or mushrooms were used. It is believed they stimulate the lower chakras and interfere with spiritual practice. ("Not that that's bad," Gopal said with a smile. "It's just not what we do here.") We had never noticed any lack in Govinda's food. The pungency of these eschewed ingredients was provided by a range of traditional Indian spices, particularly asafoetida, or hing. A foul-smelling powder also known in some corners as *devil's dung*, it was used as an antiviral during the flu pandemic of 1918. Hing requires a light touch but is very effective.

It was agreed we would watch Gopal for the first two weeks, he would watch us for the second two weeks, then we would be on our own.

It was time to become acquainted with our new crew—all of whom had agreed to stay, at least for a while. Daria was the only person on payroll. She was nineteen years old, raven-haired, short, and somewhat stocky, a reserved Goth girl. Her entire wardrobe was black, her eyes were heavily lined, and she had a few tattoos already. While her energy was appropriately dark, it did not seem sinister. Gopal had been a father figure, and we knew his departure was painful for her. We tried to put her at ease and were occasionally rewarded with a fleeting smile. Her duties were to set up the salad bar in the morning then wash dishes until 2:30 p.m., when the restaurant closed for a break.

The time between 2:30 p.m. and reopening at 5 was devoted to getting ready for dinner, cleaning, and provisioning. One day each week, Gopal shopped at both Costco and Cash and Carry, a restaurant supply store, so the entrées on those nights had to be easy ones.

During the afternoon break, a rotating crew of three volunteers (working for food) would come in and clean the dining room. They seemed pleasant and quirky. One was tall and thin, showing up in what seemed to be the same tie-dyed shirt every time. He told us showers were bad for his aura. While I have never been able to see auras, his was impossible to miss. Fortunately there were no customers around, and we were in the kitchen when he was working.

The second was short, slight of build, and intense and liked to critique the food each day. He was particularly focused on the mung bean soup for some reason. The third appeared to be normal compared to the other two and did not stay with us long.

At 5 p.m., the restaurant would reopen for dinner, and Lenny and Forrest would arrive. They were young and high-spirited; the vibe in the kitchen was generally happy, if not particularly focused. Lenny did dishes and Forrest prepped two gallons each of carrots, broccoli, and cauliflower for the steamed vegetables and diced two or three gallons of potatoes if needed, then would turn his attention to whatever else he had time for—which didn't seem to be much. Gopal paid them twenty-five dollars cash at the end of each shift.

There were no servers. Customers paid at the counter, then took what they wanted from the buffet tables. Most bussed their own dishes, and Gopal picked up the rest and cleaned tables when he wasn't needed at the cash register.

As I got to know them better, I learned Daria, Lenny, and Forrest had all gone to an alternative high school for kids who don't fit well in regular school. In my mind, there was a stigma attached to this (juvenile delinquents and slow learners), which turned out to be untrue. I would learn it was also a place to house young people who were more creative, intelligent, and independent than the conventional high school could accommodate—particularly when those students carried the burden of trauma.

Daria and Lenny had been friends at school, and Lenny's family had taken Daria in after her mother left town to be with a new boyfriend. They had eventually become a couple but claimed that was now over. They seemed an odd pair. Lenny presented as more Mexican than Goth. Unlike Daria, he was outgoing and very funny. Forrest was neither: a dude.

GET SET . . .

F inally, the paperwork was done, we had the permits we needed, and we were able to take possession. Our thirty days of official training had begun. On the first day, excited and ready, I met Gopal at 8 a.m. at Imwalle's Nursery. The morning was bright and comfortably cool, and the nursery was a country refuge on the outskirts of the city. Joe Imwalle was the third generation of his family to operate a combination farm, brokerage, and retail produce operation. His grown sons worked there too and would eventually take it over. Joe accepted me on a handshake—no application, no references other than Gopal, and we agreed he would invoice us monthly. We picked up cases of broccoli, cauliflower, and tomatoes and bags of cilantro, ginger, and peppers, then headed for Gaia's Garden.

I had been there many times before, but now I saw the restaurant with new eyes. This was ours! A broad cement walkway led to a glass double door that provided entry to the dining room—a huge space (1,200 square feet, the size of my house). I had always found it pleasing. The décor combined wood, stone, and panels of grass-textured wallpaper with a rustic, corrugated iron ceiling. A three-sided wall designed to provide more kitchen space also added interest as it jutted into the dining room, which could seat sixty-eight patrons. Four floor-to-ceiling windows provided natural light. Two buffet tables—one for hot food and one for cold—were finished with a maroon laminate that added a pop of color.

Passing the register area and the customer bathroom, we entered the kitchen. It was a typical galley setup—long and quite narrow. To the left, the front wall was barely able to accommodate a large convection oven, a six-burner stove, and a smaller one-burner stove, which Gopal called a *candy stove*, although neither he nor we ever made candy. The aisle between front and back was wide enough for two people, if they were considerate, and ended with a small sink and shelving. The back wall was the prep area with a shelving unit, a long stainless-steel prep table, a wood block–covered prep table with an industrial can opener attached to one end, and a lower metal table that held the twenty-quart Hobart commercial mixer. On the right side of the kitchen entrance, a built-in four-compartment refrigerator with glass doors (the reach-in) stood opposite a three-compartment stainless steel sink and a dish sanitizer.

Had we continued, we would have snaked around past a wall of shelves, the employee bathroom, and a utility sink and mop area and ended in the dry storage room. One wall of shelves contained #10 cans of tomato products, coconut milk, and beans as well as herbs, spices, and pasta. The longer wall was filled with large bins of legumes, rice, shredded coconut, and flours. A chest freezer was against the third wall, and a door into our landlord's space—an emergency exit and back entrance to the Market—marked the end of our domain.

By the time we had unpacked the produce, Ari and Daria had arrived. She immediately began setting up the salad bar. This entailed shredding fresh carrots, beets, and cabbage; chopping celery and tomatoes; setting out olives, garbanzo beans, and peppers; and washing, spinning, and preparing spinach, spring mix, and red leaf lettuce. Govinda's six salad dressings were among its greatest assets—Almond Blend, Tofu Dill, and Toasted Sesame being particular favorites. We felt privileged to own the recipes. Daria made these and set them out on the now vibrantly colorful cold bar.

She kept her head down and worked quickly, although I would occasionally catch her glancing at us. I wondered what she was thinking, watching the two eager but clumsy neophytes who were now her bosses.

I was there as a backup, since Ari would be doing the cooking, and I stood behind the two men, taking notes on procedures and recipes. Ari and I watched in wonder as Gopal started to make dahl. Popular throughout India, the dahl was Govinda's signature soup, beloved by customers, especially the Asian Indian workers from Medtronics. I had seen a group of them agreeing heartily when a member had suddenly shouted, "I LOVE THIS DAHL!" High praise indeed! Many had sought the recipe, but Gopal had kept it to himself—until now. This was one of the moments we had been waiting for.

As five gallons of water approached a boil, Gopal explained the menu. He had ten soups in addition to the dahl, and ten types of curry. Dahl was made fresh and served every day; the other soups were on a two-week rotation, as were the curries and dinner entrées.

We were sent to dry storage to get twelve cups of yellow split peas for the dahl, which Gopal added to the now boiling water. The split peas took a couple of hours to cook, so that would always be our first task. Next, he had us prep the vegetables for the corn chowder. Our curry of the day would be zucchini and potato, so we sliced the zucchini to add to the potatoes that Forrest had left cut and soaking in water the night before.

We watched as Gopal made three-seed whole wheat bread. The Hobart mixer made short work of kneading, and the two long loaves were soon sitting on a shelf above the stove waiting to rise. Next was corn bread, another favorite. It was dark and heavy. Sweetened with molasses, it had a pleasant moistness and was very different from the more common cakelike version.

Gopal started the corn chowder, then set out two pots for rice—one white basmati and one brown—and boiled the potatoes. Our next project was the halavah—but not the kind found in Jewish delis. Ours was a mysterious dessert made with butter, farina, and sugar formed into balls and ideally served warm, the outsides crispy, the insides succulent. It was sweet but not too sweet, and Gopal had many variations—my favorites were chocolate and berry.

Halavah (or halva, halvah, or halwa) is popular throughout India and the Middle East. Regional preferences include rolling the balls in honey and nuts or serving it as a pudding, sometimes with shredded carrots. (In line with the politics of the region, Israeli halvah is a completely different product—a type of candy served at room temperature, dense and crumbly, with a sesame seed base.)

As 10 a.m. approached, Gopal transferred the rice into hotel pans for the steam table and put them in the oven, still warm from the corn bread. It was time to complete the dahl with additions of tomato puree, cilantro, salt, and sugar, then a finish of lightly sautéed seeds and spices. It was so lovely—thick, fragrant, delicious, and nourishing. Tureens of both soups were now placed on the hot table in the dining room, the whole wheat bread was baking in the convection oven, and it was time for curry.

My experience with making anything like curry had been limited to using prepared curry powder and adding random spices in vain hopes of approaching the flavors I loved from the restaurant versions. This *was* the restaurant version, the real deal. Using a huge wok, Gopal lightly sautéed black mustard, fennel, and cumin seeds, then added chopped ginger and chilis, followed by turmeric, coriander powder, hing, and black pepper. Zucchini next, then diced tomatoes, boiled potatoes, salt and sugar, frozen peas, dried rosemary, and my old friend curry powder. While the flavors cooked in, we steamed carrots, cauliflower, and broccoli, made pasta, and heated the marinara sauce, which, mercifully, was already made. The three-seed bread had cooled enough to be sliced; chai was also sitting in the reach-in, so we heated that up. A handful of chopped cilantro sprinkled on the curry, and we had made lunch!

With ten minutes to spare, we headed to the front to prepare for the 11:30 a.m. opening. There were already a few people waiting outside.

Gopal showed me how to operate the cash register and credit card terminal, which I learned quickly enough to turn my attention to the customers. They were now OUR customers! They would make or break our venture. Who were they? In some ways, they knew our business better than we did. I felt both desperate for them to like me and confident they would. I would make sure of it.

Most of the customers knew of the transfer and expressed gratitude that we were keeping the recipes—especially the dahl—and the format. They had the option of paying $7.95 for full access to both buffet tables or $6.95 for soup, salad, and bread only. Each was billed as "all you *care* to eat," although some missed the subtlety of that wording. Most of the customers seemed to be junior college students or senior citizens—at least they said they were. (There was a one dollar discount for either.) A bowl of soup with bread for $3.95 was another option. The prices were very low, even for the times. By comparison, a burrito at the Mexican restaurant across the street was $6.95.

We needed to make sure customers always took clean plates on their return to the tables—a battle we would fight for our entire tenure. Environmentally conscious customers claimed they wanted to save water. We had to explain the policy was mandated by the health department for good reason—to avoid contamination. Even then, we would get blank stares or indignation: "But it's MY plate. I'm not using anyone ELSE'S plate!" At this point, we would act out and narrate a serving utensil coming out of the buffet pan, depositing food on their plate and touching the remains of their last serving, then going back into the communal buffet pan. Some still found it an unreasonable request and tried to transgress when they thought we weren't looking.

As I became acquainted with the customers, Ari kept his eye on the buffet tables and helped Daria refill trays as needed from the kitchen. Always meticulous, Ari stirred the food and wiped down the counters constantly, no doubt planning all the projects and changes he would implement once I relaxed a little. At 2:30, we closed for the break. Daria replenished the salad bar and covered it on her way out, waving to the volunteer who was coming in to wipe down the dining room and sweep.

Dinner was the same as lunch but with the addition of one entrée. The dish of the evening was tofu cutlets—one of the easy ones. Slices of tofu, frozen the night before, were dropped into boiling water until they floated to the top. For service, the slices were layered at a slight angle in four shallow pans. After the beautiful, healthy food we had made that morning, the sauce was a shock. Gopal pulled out jugs of commercial orange sauce and plum sauce and mixed them with a can of Snapple ("any flavor is OK") and poured this pernicious mixture over the cutlets. Into the oven they went.

We made tofu cutlets one time when they came up in rotation during training, then abandoned them. The tofu preparation method was good, though, and we continued to use that in other things. Freezing it overnight and then thawing it makes for a denser texture, useful in dishes like peanut ginger tofu and a tofu "ceviche" I would invent later.

At this point, we had time for a short break, then the setup for dinner began.

Back at the register at 5 p.m., I welcomed a smaller crowd than had come for lunch. Again, they were enthusiastic and grateful there would be few changes, and they even appeared to enjoy the tofu cutlets. Forrest and Lenny seemed happy in the back, prepping and washing, laughing and joking. At 8 p.m., we closed for the evening, and twelve hours after the day's start, I sat down with Gopal's wife, Lynn, to learn the register closing procedure. We recorded the credit card tips, then sent the batch to the processor. Leaving a $200 bank in the register, we counted out the remaining bills and put them in an envelope—which, less the cash equivalent of the credit card tips, represented our gross income for the day. Our take was about $600. Projecting, I saw $12,000 a month (the restaurant was closed on weekends). This seemed promising, even considering sales tax of 8 percent would have to be paid each quarter.

Tips from the jar at the counter and the credit cards were divided among Daria, Forrest, and Lenny. Previously, Gopal had classified them as donations to be given to an unnamed charity. Under our management, the crew was now making a few more dollars per hour, which helped our status with them.

Closing the kitchen took about an hour after the customers left. Food that could be reused was stored in the reach-in cooler; remaining dishes, pans, and pots were washed; sinks were cleaned and dried; the floor was mopped; and counters were wiped down.

In the days that followed, Ari was having a harder time concentrating in the kitchen. We were both novices at commercial cooking and had only a limited time to learn, so I was becoming anxious, as was Gopal. Ari would watch for a while, then take off to detail a cabinet or a booth or to level tables. At one point, a frustrated Gopal turned to me and said, "Well, I guess I'll teach *you*." We made the ten different curries—some with tomato bases and some with coconut—as well as lovely soups, including yam, broccoli, mung bean, Caribbean black bean, tomato coconut, chili, vegetable noodle, and minestrone. Ari came and went but seemed to be picking up the basics. True to his heritage, he was most interested in the Italian dishes and became proficient at eggplant parmesan and lasagna, which were alternately served on Friday nights. I learned the other dinner entrées, including an eggless quiche and the much-loved Govinda potatoes—a dairy bomb with jack cheese, sour cream, and curds.

Gopal was very fond of dairy. (One brief translation of *Govinda*, he told us, is "happy cow.") He showed us how to make curds and whey—a simple process of boiling milk, adding buttermilk, then straining out the chunks of curd. In Spanish, it's called *queso fresca*, or fresh cheese. The fluid that had not coagulated was the whey, and he used it in many of the soups, claiming it was highly nutritious.

During the second two weeks, I was grateful to have Gopal as a backup but became increasingly confident in my ability to follow his recipes, although time management was a challenge. There were lots of moving parts to this! I hoped Ari had picked up most of the training.

At 5 p.m., with dinner set out, Gopal and Lynn would take off to walk the local parks. Their enjoyment of new freedom and less responsibility was evident. Over time, I would develop a deeper understanding of how precious that might be. The myth of Atlas and Hercules exchanging the weight of the world would often come to mind as I got a better sense of what we were in for.

At week three, the junior college semester ended and, almost overnight, sales plummeted. Now, we were taking in around four hundred dollars a day. Subtracting 8 percent sales tax as well as rent, insurances, utilities, food costs, and employee costs gave me some anxiety, but I was confident we would find a way to build the summer business until the fall semester, when a wave of hungry students would put us over the top.

While Ari was not in the kitchen as much as I had hoped, he was not idle. He was cleaning and scraping and painting, bringing in plants and rearranging the furniture. I saw it as his way of taking ownership, metaphorically pissing in the corners. He attended a sanitation class at the junior college down the street, obtaining the certificate we needed to satisfy the health department and learning the applicable health codes and procedures. He set up an epic condiment bar with several types of vinegar and hot sauces, olive oil, brewer's yeast, parmesan cheese, soy sauce, Braggs aminos, and red pepper flakes.

On Friday of the fourth week, we hugged Gopal and Lynn goodbye. Now, for better or worse, it was really ours.

AND GO!

We had the weekend to prepare for our first day. Ari moved furniture around and cleaned. His large, high-quality sound system was installed, and so was the disco ball from our now abandoned DJ business. I worked on signage and an email blast to everyone we knew and obsessed over the procedures for getting lunch ready on time. The preparation seemed to pay off. On our first day, Ari and I made the lunch together, and it went well. I worked the register when we opened, and we had a friendly crowd. At about 12:30, as I was dealing with a line at the counter, I noticed a woman with a clipboard heading to the kitchen. She spoke with Daria for a few minutes, then left. I later learned she was the county health inspector. Daria, who knew her from previous visits, had told her this was our first day and asked if she could give us a week or two to get settled. The health inspector had agreed, and I was heartened by Daria's first show of loyalty.

A few days later, Ari was on his own—cooking while I picked up produce. I arrived at the restaurant fifteen minutes after our scheduled opening, and there was a crowd waiting on the front patio. He hadn't opened yet! Running into the kitchen, I saw Ari struggling to finish everything and Daria trying to help him. It took another ten minutes before all the food was out. Most of the people stayed, although we had lost some. Profuse apologies, to-go boxes, and free cups of chai, combined with the goodwill of most customers, got us through lunch.

"What happened?" I asked him later.

"I had to rewipe the counters—they were filthy! Nothing was where it should have been, and the rice burned while I was answering the phone!"

All In all, a difficult morning for which he took no responsibility. I remembered this pattern from the past and knew further discussion would be futile. The only solution I could see was to come in and help each morning while continuing to cover the dinner shift—except on "Italian Fridays."

During the following weeks, Ari and I would cook together, but he showed less and less interest in food preparation, focusing instead on deep cleaning and detailing equipment and furniture. His frequent absences from the kitchen were inconsistent with the requirements of the cook's job, so it fell to me most mornings. It became very clear that my vision of being the silent partner, staying home and doing paperwork in my pajamas, did not fit the realities on the ground. Now I was working double shifts and doing paperwork when I got home. I became more and more resentful with each passing day, having bitter conversations in my head with my business partner, who was neither physically nor emotionally present. I had jumped on the tiger's back and could not safely jump off—too much of my money was on the line.

One morning, prepping carrots while my brain raged with angry dialogue, I realized my attitude was unsustainable. I could not continue carrying this level of resentment: it was bad for me but worse for the food.

I had eaten in places where I could feel the love and laughter from the kitchen and had been nourished in mind, body, and spirit. I had also eaten at places where the crew was so clearly unhappy I could barely choke down the food. I needed to let go of my resentment, as justified as I believed it to be.

To the best of my ability, I focused on Ari's strengths. He had made the dining room much more inviting, and everything was very clean. He was beginning to bring in some musicians to add to the evening ambiance. He was good with most customers, remembering their names and their backstories. I was more focused on the operations, less social by nature, stressed, overwhelmed, and exhausted, so it was better to have him as our "face." In some ways, we complemented each other. Various people would remark on how much better the place looked, citing "the woman's touch." I would happily announce I had nothing to do with it: it was Ari's "Italian touch" they were admiring.

Perhaps most important was that I had a partner. I was terrified by this new venture, but it helped not to be alone. Although we were already bickering, I knew I could trust him to be truthful and that he cared about me more than anyone I could ever employ.

Before buying the restaurant, I'd had enough time and money to pursue things that interested me. I had started playing bass guitar and formed a trio with two other novices. I had enrolled in a conflict resolution program at Sonoma State University and was one class and one project away from my completion certificate. This had led to stints as a volunteer mediator for a nonprofit, facilitating restorative justice for minor crimes. I had traveled to Iran and Egypt, and Richard and I had become a couple, with plans to travel the world together. I had been enjoying some rare leisure time, having worked almost continuously for the last forty-five years.

All that, except for Richard, went by the wayside. The restaurant took everything I had. I would work ten to twelve hours a day at Gaia's Garden, then would come home and put in another two to four hours on paperwork, publicity, promotion, scheduling, and menus. At night, I would soothe myself to sleep by visualizing the menus and procedures for the next day, along with the time management strategies that went with them. Like counting sheep, this seemed to ease my anxiety.

Fortunately, I found I loved the work and was able to maintain this schedule on passion, adrenaline, and a strong constitution. Being obsessive by nature, I dove in and didn't worry about coming up for air. I no longer had time for friends and little time for family, none of whom lived locally except my mother. Over the ten years I was a restaurateur, young relatives grew up without me and friends backed off, feelings hurt. Richard, who had the most reason to be resentful, remained steadfast throughout.

Ari and I began referring to the restaurant as "the baby." Its needs had to come first. No matter how we might feel or what our plans might have been, if the baby needed us, we had to show up. We had expected this project would be hard work, but we'd had no idea what that really meant.

Some of our customers had been following Gopal for years in various locations. Most assured me the food was now as good or better. One young woman, though, approached me with a condescending smile. "Your food is still good, but Gopal's had a light. I'm not feeling that."

"I'm sorry you don't," I replied. "He trained us, and we're following his recipes exactly. Is there anything in particular we could change?"

"No, it's all fine. But Gopal used to bless the food before he put it out. I think that's what made it radiant."

That stung. I certainly hadn't seen this in the month we worked with him. (We were to learn Gopal let people believe what they wanted to believe.) I said a simple prayer every morning: "Dear God and Goddess, please let your love and healing manifest in everything we do today." Apparently, the combined efforts of my twin deities and my changed attitude toward Ari didn't make the food radiant enough for everyone.

I was especially grateful for a Japanese lady who came in often. One day when I apologized for the rice being gummy, she told me enthusiastically she preferred it that way. I wasn't convinced, but her soothing assurances and cultural authority were a balm I badly needed.

We made some changes right away, such as no longer stocking Snapple and other corn syrup–containing drinks, replacing them with high-end root beer, ginger ale, and Mexican Coke—all sweetened with cane sugar. Other beverages included apple juice, mineral water, and coconut water as well as French press coffee, teas, and chai.

I soon learned why fake nails are not allowed in the kitchen. We rarely used gloves, relying on frequent handwashing with antibacterial soap. While hand tossing a long tray of salad greens, I was horrified to discover one of my nails was missing. I examined every leaf but never found it. The prospect of a customer discovering it in their salad was unacceptable, so $50 worth of greens landed in the compost.

Ari hired a local artist to paint flowers on our windows, but there was a lack of communication, and the result was not as expected. We had pictured an elegant presentation of lavender, perhaps, in Grecian urns. What we got were huge sunflowers. Now the outside looked more like a preschool than the fine restaurant we wanted it to be. It was still a good investment, since the paint survived three seasons of rain. More importantly, it signaled to passersby that something new was happening. Many, it turned out, had avoided the place because they were offended by the Hindu art on the walls or had not been fond of Gopal. The new customers we had hoped for started coming in.

Richard came in once with a friend for dinner. That was the only time he ever ate there, being a carnivore with little interest in trying new foods. He was generous in his praise, though, telling everyone the food was terrific, and they should try it.

When the health department inspector eventually returned, Ari's excitement over what he had learned in sanitation class led to such a long conversation that she had to cut the inspection short. There were only a few minor things she noticed, and we were able to correct them immediately. Thanks to Ari, she left with confidence that we not only cared about food safety but were absolutely obsessed with it.

While everyone tends to eat more at a buffet, we quickly identified two particularly voracious eaters. Ian, a large man in his late twenties with autism, would fill his plates at least four or five times. He was very specific in how he organized his food and enjoyed displaying his creations and explaining the reasoning behind them. In between trips to the buffet, he would follow me around asking questions and making suggestions. Quite an entrepreneur, he was trying to start up a condiment business and market an invention, which had been mentioned in our local paper. Ian was very proud of his friendship with the reporter, someone I had worked with previously. He invited the reporter to dinner once and pestered me incessantly to make sure everything would be perfect—we had long conversations about the menu, the table they would sit at, and what beverages would be available. Fortunately, they had a nice evening. Otherwise, he ate alone except on rare occasions when an older woman would join him.

George was a roofer who discovered the restaurant after we took over. I was excited when we retained new customers, since we were no longer depending completely on the goodwill Gopal had generated. George, like Ian, would eat enormous amounts of food. Unlike Ian, who was portly, George was scrawny but must have had a high metabolism. He was also talkative, with a large repertoire of puns and cringeworthy jokes.

Both Ian and George came in several nights a week. Our dinners were not busy, especially after 7 p.m., so I had time to talk but did my best to look occupied since they exhausted me. When I could, I would hang out in the kitchen with Lenny and Forrest. Lenny was very funny, always joking and seeing the lighter side of things. Forrest was a willing straight man for Lenny's comedy. Still uncertain and depending quite a bit on the institutional knowledge of our small crew, I hadn't exerted much authority over them, so we got along well. One evening I decided we should have a serious talk about safety.

"If anything like a robbery happens, just exit through the back. Once you're safe, call 911."

Lenny responded immediately. "I've given that a lot of thought. I'll crouch under there with a knife." He pointed to the convection oven, which stood on tall legs near the kitchen entrance. "When he runs in, I'll slash his Achilles tendons."

I wasn't sure whether to be amused, impressed, or disturbed.

SETTLING IN

Ari and I settled into a routine. I worked most mornings, and he worked the others. I made dinner entrées while he set up for musicians, and I usually stayed into early evening, leaving him to close. Ari always made the very popular eggplant parmesan and lasagna on Friday nights, giving me a welcome break.

Evenings and weekends at home were taken up with paperwork: creating menus for the week, making promotional materials for our growing list of entertainment, compiling an email list, maintaining our website, answering calls and emails, paying bills, and doing the bookkeeping needed to make monthly deposits and file our quarterly returns with the IRS, the Franchise Tax Board, and the Board of Equalization. At that time, I was also doing payroll by hand every two weeks.

Daria was a godsend. She was still reserved but also observant, and she saved us from many mistakes. ("Didn't you already add the salt?") She was able to answer many of the questions we hadn't known to ask Gopal. Daria, Forrest, and Lenny were our core staff, but almost immediately, others started coming (and going).

Ari and I were butting heads over a homeless man, Ed, whom Gopal had brought in to help prep once or twice a week in exchange for food. On breaks, Ed would sit with his German shepherd on the patio and entertain a group of lovely college students who found him sweet and wise. Ari was appalled by Ed's lack of hygiene and didn't want him in the kitchen. This became a bone of contention, since I saw Ed as a kind man who belonged at Gaia's Garden. And, I pointed out, he spent a lot of time in the bathroom cleaning up before his shift. Ari argued that Ed was constantly going out to visit his dog, then returning to the kitchen, washing only his hands but having picked up dog hair and whatever else. Plus, he stunk of tobacco. My hippie values favored inclusion and generosity. I cringe now when I remember referring to Ed as "the spirit of Gaia's Garden." Ari had hippie values too, but in this case, they were overridden by his concerns as the restaurant's sanitation officer. We bickered about this for a few weeks until I learned Daria, who was very fond of Ed, would not eat any food he had prepped, nor would Lenny and Forrest. It was particularly sad because he had gotten one of the students pregnant and was determined to get his life together. Still, I agreed Ari could let him know we would not be part of that plan.

We lost our quirky and only marginally reliable volunteer cleaning crew to summer fun and festivals, which was a relief. I hired a friend, Carrie, although I had some initial trepidation about becoming her employer. She had proven to be a loyal and entertaining friend, down to earth and practical. Still, she was the only person I'd ever met who carried a letter with instructions on what to do should she have a psychotic break, so I had some concerns. As an employee, she was a solid, mature, and cheerful presence at the restaurant and knew how to clean efficiently. Ari was much happier when she was on shift. He respected her abilities and work ethic, and she was accepting of what I was beginning to suspect was his ADD or OCD—or both.

As we started to gain some mastery and relax into a routine, preparing the buffet and managing the restaurant became a joy. It took everything I had, physically and emotionally, but it was worthwhile. I'd had many jobs in my life, apparently unrelated. Now I was using skills from all of them. I had been both an employee and a supervisor, a waitress, a masseuse, a welfare worker, a banking consultant, a clerk typist, a research assistant, and a mortgage broker. Early on, I had lived among street people, johns and pimps, then later in life spoken at professional banking and real estate conferences. Now, I needed all the skills I had gained. My patchwork history finally made sense. My biggest regret was not having started when I was younger.

I did enjoy cooking, it turned out. Some of my experience as a home cook over the years was helpful, but cooking in quantity with consistency while meeting deadlines and satisfying customers requires a specialized skill set that I developed and enjoyed much more than working in my kitchen at home. I'm not a good housekeeper, but organization and cleanliness were essential at the restaurant. Gopal had trained me well on his system and left us supplied with shopping lists and all the utensils we needed. I had long counters to work on, a lot of prep done for me, and someone else to do the dishes!

Working with the Indian spices—cumin, coriander, fennel, and carda-mon—with their fine aromas and exotic tastes was sensually satisfying, as were the colors displayed on the finished buffet: a fresh, beautiful array of green, yellow, red, purple, and orange. Because I was making the same dishes every ten days, I became adept at them. While still using the recipes for some, I became able to judge doneness just by sight and smell.

Once I had become proficient at time management, I enjoyed the dance, moving from one project to another—tasting this, adding that, bringing everything to fruition at just the right time. I came in early, preferring to be in the kitchen alone, but Daria was easy to work with when she came in later. As we got better acquainted, we talked more, and I would occasionally become distracted, so I purchased a fancy timer that could be set to oversee four projects at once.

It helped that I loved vegetables. One of the most memorable meals I have ever had was in a small French restaurant where I was served an expensive bowl of small raw turnips—each one perfect. I prefer simple food, where the taste of the vegetables, rather than the artistry of the chef, takes center stage. (Crema seems ubiquitous on vegan food now, zigzagging over everything. For the record, I deplore it.)

We eliminated white rice and served only brown basmati, naming the freed-up space on the hot table "the mystery spot." This was the place for plain vegetables of the day—a rotating feast of green beans, corn on the cob, greens, roasted yams, potatoes, turnips, parsnips, or Brussels sprouts—seasoned lightly if at all.

We discovered purple and yellow cauliflower, which made a beautiful presentation when steamed with carrots and broccoli. The buffet tables popped with color (aided by Ari's new full-spectrum lighting), and the food was fresh, tasty, and nutritious.

There were mistakes, of course. Dahl without salt or sugar tastes like dishwater, which I found out after having served it for an hour. I think that error cost us the Indian group from Medtronic. Rice was a challenge at times, but for reasons I no longer understand, I stubbornly rejected Ari's plea to buy a rice cooker. Burning the spices for the curry ruined the whole batch no matter what steps I might take to rectify it.

As I became more confident, I started developing recipes of my own—stuffed cabbage, "Bubba Q Sauce," pesto rigatoni. Some of them were good; others were less so. A halavah variation made with rose water and dried petals and colored with beet juice was pretty but tasted like soap. I'm sure it can be done well, but I became discouraged and abandoned that project.

One of the regular customers, whom we nicknamed Poodle Lady due to her haircut resembling that of her two dogs, had a series of complaints. There was too much salt in the soup. The garbanzo beans were too hard. The steamed vegetables were too hard (or too soft). The chili was too thin (or too thick). I would take each complaint as proof I was blowing it. Then it hit me: while she complained every day, she also came in every day! At that point, I listened politely but took her less seriously. All in all, though, we were doing well. It was a joy to hear a buzz of happy conversation and laughter in *my* dining room.

Working together in the mornings, Daria and I became better acquainted. Her father wasn't a presence in her life, and her mother was still in the Midwest with the boyfriend. We talked about everything, from childhood experiences to our relationships, Goth and punk culture, and my youth in the '60s and '70s. She was having her entire back tattooed with a classical mural. This was being done in stages as she could afford them, and I was charmed she trusted me enough to bare her back and show me. The entire project, she estimated, would cost four thousand dollars. I grew to love her and to respect her formidable strength, skills, and intellect. She also worked well with Ari and seemed to understand our very different work styles, and she accommodated us accordingly.

While things were going well, I still felt like an imposter next to "real" restaurant people: competition scared me. Initially, we were the only plant-based option in Santa Rosa. A restaurant opened to great fanfare downtown, specializing in local ingredients and offering seafood and vegetarian items. They didn't last long, as the carnivores wanted more variety in their protein and vegans abhorred the smell of frying fish. Shortly after we took over as Gaia's Garden, a religious group leased a store to the north of us with the intention of serving plant-based meals to schoolchildren and their families. Their focus was on comfort foods, such as burgers, fries, mac and cheese, smoothies, and shakes. The manager ate with us frequently as they were getting set up. She was a big fan of our Almond Blend dressing and kept asking me for the recipe. I refused all such requests, having paid quite a bit to acquire that knowledge. At the time, I naively assumed she had taken no for an answer.

The junior college reopened for the fall semester, and as expected, our lunch business increased significantly. It seemed like we might be making money, but it was difficult to tell. By the time I got home each night, I was exhausted, although at least the pile of paperwork awaiting me offered a change of pace. There was so much of it that I rarely found the energy to detach and take in the bigger picture. I was also trying to be a good companion to Richard and a comfort to my aged mother. There seemed to be no time for analysis.

In retrospect, I wish I had found the time. Not being on top of costs to determine pricing was a serious error. There are formulae for pricing individual restaurant meals. Generally, it's 30 percent food cost, 30 percent employee cost, 30 percent overhead (insurance, rent, utilities, laundry, cleaning, etc.), and a 10 percent margin. It was difficult to apply this to a vegetarian buffet.

We knew how much food we put out each day, and how much was left over, but the breakdown for each item eluded us. I purchased a computer program that promised to sort it all out for me, but the amount of time and effort required to input all our information and learn the program's operations became too cumbersome. I sent away for a book on buffets that suggested each customer averages one pound of food. I had no idea how many pounds we were making, so that was less than helpful. I could have figured it out but didn't think I had the time. This was probably the biggest mistake of my restaurant career.

Many of the returning students were vegan, and there were frequent requests for a vegan dessert, since the halavah contained butter. I had veganized a lot of our recipes, but the price difference between a pound of regular butter and a pound of nondairy butter was significant. I made a few batches of vegan brownies, which were *too* well received. In addition to those consumed with the meal, more would disappear into pocketbooks and wrapped indiscreetly in napkins. One man, who had finished his meal, announced the brownies were so good he was taking a couple for his girlfriend. I told him they were for our customers to eat onsite only. He gave me a charming smile and took them anyway. We needed a dessert that would not be so easily pilfered! Pudding seemed like a good option, since it could not be stuffed into a coat pocket. I found a chocolate pudding recipe using cornstarch instead of eggs and experimented with flavors—orange chocolate, Mexican chocolate, and "after dinner mint." Coconut tapioca was delicious and popular and became a staple. Ian, our voracious customer with autism, suggested a chai tapioca, which turned out to be wonderful.

The coconut tapioca taught me an important marketing lesson. While adding pineapple juice and chunks on one occasion, I burned it slightly. Adjusting and diluting to the best of my ability did not eliminate the singed taste of the Piña Colada Tapioca, and it did not get consumed as enthusiastically as the others. On the third day, unwilling to throw the batch out, I renamed it Roasted Pineapple Tapioca, and it was gone within a few hours.

In response to customer requests, we substantially veganized the entire menu. We were not aware of a large vegan presence among our customers, but they seemed such an important part of our target demographic, we wanted to accommodate them and attract more. Unfortunately, like many activists, a lot of them couldn't afford to eat out much, even with us. Others objected to us on principle, since we were not 100 percent vegan, while encouraging their community to begin patronizing any meat-serving restaurant that added a vegan dish to their menu. The goal was to encourage other restaurants to use less meat while we were held to a higher standard and being penalized for the few dairy-containing items we still offered.

We no longer used whey, as Gopal had, adding coconut or soy milk to the soups instead. They were richer and creamier—and more expensive to make. The spinach curry had been made with sour cream, and we found coconut cream worked just as well. We also found the curries and most of the soups didn't need sugar to taste good and eliminated it from all except the dahl and the carrot soup. Over time, we would phase out the entrées that contained dairy until the only nonvegan items were the halavah, butter pats and cheese on the salad bar, and three salad dressings that contained honey. This failed to satisfy some of the area's vegans, but most were appreciative.

In fairness, vegans receive a lot of condemnation ranging from ridicule ("How can you tell if someone is vegan? Don't worry, they'll tell you.") to outright hatred. While some may seem to bring it on themselves with abrasive and sometimes silly public displays, there is one inescapable fact: they're right, particularly when it comes to industrial meat production. The public prefers their meat neatly cut up and packaged in stores, with no reminders that these are body parts of sentient beings. Consumers prefer being spared the evidence of these animals' misery, terror, and screams of agony. It's easy to look away, but vegans can't. They are the best of us. I tried to remember this when they got on my nerves, which was often.

When customers would ask what was vegan, I would first need to define terms with them. Probably 80 percent meant no meat, eggs, or dairy. More strict vegans would not eat honey. One regular informed me that since there was sugar in the carrot soup, it was not vegan. That came as a surprise, but she was right. To make white or brown commercial cane sugar, sugar cane syrup is strained either through charred animal bones or seashells. For brown sugar, molasses is just added back in. True vegans eschew anything derived from animals, living or dead. Organic sugar is much more expensive, but it's vegan, so that was an investment we needed to make.

Another customer was constantly extolling the benefits of sea salt and the dangers of iodized salt, so we also made that change. Likewise, canola oil is considered poisonous by some, so we replaced it with the more expensive rice bran oil.

Organic, non-GMO produce was another issue of importance to our community, but we were limited because our people were also very price conscious. We sprung for organics for the most heavily sprayed produce (potatoes, spinach, spring mix, strawberries—all among the "dirty dozen") and bought our rice and grains from companies that used neither sprays nor GMO seed. Fortunately, Imwalle's also met those criteria for their own produce when in season. We couldn't guarantee the rest, which came primarily from the Central Valley of California and Mexico. We switched from soy sauce to the very expensive, non-GMO, gluten-free tamari.

My description of the sourcing was usually more than enough to assure inquiring customers we were conscientious. By the time I was done, their eyes would be rolling back in their heads, and they were anxious to move on to their meal. I would tell the employees, "The best thing about our customers is they care what they eat. The worst thing about our customers is they CARE what they eat."

Recognizing the varied dietary preferences of our customers, Ari teasingly put two covered empty trays on a counter and labeled them "Breathetarian Dessert." Most people got the joke when they found nothing but air, but one customer asked when we would be refilling it.

BUILDING COMMUNITY

Most of the friends, acquaintances and former coworkers we had expected to support us didn't show up—wishing us well but eating elsewhere. We had misjudged how important a bar atmosphere and meat are to some people, and perhaps we had misjudged the strength of those relationships. At the same time, we were finding our new community among vegetarians, vegans, seniors, students, and others looking for cheap, healthy food and with tradespeople who appreciated our menu and our efforts. Artists and musicians, some of whom became customers, helped fulfill our vision of a vibrant, happening cultural oasis.

Our regulars included a couple who brought their own garlic, since we didn't use it. A single man seemed abrasive at first but proved to be a solid supporter, coming in nearly every day for ten years. Several medical practitioners dined with us, and I was told by a customer, whose boyfriend was a health inspector, that they often saw other health inspectors when they came in. Many students presented smelling of pot, but I didn't begrudge them the huge meals they took, knowing that for some it might be their only meal of the day.

There was a charming pair who would come in often. The girl was both deaf and blind. She and her older companion communicated by tracing signs on each other's hands. The companion told me they visited when the girl asked to go to the "many foods and little cakes restaurant," referencing our buffet and halavah balls.

One of our customers was a psychologist who came in one day with six very thin women. "I'll just have a salad," whispered one of her guests.

"NO!" declared the psychologist, "YOU'LL HAVE THE FULL BUFFET!"

She did not have to breach confidentiality for me to discern that her group was composed of recovering anorexics.

Oddly, two women came in within weeks of each other to make amends. The first told me she had lied to get the student discount and that she owed us a dollar. She was newly sober, she said, and it was necessary that she conduct herself with rigorous honesty. I took her dollar, gave her a hug, and told her I knew her recovery program, since I had thirty years in it myself. That was a moment.

The second woman arrived a few weeks later and was much less composed. Through tears, she also told me she had lied about being a student. "I did that in front of my daughter! What kind of example is that? I'm supposed to be a Christian!"

I came around the counter to hug her. "You're the best kind of Christian! Everybody makes mistakes, but a real Christian tries to make them right."

She was still sniffling as she handed me a crumpled dollar for our coffers.

Most of our customers were kind and grateful. One particularly supportive patron was Rae, a young woman whose head was always covered with a turban. I suspected she was undergoing radiation, but she never mentioned it. Instead, she noticed every single change we made and always had something nice to say about it—whether it was signage, a new plant, or a minor adjustment to a recipe.

She asked me one evening what I thought was needed to boost business, which was slow on winter nights. I said I was considering better signage, since many who drove by weren't aware we were a restaurant. She pressed twenty dollars into my hand. "Please take this, then, and put it toward signs." I tried to refuse, but she was insistent, and I was deeply touched. I never saw her again. I heard from a mutual friend that she had gone to stay with her brother and had died of breast cancer a few months later.

We were also blessed with key people who worked for trade. Actually, Willie was a *mixed* blessing. A senior who bore some resemblance to Willie Nelson, he took over the garden, bringing in plants from other projects and creating a colorful yet wild landscape in front of the restaurant. I liked it, but what Ari called "the hippie jungle" decreased our visibility, and broken pieces of tile used as mulch seemed sloppy to him. We had to insist Willie wear shoes inside and use our plates rather than the wooden bowl he preferred. Occasionally, he would present us with a handful of silverware he had accumulated—some ours, some not. His two dogs roamed the property unless we reminded him to keep them locked up. He was very talkative. I did my best to dodge the long conversations and to divert him to Ari, who also liked to talk. Still, I appreciated what he was doing for us and the money and labor we were saving. He didn't ask to be paid, but every so often we would feel compelled to slip him a fifty.

Mike was a handyman at the Market next door. He was willing to trade for half of his labor, which was convenient and saved us a lot of money since he could handle emergency plumbing and electrical jobs as well as carpentry. Ari took the trade aspect to be carte blanche for his pet projects, and I had to tell them both all such jobs needed my approval. Ari bristled, but Mike understood. Mike, I learned, had been an executive and a training manager for two nationally known food companies. Ready to retire, he had been wiped out by the recession of 2008. Fortunately, he had manual skills and a positive attitude. I would introduce him as "our handyman and marketing consultant." He had good ideas about adding variety to the salad bar and the hot table, but it was a few years before I had the energy to implement them.

A longtime friend, Ken Risling, an electrician, did a lot of work for us on trade. Our building was old and had dubious wiring. He found we had been paying to run one of the computers next door and providing heat for an adjacent business.

One morning, the electricity to the buffet tables shut off twenty minutes before opening. That very day, a customer who was also an electrician arrived early for lunch and had us back on track in time to open. There were many "coincidences" like this, shoring up my hope that this project might really be blessed by a Higher Power.

In addition to generous supporters who helped with the property itself, many artists and musicians came forward to contribute to the creative aspects that were so much a part of our dream. Décor was enhanced considerably (and cheaply) by the willingness of artists to exhibit their work with us. The shows lasted two months. Proceeds, which were rare, went directly to the artists. We set out fruit, crackers and goat cheese, chocolate, wine, and sparkling water for their receptions and in return had colorful pieces on the walls. Our biggest sale was a mosaic by Victor Jorgensen, a master stained-glass artist. When his show was over, he insisted we keep another of his works—"Bacchus with Chocolate Bar"—and made us a ridiculously generous offer so we could purchase and display it.

I invited a friend, Michael Ramos, to exhibit with us. His paintings are wonderfully executed, surreal and very complicated. It was his first show, and we loved having it. For several months afterward, he would bring in new paintings to show the crew, who always gathered around in sincere admiration.

One memorable show was by a woman who was both an artist and a neurophysicist. She'd had a near-death experience, which she memorialized on a series of huge, bright canvases. My favorite was completely yellow with one white squiggle. I wasn't taken with the artistry but loved the bold color on the walls. She priced it and the others at $5,000 each, which was certainly too high for our clientele and a source of some amusement. I'm not sure she even wanted to sell; the series was so personal to her.

Perhaps our most successful art event was a show by elementary school students. They priced most of their works at five or ten dollars, and the customers were enthralled with them. Some—and not just relatives—bought several pieces. The most expensive was a drawing of a lion's head that was exceptionally well done. This brought the young artist fifty dollars.

It didn't take long for Ari to assemble a full calendar of music. In keeping with the international offerings on the buffet, we had jazz, reggae, blues, solo guitar players, Celtic groups, French music (cabaret and traditional), and African kora players and drummers, among others. Some of the best musicians in the area played for food, tips, and whatever we could spare from the night's receipts. For many, their performances served as rehearsals, preparing them for better-paying gigs. Most of them came out of respect for Ari, who was a superb saxophone player and entertainer with whom they had history. He knew as well as anyone that the musicians deserved more money than we had, and he went out of his way to show them consideration and appreciation in other ways—food and beverages on the gig, of course, but also tokens they could use later as regular customers.

In November, I received a call from BMI, a huge company that licenses the rights to play copyrighted music and that purportedly pays royalties to the musicians. They had seen our website with promos for shows, and they wanted their cut. Three hundred thirty dollars, the agent told me, would cover the next six months. Appalled, I told him I would get back to him. Research showed I had no choice. A club in an adjoining county had bucked them and lost $20,000 plus court costs. I thought of trying just to pay for songs we played, which was impossible. Their catalogue included over 100,000 titles and at least as many arrangements. I would be better off paying the $330, which I did. It took a few months more for ASCAP and SESAC to catch up with us, but I had to pay them, too. This fly in our soup meant that just for the right to host live music and play background CDs, we now had to shell out $150 a month. Since they didn't know what songs we were playing, I doubt the individual musicians were compensated, but that was not my battle to fight.

BLOWUP

About three months into our tenure, Forrest cut his finger badly while slicing yams. They require a lot of force, but if that force is applied to a body part instead of the root vegetable, the result is likely to be a deep cut that won't stop bleeding. Forrest called his mother, and I gave them the information for urgent care. His mom asked if I wanted to just pay instead of filing for worker's comp. I thanked her for the option but declined, glad I had put him and Lenny on payroll early on, so I could make the claim.

In this new venture, I was determined to do things by the book, having previously been a mortgage broker, where rules were just part of a big game. No more looking over my shoulder! Forrest had some stitches and was out for a week. There was a lot of paperwork but no regrets on my part.

Ari was having increasing problems with Forrest and Lenny. He had taken on the authoritarian role I avoided and was becoming frustrated with their lack of compliance. Forrest's sloppy vegetable prep resulted in inconsistent sizes, which in turn made it difficult to cook everything properly. Lenny was not very conscientious when cleaning his area, bounced out of work as early as possible, and was guilty of the cardinal sin of not putting tools back in their properly labeled niches. They both often left closing tasks undone. I tried to be a buffer, presenting Ari's complaints in a more tactful manner, but nothing changed, and Forrest's resentment became palpable. So did Ari's.

We were all in the kitchen one night after the restaurant had closed, putting food away and cleaning up. Lenny and Forrest were joking around more than working. Ari examined the carrots Forrest had prepped for the next day, and his building frustration erupted in rage. I had seen Ari in this state before but never with anyone but me. Giving credence to the dual nature of Geminis, this seemed like a different person. His skin actually darkened as he screamed, "I AM SICK OF THIS SHIT. YOU'RE PAID TO DO A JOB, FUCKING DO IT! I'M NOT YOUR NANNY, I'M YOUR BOSS, AND I'M SICK AND TIRED OF TELLING YOU THE SAME DAMN THING EVERY GODDAMN DAY! YOU'RE NOT BEING PAID TO PLAY! I'VE SHOWED YOU FIFTY TIMES HOW TO CUT THE FUCKING CARROTS! THIS IS A BUSINESS, NOT YOUR DAMN PLAYGROUND! AND LENNY, YOU BETTER LEARN TO USE A BROOM AND MOP! HOW HARD IS THAT? MOST NIGHTS, YOU LEAVE THIS KITCHEN FILTHY!"

The three of us were stunned. The two young men, formerly full of swagger, were now two frightened boys. I didn't know their histories but suspected they were no strangers to male rage, and it hurt my heart to see the fear in their eyes. As they cowered against the walls, I tried to mediate without undercutting Ari too much. This was impossible, so I suggested they call it a night, and they fled out the back.

Once they were gone, I turned on Ari. "YOU CAN'T TREAT PEO-PLE LIKE THAT!" Then, more calmly but through clenched teeth,

"What were you thinking? This . . . will . . . never . . . happen . . . again!" He had lost some of his fire and seemed surprised at himself. We reached no agreement, but it was a few more years before it happened again.

I had never experienced this kind of blowup in a kitchen, although I have since learned it was relatively mild compared to some and that, in retrospect, it was deserved. Most of the kitchens I had worked in as a server had been small operations with the same tried and true menus day after day, well-established standards and procedures, and a certain complacency toward quality—diners, truck stops, a spaghetti house, a midrange steak house. None was innovating as we were, nor were they run by novices. Still, I'd had enough bad experiences to be fond of saying "all restaurant owners are pricks." Now that the shoe was on the other foot, I had more compassion for those harried entrepreneurs but didn't want to emulate them.

I was appalled at the blowup and that Ari would be so unprofessional. Unfortunately, we were setting up a dynamic where I became overprotective of the crew and saw Ari as overly critical. In the coming years, we would spend a lot of energy reacting to each other rather than uniting to move our venture forward.

I was surprised when Lenny and Forrest showed up the next day. I apologized to them on the restaurant's behalf for the way the message had been conveyed, and they mumbled an acknowledgment. The vegetable cuts were a lot more consistent for the time Forrest stayed with us.

FIRST YEAR WRAP-UP

One afternoon in November, an elderly Mexican woman came in with her two teenage grandsons. Pushing the older one forward, she prodded him to ask if we had any openings. Shyly, but with fair English, he said he had worked at a Mexican restaurant. I told him we needed someone to clean and pick up some dishwashing shifts, since we were now open on Saturdays. I sensed their desperation and was gratified when David showed up the next day and was able to produce a Social Security number. He worked very hard. I loaded him down with leftovers the first night, which he took eagerly. That was probably the last time he ate our food. Apparently, neither he nor his family liked it. He was a good worker—focused, fast, and efficient. Forrest and Lenny resented him, since he showed them to be the slackers they were.

We decided to close for two weeks over the winter holidays since the junior college was out of session. Ari and his girlfriend paired with an artisan and his girlfriend to decorate the dining room walls with trees made from cob—a durable, natural material similar to adobe. The results added a lot to the ambiance once the trees were trimmed with fake foliage and lights, probably worth the $1,250 we spent. At the same time, it reinforced our hippie vibe, which undercut our efforts to be seen as a respectable restaurant.

David and a friend came in to clean up the huge mess the creatives had left behind. When Ari asked David why he had come to *El Norte*, David responded that his only option in Mexico was to join a gang or be killed. This explained the serious manner of one so young, why he seemed so driven. We were glad to have helped him start a new life here. I didn't ask his age; I suspected he was fifteen or sixteen, but he was willingly doing a man's work.

The cob sculptor built a pizza oven outside, with the idea that his girlfriend would make and sell pizzas on Sunday nights. She had difficulty assembling the ingredients and working in a strange kitchen. Customers pronounced the pizzas good but were not thrilled with waiting up to an hour to get one. We couldn't even placate them with beer or wine. It was time to get that license.

As the year ended, I knew we had lost money, despite having improved the buffet and décor significantly. There were a lot of expenses in addition to the increased costs of better ingredients and a larger payroll. Credit card processing cost us about $325 per month in the beginning, then rose to around $800 as our transactions increased.

Our facility costs were high. Gas and electricity averaged $1,200 per month. Fortunately, the Market paid for water. There was also liability insurance ($157 per month), alarm service ($46), water filtration service ($40), dish sanitizer rental and chemicals ($120), phone and internet service ($72), and laundry ($44), plus the unexpected $150 per month for music licensing. Every six months we had to have the hood over the stove cleaned and had to pay another company to service the Ansul (fire suppression) system and fire extinguishers. Those expenses worked out to another $150 monthly. Our license from the health department was $1,000 annually.

The triple net lease (tax, insurance, repairs in addition to rent) started at a manageable $2,374 per month but increased each year by 3 percent, which became significant. I consulted one expert who asked me what percentage of our gross we were spending on rent. It was close to 25 percent, and he refused to work with me. "You have no chance. You should shut down now. You'd have a hard time if it were 12 percent; it should be 8 percent." I was dismayed but only temporarily. We had a fantastic location and—for the moment at least—were one of only two plant-based restaurants in a county known for its health orientation and appreciation of fresh produce. We would just need to increase our income so the percentage going to rent would drop significantly. And I still had plenty of money.

People complaining about our prices—a healthy, unlimited buffet for the ridiculously low price of $7.95—never thought about all these expenses when they would announce, "I could make this at home for three dollars." Ari joked that our motto should be "What you would make for yourself if you cooked four hours a day."

In our first six months, we had taken in over $90,000 gross income and were showing a $23,000 loss. I had been prepared for the fact that most restaurants lose money at first. This wasn't what my projections based on Gopal's numbers had shown, but it was reality, which I did my best to ignore as we went into the new year: 2010.

GREED

I spent most of the holiday break working on the beer and wine license and designing new menu boards to reflect some needed price changes. Ari always pushed for larger increases while I feared losing the customers we had. There was some compromise, but the results were more reflective of my instincts than his. We raised the price of the full lunch by $1, to $8.95 for "all you care to eat," and dinner was increased by $2 to $9.95. We dispensed with unlimited soup, salad, and bread, offering a one-time-through option for $7.50 along with some even lower priced one-serving options. Most customers took it in stride, but thus began several years of policing.

Anyone researching the phenomenon of greed need only watch the activity at a buffet restaurant. Even the nicest people succumb to the allure of abundance. Many would pay the lower price for one serving of soup, salad, and bread and then define these items to include curry, hot pasta, and dessert—pretty much anything else they desired. Wanting to ensure their money's worth, they would pile the plates ridiculously high, usually taking much more than they could eat. One enterprising architectural student used corn bread to build walls around his plate so he could pile the food even higher. Others would try to reuse their plate to get more food, claiming they hadn't seen this or that item before.

It was always a difficult situation for us, not wanting to alienate customers yet not wanting them to further stress our burgeoning food budget.
When we did confront a customer, we would usually frame the situation
as a misunderstanding, our fault for not having made the system clear. "So,
next time...." I often didn't say anything at all—until one woman put me
over the edge.

She ordered the full buffet—"all you care to eat"—to take out. This was
foolish on our part but a popular option, and we provided a ridiculously
generous number of containers—a three-compartment nine-inch-square
box, a smaller clamshell, eight-ounce and sixteen-ounce hot cups, and
a small bag for bread. (These containers alone cost us nearly a dollar.)
Everyone seemed quite happy with the arrangement, which provided them
with a lot of food.

This customer informed me she would be eating some of it in-house
and taking the rest with her, which was fine. We had many customers on
short lunch breaks who would do the same. She ate everything in the large
box, the small clamshell, and the sixteen-ounce cup, then headed back to
the buffet to refill them. I was busy at the register and couldn't get to her
so decided to let it slide. The last straw was seeing her at the bread box
emptying its entire contents into a shopping bag.

I ran to her. "Stop! What are you doing? You've already had a lot more
than you paid for!"

"It's supposed to be all you can eat!"

"Yes, but not for your entire life!"

Her mood shifted from injured to outraged. Gathering up her containers, she pushed the smallest one toward me—"Here, I don't even want
this!"—and she flounced out. Shaking my head, I went back to my post,
thinking that was the end of it. It wasn't.

The next day, she came in during Ari's shift and demanded he fire me. She became even angrier when informed that I, as the owner, could not be fired. She left, yelling she would tell everyone what a horrible person I was. She never came in again, but—true to her word—she accosted Carrie and, later, Jim when they were working outside, telling them and everyone within earshot that they were crazy to work for such a terrible person.

A customer told me about a class at Sonoma State University where senior business students would form teams and consult with small companies. We needed help moving forward, and this seemed like a godsend. I attended with other owners, and we all made our pitches to the class. Four students signed up to work with us. We met once, and they strongly suggested working on a logo and a tagline. They had some suggestions for the latter, none of which resonated with me. I ended up with "Food, Music, Art, and Community." The logo would come later, but I started using a picture of the steamed vegetables—bright-green broccoli, orange carrots, purple and yellow cauliflower.

After the first meeting, they disappeared, despite having promised subsequent meetings, analysis, and a report. I later saw the report they handed in to their professor, indicating several meetings, conclusions, and recommendations—none of which had actually happened. Their results had little relation to the operations of our restaurant; they had just made stuff up. I guess they thought I wouldn't find out or report them to the professor. They were wrong on both counts, but these future captains of industry had already graduated, ready to take on the wider business world.

SPECIAL SITUATIONS AND CROSS-TRAINING

Forrest gave notice in January, two months after his fight with Ari, and so did Carrie. We needed a prep person and a janitor. I expanded David's shifts to cover cleaning and some prep. He was a willing worker whether cleaning, washing dishes, or preparing vegetables. He had trouble cutting the vegetables in uniform sizes, but, unlike Forrest, he was clearly trying, and his skills improved significantly as Ari worked with him. We needed more help on that side, though, so we started interviewing.

One junior college student had minimal experience and was vegan with a charming personality. A redhead, her passion was art, and she looked the part in a pleasantly Bohemian way. She told us at the interview that she had Tourette's syndrome, but her symptoms did not include the stereotypical shouting of obscenities for no apparent reason. Instead, she suffered from physical tics and would sometimes have to arch her back or adjust her position in what might seem an awkward way. I was concerned she would have difficulty handling sharp knives, but her assurances to the contrary proved true. She moved away in the spring, at the end of the semester, but would stop by and visit when she was in town.

A dishwasher, an exchange student from France, was 6'6" tall. I expressed my concern that bending over the sinks would seriously strain his back. His response: "I've been living in your world a long time. I know how to adjust." Taking him at his word proved to be the right decision. Another was so rotund he could barely clear the narrow aisle in the kitchen, yet he moved with considerable grace, never getting in anyone's way. I was impressed by these young people and how they handled their physical challenges and did excellent work without complaint. Unfortunately, because they were students, they did not stay long.

We hired a janitor. After about six weeks, he came in early for his paycheck, said he'd be back to cover his evening shift, and never returned. We hired Paul to replace him. Everybody loved Paul. He was good-natured and kind as well as funny. Unlike the rest of the crew, he had a BA degree—in gender studies. His work was impeccable, whether cleaning the dining room or prepping vegetables. He moved gracefully and worked with an easy efficiency. Noting his relaxed demeanor, I would be pleasantly surprised to find he had knocked out gallons of prep and that everything was cut perfectly. He took particular pride in producing identically sized small dices of carrots or potatoes for the soups. Ari and Daria were over the moon, having finally found someone who met their standards. Paul was forthcoming about his love for travel and let us know work was his means of financing trips to exotic places. In the three years that he worked for us, he took trips to Bali and to Thailand that lasted a couple of months each, as well as some shorter domestic ones, but he gave us lots of notice, and we always welcomed his return.

Paul was the perfect "utility guy." He excelled on the kitchen side but would jump in to do dishes or clean if needed. It was easy to train him on the register and other front-of-house tasks, and it was a great relief to know that when Paul was on duty, we could finally leave the restaurant with no worries. Cross-training was a priority with the other employees as well. We had a small crew, and if someone was sick or just didn't come in, we needed to be able to allocate their duties to others.

I started training Daria to cook for the buffet, and she was able to take over within the month. All her years of observation were put to good use, plus she had a natural ability. She was creative and developed an oil-free salad dressing as well as an easy polenta, which held up better on the hot table than did pasta. I suggested she take some classes at the culinary school down the street and was gratified when she did. We began a program of paying fifty dollars a quarter to culinary students to help cover books and uniforms.

One morning, Daria called in sick, and I was glad I had trained Lenny to do the salad bar. He was working happily, we were talking and laughing, when I heard a crash followed by clatter behind me. Lenny had fallen to the floor, knocking over the cart containing all the prepped salad ingredients. I rushed to him, remembering he had epilepsy. Ascertaining he was conscious, I headed to the house phone in the dining room to call 911. Suddenly, he rose from the floor, then fell again. "Stay down, Lenny!" I ordered. He started to get up. "LENNY! STAY DOWN! I NEED TO CALL 911!" He got up anyway, hitting both the prep table and the oven across from it as he fell again. "STAY DOWN, LENNY!" This time, as he lumbered to his feet, he threw his arms around me. I didn't feel threatened but was increasingly concerned about my inability to get to the phone. I was screaming; he was bouncing around the kitchen. Finally, a young woman from the Market next door poked her head in.

"Is everything alright?"

"NO! CALL 911!"

She did, and we teamed up to keep Lenny from injuring himself until the paramedics arrived. By the time they did, Lenny was nearly comatose. It occurred to me I should call a family member, but having taken over his employment from Gopal, who didn't keep records, I had no records. Fortunately, my tech-savvy assistant went through his phone and was able to call his mother. As Lenny was taken out on a stretcher, I thanked the young woman for coming to our aid. "Well, we heard you over there but thought Ari was having a heart attack." I was too flummoxed to have that statement clarified and went to work re-creating the salad bar and finishing lunch. That night, I made up employee forms and started an HR department in a file drawer. When he returned, Lenny's file included a doctor's note and his pledge to take breaks at the first sign of trouble.

MOVING RIGHT ALONG

The beer and wine license was a priority. I had started the process during the winter break and filled out the usual documents about my financials, our business plan, and the layout of the restaurant. Fingerprints were taken, although between dishwashing and constant handwashing, I barely had any ridges and grooves left. In addition, we were required to send notification letters to every residence within one thousand feet. There were a lot of apartments near the college, so we had to appeal to two hundred households. Only one voiced a concern—that they would be disturbed by loud music in their home, which was near the end of our zone, across a main street and halfway down the block. I tested their theory with the Neil Buckley Octet—trumpet, trombone, three saxophones, guitar, string bass, and drums. They were definitely our loudest band. Leaving the front door open and walking across the street, I could barely hear them, so I was able to assure the neighbors they would not be inconvenienced. They withdrew their objection.

The Department of Alcohol and Beverage Control (ABC) was concerned about the character of the neighborhood and whether our alcohol sales might add fuel to existing urban blight. I requested a printout of recent police calls in our area and received a stack an inch thick. We were in an area designated as "high crime"! I'd had no idea. Most of the calls were from a liquor store across the street and down a block, with the rest from a nearby motel. A letter of explanation was required and proved satisfactory. I also had to provide a letter making the case for our positive contribution to the community. That was easy. In our first six months, we had not only provided affordable, nutritious food but had presented excellent musicians and fine art, and we had held a benefit for a woman with cancer and another for a very sick child. There had been three workshops about healthy eating, and we were planning a series of dinners with local authors.

Another requirement was a conditional use permit from the city—more fees ($2,500) and forms to fill out. I had to go before a board and make our case. It was a friendly meeting, and we received our permit within a few weeks. They were viewing us as a nightclub, and no matter how hard I tried to distinguish our mature, community-minded, health-oriented evening clientele from standard bar folk, they were unmoved. We had to serve beer in glasses, not in bottles.

"Why?" I asked.

"If a fight breaks out, someone might use the bottle as a weapon."

We were allowed to serve wine in large bottles, which would have made far better weapons, but resistance seemed futile. We were limited in the size and positioning of the stage, and they were quite concerned about exits in the event a band set our vegetarian restaurant on fire. Dancing was forbidden, and that was the one rule we chose to ignore.

Finally, it all came together, and we got our beer and wine permit from Alcoholic Beverage Control ($500). Gopal was relieved, since he had been waiting for the additional $5,000 I had promised. Ari started sampling high-end beers and wines that I, as a nondrinker, knew nothing about. (When I had consumed alcohol back in the day, it was usually in a box or a red, white, and blue can.) Fortunately, Ari knew about quality beverages.

It was also a requirement that all alcohol be purchased through a registered distributor. Three more applications. I was losing my enthusiasm for paperwork. Soon, we were getting cases of beers—ranging from light to dark—and a selection of white, red, and rosé wines as well as sake and port.

David, the Mexican teenager who had worked so hard for us, gave notice. He had a job at a meat processing plant in Petaluma, which paid better. We later heard he had put on a massive amount of weight. Ari thought it was to insulate himself from the soul-destroying horrors of that work.

Daria suggested a replacement dishwasher—Butch. He was a punk rock star with a local following and was in need of a stable income. Among his many visible tattoos, one of a percolator caught my eye. He explained that a tattoo parlor had been running a special: for fifty dollars, customers could choose to take what they got from a grab bag, and he had gone with it. This casual approach to a lifelong decision amazed me, but he seemed fine with it. Beautiful young women would appear at the kitchen door just to get a glimpse of Butch, and his presence definitely added to our "cred."

Butch was energetic and charismatic and did a decent job on the dishes, although Ari found many shortcomings in his performance, particularly regarding his attention to protocol. Determined to organize the kitchen more efficiently, Ari labeled just about every slot, shelf, and drawer, expecting utensils would be properly returned to their designated spots and produce would be easily found and inventoried. This system was far from foolproof. At times, it wasn't practical—particularly when we were cramming an abundance of leftovers in the reach-in. Other times, the dishwashers would just get careless, or mistakes would be made in the heat of the moment. There were enough people in the back of the house that it was usually impossible to identify the culprit(s), and Ari's frustration mounted daily. I tried to inject some levity by suggesting he was trying to save the world with labels, but this did not amuse him.

Ari was becoming more and more dissatisfied with our employees, and his complaints seemed relentless, although—in retrospect—many were valid. I thought we were all doing the best we could and that his demands were unrealistic and annoying. His frustration only increased as I began tuning him out. He and I dealt with stress differently. I went behind a wall, unable to process more input. He expressed his outwardly. Neither approach was productive, especially in combination, and it became increasingly difficult for us to manage effectively or work cooperatively. We continued on in this way, often reacting rather than acting—to the detriment of our business and the frustration of the crew.

Our next hire lasted only a few months. On his last night, I saw him attacking the dishes and cleaning the area around the sinks with a ferocity unmatched by any previous employee, even David, whom he had replaced. A couple of warnings to stop banging the plates went unaddressed. Around 8 p.m., two hours before his shift was to end, he came out to the register.

"Is it OK if I go home for an hour? There's a basketball game on, and I want to catch the last half."

"No. Of course not. You need to work your whole shift."

He glared at me, stomped back into the kitchen, banged a few more pots, then stormed out.

The next afternoon, he showed up to apologize. "Look, I'm sorry for last night. I have a problem with amphetamine. I'm going to rehab today. Sorry to leave you in the lurch, but. . . ."

"No, no. I'm so glad you're doing that! I've had my issues too. Take care of yourself and please stay in touch. Let me know how you're doing."

We hugged, and I never saw him again.

OUR PLACE

Despite our escalating disagreements, both Ari and I loved having our own venue. In the past, I had often amused myself on road trips by building imaginary public spaces with great coffee, healthy food, and support for and from the local community. Ari had fond memories of time spent with the Illuminated Elephants—a communal, nomadic band of artists and musicians from Mexico—and had envisioned hosting a permanent *peña* where music and art of all kinds could be showcased in combination with good, healthy food. We had both enjoyed the community nurtured by the Old Vic in Santa Rosa, a pub run by a sometimes charming and reliably cantankerous Brit who hosted a community of performers and diverse patrons from the British Commonwealth. We had aspired to create such a place and had done it!

Ari as a musician and I as a mobile DJ had facilitated other people's events, but now we could produce our own, hoping to incorporate the best of these past experiences. Anything we thought would be fun, we could at least try. Ari had complete say over music, entertainment, and benefit events. He had a good sense of what type of music would be compatible with dining and conversation and the professional experience needed to select and monitor performers. While he was often short-tempered with the kitchen staff, he was extraordinarily tactful and kind to auditioning musicians, even when their skills weren't at the level we needed them to be.

For Valentine's Day, I finally realized my fantasy of having a Love Sucks party. Getting back in DJ Mama persona, I assembled a playlist of songs I hadn't been able to play at weddings—"Love Sucks," "Love Hurts," "Love Bites," "Chain of Fools," "Goodbye Earl," "It Wasn't Me," and "Call Tyrone," among others. Black tablecloths, wilted roses, and chocolate hearts graced each table. Despite good promo, it was sparsely attended. Having spent some lonely Valentine's Days myself, I had thought this event would fill a huge void. Instead, there was one enthusiastic dancer, a couple of women playing backgammon, and a few other couples. Ari kindly suggested I was ahead of my time.

Better attended was a workshop on senior sex by the irrepressible Joan Price. We scheduled her for a slow weeknight and put her group on the far side of the dining room. About fifteen seniors showed up, eyeing each other shyly. Joan immediately launched into a spirited discussion of lubricants, handing out samples and challenging most people's comfort zones. One who did not meet the challenge was our regular with autism, Ian. Although he sat on the other side of the restaurant, he heard more than he could handle and informed me he had lost his appetite and would be leaving. That was probably the only night he didn't cost us four times what he had paid.

Before we knew it, it was May 2010. We had been doing this for a year! Ari and I had had many fallings out. Other times, we bickered with such practiced ease that people assumed we were married. All of that aside, I appreciated the many improvements he had made to our restaurant—many over my objections initially—and the care he put into the décor and the quality of our food. I also knew that of all the people associated with Gaia's Garden, he was the one who would always have my back and who would never lie to me.

To celebrate Ari's birthday—also in May—I hired a singing telegram with the theme "You bring the magic." During our stint as DJs, I had done at least 80 percent of the work, yet Ari the entertainer was the one who made people jump and shout and leave smiling. My few solo gigs were competent but lacked that electricity, and I depended on him to bring it to the restaurant experience for our customers. Despite our differences backstage, he was doing well in the front with music, art, and a charm that most (but not all) appreciated.

Ari continued to schedule an impressive calendar of music. We had entertainment most nights—singles, duos, trios, and full bands presenting standards, jazz, Celtic music, Americana, Africana, boogie-woogie piano, and French café. Each had their fans, and our customer base was slowly expanding. We asked for a four dollar minimum purchase, which some people actually resented.

We did not charge a cover for most of the music. Ari was cynical about the local scene, having spent decades there playing his heart out for the equivalent of gas money. I think he had warmed up to me in clubs because I always dropped five dollars in the tip jar. Unfortunately, this distinguished me from other patrons who considered live music to be their God-given right or thought the pot of tea they nursed throughout an evening served as sufficient financial participation.

An exception was made to the "no cover" policy when we were contacted by an agent for Fantuzzi about performing at Gaia's Garden. I was thrilled, remembering him from my New Age days—a fabulous performer who brought the funk to sold-out crowds of flower children, many of whom had settled locally. We agreed on a ten dollar cover charge and braced ourselves for an overflowing house. About twelve people showed up. Fantuzzi took it in stride, possibly because Ari made sure the wine flowed freely. Fantuzzi was willing to try it again in October, even throwing in a Burning Man slideshow. We recommended a five dollar cover, but the band demanded and deserved ten dollars. The result was again disappointing.

On another occasion, we presented David Rovics, a singer-songwriter popular with our left-leaning clientele. While his performances easily command twenty to fifty dollars elsewhere, ten dollars was apparently a bridge too far for our customers.

These experiences were disappointing on their own, but they also reinforced our perception that our clients—who might cheerfully spend money elsewhere—were reluctant to do that with us. We weren't sure why. There was the buffet mentality coupled with the hippie vibe we couldn't quite shake and the fact that our base of students, activists, and seniors were on the low end of the income spectrum. Whatever the reason, our customers were pinching pennies with us, and this fed our fears of increasing prices for food, despite knowing we were losing money. We were in a bind but still optimistic, confident as we were in the quality of our food and entertainment. "Build it and they will come" wasn't working out yet, but surely if we could hang on, word would spread, and the public would realize what a tremendous value and worthy experience Gaia's Garden offered.

HEALTH AND SAFETY

To save money, Ari had taken on the task of cleaning the grease trap. This is a large metal box under the sinks that catches grease and bits of food before they can go into the wastewater. About once a month, it needed to be unhooked and pulled out, then drained and rinsed—a nasty job because the accumulated debris had a horrid smell. If it got too full, it "blew." This happened one day, and the kitchen floor became a noxious pond that smelled like a baby diaper times ten.

As Daria and I were watching the expanding pool of sludge in horror, Ari rushed in to let us know the health inspector had arrived for her quarterly inspection. She would have to shut us down until a reinspection if she knew, so I ordered him to keep her talking in the dining room. Talking is Ari's strong suit, and it bought enough time for Daria to pull out the shop vac and clear the floor while I boiled a pot of water with cinnamon, cloves, and half a bottle of orange extract, hoping to overcome the stench. Perhaps another sign of God's grace: we pulled it off—each using our superpower. By the time the inspector got to the kitchen, Daria and I were casually prepping vegetables, enjoying the pleasant scent of my aromatherapy. After that experience, we signed up with a professional crew to come in every three weeks. Another $130 a month.

One evening, Ari was informed by a customer, an attorney named Jack Buttons, that the knob on our customer restroom door was not compliant with the Americans with Disabilities Act (ADA). He said he had problems with his wrist and could not turn the standard round knob; it was necessary to have one with paddles that could be pushed. Ari apologized and offered to assist—although Mr. Buttons had apparently been able to manage. The next morning, Ari purchased the proper handles and changed them before the restaurant opened. Nonetheless, Mr. Buttons called Ari and threatened a lawsuit unless we paid him $500.

I spoke with a manager at the Market—our landlord—who laughed it off. She knew him, and he had been threatening them for years. She considered him nothing but an annoyance. They never paid him anything, and he always went away. Nonetheless, I began researching and was shocked at what I found. The ADA, a federal program, was reasonable. They considered a business's ability and willingness to make changes and allowed time for a plan to be implemented. California was another matter. There was no grace period, not even the overnight hours it had taken Ari to remedy our oversight. Mr. Buttons, with his time-stamped picture of our round doorknob, could sue us and would automatically be awarded a minimum of $4,000 plus court costs. He was not the only one aware of this law—I found articles about several attorneys with a range of disabilities who specialized in these cases, seemingly for their own benefit. One had seventy suits pending in various states! Ari had an attorney friend who met with Mr. Buttons on our behalf and negotiated a contract whereby we would pay him $250, and he would waive all present and future claims against us for anything.

We had to meet with him to sign the contract and managed to remain civil until everyone had signed. At that point, as we were getting up to leave, he insisted on telling us how much he loved our restaurant and wanted us to be successful, extending his hand. Neither of us took it.

I approached the Market about splitting the cost of hiring someone to do an ADA inspection—about $1,000. They were not that concerned, so I reviewed all the ADA guidelines myself instead. Mike, the handyman, came in and adjusted the heights of the bathroom mirror and sink by about an inch. We put signs in braille near the restroom door and made sure all the plates and utensils were accessible from a wheelchair. After that, either we were fully compliant or the other predators were not sufficiently fond of vegetables to bother us.

Butch's band was going on tour for three weeks, and he suggested that his friend, Mason, could fill in for him in the dish pit. Mason already had restaurant experience, and this seemed like a good arrangement. I liked him. Tall and thin, he had significant body art and some piercings, a cheerful confidence, and a good work ethic. As I got to know him, I learned he had been headed down a dark path but had stopped to take stock of his life, consciously visualizing the better man he wanted to be and following through with right action. He had a steady girlfriend and was very devoted to her. I found this impressive, particularly in a lad of twenty-three. When Butch returned, we moved Mason over to the prep side, since he had good skills and worked well with others. They hadn't told us initially that he, too, was in a punk band. Fortunately, he and Butch were able to coordinate band practices, shows, and tour dates most of the time so that we had coverage. I gave up scheduling either of them for Saturday nights.

Butch got us our only mention to date in either of our local newspapers. In an article about his band, he expressed appreciation that we allowed him to tour while keeping his job. Later, he was delighted to see the policy memorialized in our employee manual:

Reasonable effort will be made to accommodate school schedules, tour dates, and other productive activities.

"Other productive activities!" he repeated gleefully several times.

WHEN THE SAINTS GO MARCHING IN

My mother was ninety-six and, though frail, seemed ageless. When I'd visit her on Sundays at a care facility about forty-five minutes away, we'd talk about politics and her latest interest—how water forms different types of crystals depending on the moods of the researchers. While receiving twenty-four-hour care, she suffered a fall and was taken to the hospital. I visited her there each night, and she seemed less and less present; still, she always recognized me and would speak sharply to any nurse who dared treat her like an infant. The nurses indicated she could go home once she got over a bladder infection.

One night, I decided to give myself a break and spare myself the long drive. I had just worked a fourteen-hour shift and was tired. "I'll go up in the morning," I thought. Fortunately, I listened to the inner voice that told me to go anyway. She was agitated, and I rubbed her legs until she fell asleep. She died later that night.

Ari, Daria, and Paul took over the restaurant while I spent the week grieving and planning her memorial. Ari had been very fond of

Mom—they were both Gemini music teachers. I placed all her percussion instruments near the podium, and after the speeches, songs, and reminiscences, her students and great-grandchildren used them to accompany "Give Peace a Chance" in a joyous cacophony. Ari brought out his saxophone and, though more tearful than I was, led us out to the reception hall with "When the Saints Go Marching In." Mom would have loved it. Richard, who had also loved Mom, was my rock, quietly present and lovingly attentive.

I had been twenty-one before attending a funeral and had been to only a few in the intervening years. My parents hadn't found them important. It was my nieces who taught me the benefits of honoring the dead, the bringing together of family and friends and the comfort of ritual, having endured many losses in their young lives. The three daughters of my late brother Leslie came from long distances along with five of their children. My eldest niece flew in from Connecticut and was so far along with her pregnancy that air travel would have been too dangerous had we waited another week. My stepson from a previous relationship left his busy dental practice to fly up from San Diego.

Their commitment to family was heartening, yet I also felt pangs of guilt and regret. My stepson had embraced me as a grandmother to his children, but they were growing up without me as I devoted all my energy to the restaurant. My nieces' children were also strangers. Everyone was facing their challenges with love and resiliency, but without me for the most part. I had no children of my own. This was my family, whom I rarely saw any more.

The day-to-day operations of Gaia's Garden took all the time and energy I had. And I had my other family at the restaurant. They frustrated me often yet inspired me; our employees, with their courage, vulnerabilities, resilience, and youthful energy, took most of my attention. Someday the restaurant would be over, and my crew would move on. Seeing my actual family and admiring their commitment, which was greater than mine at the moment, caused me to examine my priorities enough to be uncomfortable but not enough to change. I had a restaurant to run and had already spent a week away. I needed to get back to it.

THE NICEST PERSON I EVER MET

Now that Daria was cooking, we needed someone to work the salad bar. Angela was an enthusiastic vegan and gushed that she would be thrilled to work for us. After a week, the luster had worn off, and she showed herself to be slow, unskilled, and uncooperative. I had hopes of bringing her along until one evening when Ari and Carol came in for dinner.

When Ari and I had been a couple, I had heard a lot about Carol. She had been his high school sweetheart and, although they had both married and divorced others, there was an enduring love and passion between them. I had never met her, but when Ari and I were together, my jealous mind had viewed her as my nemesis—possessing all the qualities of beauty, seduction, and charm I perceived myself lacking. Now they had reconnected yet again, and she was visiting from Ohio. I was amazed to find she was a pleasant but normal looking woman, not the blonde bombshell of my paranoid fantasies. I liked her a lot. She was down to earth, friendly, and funny.

When she and Ari came in for dinner that night, the three of us were conversing and laughing as Angela walked over to us.

"Oh," Angela said to Ari, "is this your mother?"

Carol had the grace to act like nothing had been said while Ari jumped in.

"Certainly not! Carol is my dear friend!"

I didn't want to amplify Angela's faux pas by discussing it further, but, as an older woman myself, I felt personally wounded and protective of my new friend. That's when I decided lack of good judgment, when added to her other shortcomings, tipped the balance against Angela's continued employment.

When she came to work the next morning, we sat down, and I presented her last check, which included a week of severance pay. Without citing the Carol incident, I referenced the other areas in which she needed but had not demonstrated improvement.

"What? You're firing me?"

"Well, yes. It's simply not a good fit. I'm sorry it hasn't worked out."

Just then, Daria came in from a break. Angela's malevolent stare followed her across the dining room. "So, that's your pet."

"She's not my 'pet.' She is extremely competent."

"Well, so am I!"

Realizing there would be no peaceful resolution if I responded truthfully, I stood up, wished her well, and headed for the kitchen.

"I'M THE NICEST PERSON YOU'LL EVER MEET!" she shrieked on her way out.

To replace Angela, we hired Jim. He was a young man in his twenties with a rather rakish air and a well-crafted resume showing considerable food service experience. Daria said she liked working with him, which was all I thought I needed to know. He set up the salad bar in the morning and did some prep and cleaning. We tried having a barbecue outside during the afternoon break and put him in charge, but we never could make money at it. The final straw was when he sold out of everything we had, yet after food, labor, and propane costs, our entire day's profit was twenty dollars. I was done subsidizing the barbecue in hopes of building it up and too distracted to question the numbers. Having one less thing on my plate was a huge relief.

Jim lived with his mother, who was disabled. They were having problems making ends meet, so I was generous with advances. Every day it seemed he would need twenty or forty dollars. It was paid back with each paycheck, but he wasn't netting that much by payday, so the cycle would continue. I felt bad about not being able to pay our employees more—most were at minimum wage plus a few dollars from the tip jar, but the money just wasn't there. To compensate, I was flexible with advances and scheduling. Most employees were appreciative, but in Jim's case, this was a mistake I should have recognized.

Neither Ari nor the usually jovial Lenny shared Daria's high regard for Jim. Both described him as disrespectful and lazy. I was so glad he and Daria were compatible and could get the buffet out on their own in the mornings that I overlooked those comments. I was already tuning out Ari's relentless complaints and thought Lenny might be jealous, since he and Daria had been a couple. ("I just want to punch him in the face," he told me once, then assured me it was only a fantasy.)

GROWING THE BUSINESS

Ari and I constantly butted heads about the employees. He cared, but only if they met his standards. In other words, if they were like superstar Daria or our utility guy, Paul. Everyone else he saw as slackers, and he took their shortcomings personally, as a sign of disrespect to him. This created a lot of daily tension—between us and with the crew.

We saw our roles differently, and the best answer was somewhere in the middle, although we couldn't seem to get there. My priority was to support the staff so they could do their best. As I saw it, my job was to make sure they had the training, support, and materials they needed—which meant running to the store on a moment's notice, washing dishes, or jumping in on the cooking and helping them navigate the rough spots. I took pleasure in working alongside them. Ari seemed solely focused on performance. I sensed he was working with images from the movies, where the owner sits in a corner drinking with some important guest while the invisible employees do the work necessary to make everything run smoothly. "That's what they're paid for! If they don't like it, they can leave!" he would tell me.

Turnover of employees is common in the restaurant business, but I wanted to retain anyone we had seen fit to hire. We had over eighty employees come and go during our ten-year tenure. Some stayed a few days, others three years or longer, and the process of attracting, interviewing, auditioning, and training new people was exhausting, as was dealing with sudden holes in the schedule when someone didn't show up and the intense drama others brought with them. We seemed stuck with hiring marginal people with potential, and I wasn't confident in most cases that we could afford anyone better. We couldn't even afford ourselves! I had yet to draw a paycheck, and Ari was getting only enough to cover his rent. It still seemed our solution would be to get more customers so we could benefit from economies of scale.

We were diversifying our customer base—including workers from the nearby county offices, health-conscious families, members of the recovery community, and some of our musicians, writers, and artists and their audiences. This had come at a cost—thousands in radio and print advertising—but seemed to be worth it. I sent out frequent emails and maintained a presence on Facebook vegan groups as well as on entertainment pages and, of course, our own. I posted flyers at the junior college and at the Market. Once we acquired Wi-Fi for customers, I subscribed to a program that would capture data and allow me to send notices to the 1,500 or so people who used the service. I could ignore the frequent solicitations from people promising to put us at the top of the online search engines. A simple Google search for "Vegetarian Santa Rosa" or "Vegan Santa Rosa" always placed us in the premier spot.

When the junior college closed again for the summer, business fell—but not as drastically as it had the year before. In anticipation of another large dip, I had signed up with Groupon, a popular online discount program. The five hundred two-for-one coupons we had made available sold out in a few hours. Some went to existing customers, but the promotion brought in many new ones.

Daria's mother was coming to town, and Daria's excitement seemed un-characteristically girlish. They hadn't seen each other for years since the mom had left her on her own at sixteen. Daria needed two extra days off to prepare, planning outings they would both enjoy while catching up. I was excited to hear all about it. When Daria returned to work, she looked dour.

"So, how was it?"

"Oh, it was fine until she got arrested."

The story involved alcohol and warrants—and a vulnerable young woman being wounded one more time. I expressed sympathy but kept my opinions to myself, knowing how powerful a child's longing for even the most dysfunctional parent can be. We cooked together, mostly in silence, and made it through.

Ari had the idea of "Dining with Authors." This came to fruition when we were approached by Jeane Slone, an author and entrepreneur who represented eighty other Sonoma County authors. She was hoping to display some of their books in the restaurant, as she had at other restaurants and coffee shops. Ari pitched his vision of bringing in a few authors and inviting the public to dine at their tables and talk about books, writing, or any other topic. The social and dining hour would be followed by short readings. Jeane embraced the concept and organized the events, which happened regularly for several years. I would describe them accurately as literary salons with lively, intelligent conversations.

The authors' readings were delightfully diverse, but it's amazing how clueless some people can be about the suitability of their material. We didn't think to control the participants, and some of the short readings were horrendous. One woman selected a description of her son's stinky gym shoes. I'm sure everyone was struck by her mastery of craft, but it was hard to consider eating after hearing her. Another was a war veteran who chose to read a piece replete with cursing, shouting, and painfully graphic carnage. I believe Jeane cautioned her authors after that.

These evenings were a boon for the restaurant: We could always count on a full house. Books were also on a shelf unit for sale. I was amazed none was ever stolen.

In November, we extended an invitation to Veterans for Peace, composed locally of fifteen men and one woman who had served in Vietnam, to be our guests for dinner on Veterans Day. In anticipation of their visit, I purchased a journal and placed it on a table with a vase of white carnations and a sign inviting customers to write messages to the veterans. I wrote on the first page, ending with, "You were my boys of summer. I loved you then, I love you now. Thank you for your continuing service." It was interesting to see what others wrote. Most were brief: "Thank you for your service." One man, who had been a regular customer, wrote several rageful paragraphs on how they should have gone to Canada, as he had, rather than participate in the war machine. There were heartfelt messages from fellow vets, saying, "You were right. Thank you for telling the truth." Others wrote of their fathers lost in that war or forever damaged by it. One younger man, possibly a recent war veteran, sat in front of the book for a very long time, just staring at it. Finally, he scrawled something and left quickly. Of course, I rushed over to see what it was. It simply said, "Thank you." The depth of emotion still felt, over four decades later, came through poignantly on those pages.

We prepared a nice table for the vets, with red, white, and blue flowers and wine. Although some of them may have missed meat, they enjoyed the acknowledgment and the chance to socialize and were touched by the journal. As pacifists, they told me, they did not feel welcome at the American Legion and VFW dinners. They left a large pile of cash on the table, probably more than we had expended on their behalf. I was happy to share it with Paul, whose work continued to be stellar in any position, but was less so with Lenny.

Lenny was tired of doing dishes, and we were moving him over to the prep side. As we had prepared to host the Veterans for Peace, we were horrified to find the day shift had left us with shortages, and Paul and I scrambled to fill the tables before the vets arrived. Paul had set right to work, making fresh steamed vegetables, brown rice, ginger-chili salsa, and pasta; topping up the salad bar; heating more marinara sauce; and replenishing the bread and pudding. Meanwhile, Lenny was making halavah for the next day and taking up two-thirds of the precious prep table space in the kitchen. He had stressed the motor on the blender by adding too many figs at once, despite previous warnings, and he had added two gallons of water to the mix instead of three quarts. I told him to dump the batch and start over. He repeated both mistakes—with the figs and with the water. The next morning, the new batch of halavah was inedible—much to Daria's disgust.

I couldn't justify keeping him on anymore. He was burnt out on dishes yet was a liability on the prep side. He had skated on his humor and considerable charm, but that had worn thin, especially when we found out he amused himself by throwing our knives into the butcher block table, points first. Ari and I agreed to let him go; it was hard for both of us. He had been with us from the beginning, and he was lovable. Ari, despite being exasperated by Lenny's inefficiency and overly playful approach to work, was fond of him. We didn't know then that he was dyslexic as well as epileptic, which might have accounted for his difficulties following recipes. Even so, there were enough other things. We were done.

I barely slept that night, dreading the confrontation to come. Firing Angela had been relatively easy, but Gaia's Garden had been Lenny's home in some ways, and his first job. He was part of our original "family," and I loved him for his humor and optimism, but we were clearly at the end of our road. I placated my sense of guilt by preparing a generous severance package.

Waiting until the end of his shift the next night, I asked him to stay after. "This is hard, Lenny, but it's time for us to move on separately. You're burned out on dishes and not ready for prep. I hope you find a job you really like, but this isn't working for either of us. There's a month's pay here to buy you some time." As I handed him his last check plus four weeks of severance pay, I assured him I would not contest his unemployment insurance claim.

Lenny was shocked, then enraged, screaming, "WHAT? YOU'RE FIR-ING ME? I CAN'T BELIEVE YOU WOULD DO THIS!" He grabbed up the paperwork and his skateboard and stormed out. Butch saw him later that night and reported he was still infuriated. I was concerned Daria might be upset when I told her in the morning. She said only "OK," but her expression said, "What took you so long?"

(We didn't see Lenny for another couple of years. When he finally came in, we shared a hug, and he showed me a zine he was working on. Ari saw him a few times later at other places and always had pleasant interactions. The last time he saw him, Lenny had matured and seemed happy. He had a cooking job he loved. As Ari said, "A lot of these kids grew up at our place.")

I was now pleased with our crew, for the most part. Daria, Paul, Butch, and Mason were solid. There was a lot of laughter and joking in the kitchen as well as more personal, trusting conversations, and we were turning out wonderful food. I loved working with them and took advantage of my position to make sure every new hire listened to the Carrot Joke. I told them it was part of their orientation. Gather 'round, children:

(trigger warning: punchline is funny but not politically correct)

The Carrot Joke

Farmer Brown was harvesting carrots one day when he came across the largest carrot top he had ever seen. Pulling it out was impossible, so he started digging around it with a shovel. It took him most of the day, but finally he gave it one last pull, and out it came, with such force that he fell over backward. It was nearly six feet long!

To his amazement, the carrot stood up on its pointy end, shook off some dirt, and exclaimed, "Thank you! I'm so glad to be out of there!"

"What? You can talk? You're a talking carrot?"

"Of course I am," replied the carrot. "What would you like to talk about?"

Farmer Brown lived alone and was glad to have company. He took the carrot home, and the carrot became like the son he never had. The carrot loved music, especially rock and roll, and he had natural ability. Farmer Brown bought him an electric guitar and an amp, and the carrot would play amazing riffs with his tendrils.

Soon word got out about the amazing talking, rocking carrot, and he became famous. He went on tour, and his shows were always sold out. At the pinnacle of his career, he was performing on the rim of the Grand Canyon. This momentous event was covered by all the major networks. The carrot was rocking out so hard that he lost his balance and fell over the edge into the canyon below!

Farmer Brown raced to the bottom and found the paramedics already there. They were scraping up carrot parts and carrot pulp and putting them into the ambulance. Farmer Brown, his heart in his throat, followed them to the hospital.

Finally the doctor came into the waiting room, where Farmer Brown had been pacing anxiously for hours.

"Doctor! Doctor! How is my carrot?"

"Well, I have good news and bad news."

"Give me the good news!"

"Your carrot will live."

"Oh, thank God! My carrot will live! What could be the bad news?"

"For the rest of his life, he'll be a vegetable."

Everyone seemed to enjoy it as much as I loved telling it.

Jim seemed like a weak link, but Daria liked working with him. I was concerned with the frequent advances on his paychecks and his bad habit of loudly inhaling snot when working in the dining room. This certainly didn't enhance the customer experience, and although I mentioned it to him, he continued. Ari was constantly reminding him to pull his pants up; his response was that he was built "weird" and they kept falling down. Ari introduced the concept of a belt, but apparently that was a bridge too far.

One dark, rainy morning, when Jim, Mason, and I were scheduled to work together, Jim called out with a "stomach flu." Mason wasn't buying it. "*I* woke up hungover, next to a woman, and *I'm* here."

Ari and another musician—Doug Jayne—made plans for a New Year's Eve party. Projects like this inevitably involved more work on my part than on Ari's, but it still seemed like a good idea. Doug's band, Stupid White People, had a good draw, and Doug, with his characteristic dry humor, had prepared promo that included "Ask your doctor if healthy eating is right for you!" We had a full house that night.

I was concerned about alcohol consumption, remembering my own past. So far, sales had been slow. Ours wasn't the kind of place where people just sat and drank, but this was New Year's Eve. To me, it had always been about alcohol, a welcome excuse for bacchanalian excess with normal drinkers imbibing like I did every day. We would be liable if we overserved anyone who got into trouble.

In addition to dinner, I planned snacks to be distributed throughout the evening and a simple but hearty buffet of black-eyed peas, greens, and corn bread at midnight, making sure we had plenty of sparkling water and apple juice in addition to champagne. The band and the party were upbeat and fun. I was surprised at how moderate the guests were in their drinking—nothing like how I remembered my own socially sanctioned annual blowouts. Many turned down the champagne or had a couple of flutes full, then switched to water. No one seemed to be overindulging, although the ticket price had included unlimited food and champagne. When it was over, I stood by the door—thanking everyone for coming but also making sure they seemed steady enough to drive. They all passed my scrutiny. Picking up glasses later, I was amazed to see how many were still half full.

Our gross for the year was $186,000, and our net was minus $27,600—a significant loss but proportionately less than the year before. Maybe we were going in the right direction. I had heard it was not uncommon for restaurants to take three years before becoming profitable but saw no reason why it would take us that long. We had a good crew, great food, and loyal customers. Surely 2011 would be better. I was running short of cash but still had assets. I hoped I wouldn't have to liquidate them. I thought it was all about staying the course, believing in our mission, and relying on our employees. I had yet to learn it wasn't that simple.

SNAKE

P aul, our globe-trotting utility guy, was in Bali, and we all missed him, especially since Jim's work was deteriorating. Daria liked working with him, though, and he had good prep skills, so I thought we needed him. I spoke with Jim often about taking long, unauthorized breaks, being tardy, working slowly, loudly banging tables and chairs next to diners, and leaving cleaning supplies where people could trip over them. He would promise to do better and would for a while, then he'd sink back into the same bad behavior.

Things came to a head toward the end of March. On a Thursday, Mason reported to Ari that he had seen Jim around the register and thought he had taken money. When Ari counted, he was fifty dollars short. We'd had a recent series of shortages, but I hadn't been too concerned. Ari was inept as a cashier, and I knew that neither he nor I were stealing. I hadn't considered that anyone else would have the audacity to go into the register.

I was wrong. A belated analysis showed the major shortages (as much as fifty to one hundred dollars each) coincided with Jim's work schedule. We agreed to fire him for other causes and cut our losses, since we couldn't prove the thefts. At the time, we were seriously short-staffed. We decided to keep him on for two more days, until Saturday, and contain him—making sure the keys to the register were always on our persons and inventorying the beverages constantly, since we knew he had taken some of them without paying.

The next day, Friday, an employee from the Market told us they were missing $300 and suspected Jim. He seemed too comfortable wandering into their offices from our back exit, which led into their auxiliary office and then to the street. We had suspected he was using that route to take unauthorized breaks and had become sure of it when he set off the alarm the night before—although he had denied doing it. The Market's motion sensors indicated he had headed for their main office, where the money had been left out by mistake, rather than to the street for an illicit smoke.

We were still planning to fire him but wanted to do so at the end of his shift on Saturday, since he was the only one available to work with Daria in the morning. At 9 a.m., Ari called me. He had found a tackle box in the employee bathroom containing drug paraphernalia. What should he do? Confiscate it, I told him, and tell Jim to hit the bricks; I would come in and finish the shift. When Ari headed back to get the box, Jim was bringing it out of the restroom. Ari asked him about it and was told it contained "art supplies." Citing privacy rights, he refused to let Ari inspect it. Ari told him he was fired and to leave immediately—which he did.

We filled Daria in on what we had learned from the Market and our concerns about the register. I was also finally connecting the dots to include the constant advances, the snotting, and the supposed failure of our barbecue project. She heard us out, then said she'd had no idea any of this was happening.

After she left for the day, I received a call from Jim. He stated the "allegations" were "pretentious" and knew every detail we had shared only with Daria. I told him he was barred from the restaurant and that I would meet him across the street to give him his final check. When I did, I noticed he resembled Beetlejuice in his black-and-white vertically striped pants. He started to plead his case. "Get help," I told him and walked away.

Shortly thereafter, Mason brought in a flyer from a local gas station. It was a picture of Jim from their security camera and the accusation he had stolen from them.

Daria's involvement was problematic. Other employees were now letting it slip that she and Jim had been intimately involved. Daria and I hadn't had much private time in the kitchen as our staffing increased, and she had always been reticent about discussing her romantic life, if she even had one. She and Jim had had a lot of alone time since I wasn't there as much in the mornings, and apparently more had been cooking than I'd thought. I hadn't suspected a thing, assuming she had higher standards. She was so wise, so capable, that I had overlooked the penchant of troubled young women to seek lower companions—just as I had in my tumultuous youth.

Still, she had proven her loyalty to us again and again. Was it possible she hadn't known? Maybe she had known about the drugs, which she should have told us about, but not the stealing. We assumed that, with her having the whole story, her relationship with Jim would be ending.

Desperate to fill out our staff, we hired two young women whose tenures were short and not memorable. Another short-termer, Cirak, was different. He came in to see if he could work in exchange for food that night, so we traded him an hour of dishwashing for a meal. He was soft-spoken and intelligent and had a pulse, so we hired him.

I heard from a few mutual acquaintances that his family and friends were delighted that Cirak had a job. Unfortunately, it lasted only a month. He became disoriented amid the hustle of the kitchen, which got very intense and was better suited to the energy of testosterone-fueled punk rockers than that of more gentle souls. Also, he spoke so softly that the only way to communicate with him was to drop everything and stand close. Ari saw it as a power trip. Mason and Butch told me he gave them the creeps. I saw that it disrupted the flow. I told Cirak we had no more hours to give him, which was a lie but the kindest approach I could muster.

I would see Cirak occasionally when downtown; he remained shy but friendly. Five years later, on June 28, 2016, an article in the Santa Rosa *Press Democrat* started with the following:

Cirak Tesfazgi appeared to have set up camp around midnight Monday morning in a downtown Santa Rosa doorway alcove....

A college graduate with a love of poetry, for years a fixture at downtown cafes, a first-generation American whose wide smile was readily recognized by strangers, Tesfazgi suffered more than 50 stab wounds early Monday morning, likely caused by a bent chef's knife police found on the ground near the alcove at 418 Riley St.

Accompanying the article was a collection of Cirak's poems. His assailant was later caught when he randomly attacked another man in a movie theater.

His mother had tried to protect Cirak from the streets, her door always open, but he preferred being outside.

Several years later, I would learn Cirak as a younger man had been a very different person – outgoing, athletic and ambitious. A major car accident had profoundly changed him, and the aftermath had brought him to this horrific encounter with a crazed stranger.

We didn't know all that then, of course, and were focused on our rapid turnover, which was becoming exhausting. Fortunately, the restaurant gods took pity on us and sent Eric. His resume indicated managerial experience, so I let him know our opening was for a dishwasher, which might be too far down the scale for him. His response was that work was strictly a means to an end. His real interests were in the arts, and he only needed to sustain himself. He was meticulous, cooperative, focused, and congenial. In a short time, he became another valuable utility guy—moving easily among the dish pit, the prep tables, and the register. His managerial skills were evident, and I appreciated the humility with which he used them to support rather than overtly judge us. His detachment from the job probably served us all well.

One day I was showing him how to transfer flour from a fifty-pound bag into a large plastic container. It didn't go as planned, and I ended up dusted with flour from head to toe. Just then, I was called to the dining room to meet someone's parents. Still powdered, looking like the Ghost of Gaia's Garden, I spoke with them briefly, then excused myself: "I have to see if Eric needs me to show him anything else."

I thought that was one of the funniest things I had ever said, but their blank looks indicated I wasn't connecting with the house.

Millennials like Eric (and Gens X and Z) get a bad rap for lacking proper work ethic. This was not our experience. Some employees of all ages were slackers. Our crew of young people did not equate their identities with their jobs as generations before had, yet they showed up and offered a fair exchange of labor for money. In some ways, it was more than fair. At their ages, when I worked "throw-away" restaurant and clerical jobs, I could afford my own apartment, food, a car, alcohol, pot, and an occasional movie. These young people could only dream of having their own places; they had to contend with roommates or live with their parents. Most rode bicycles, walked, or took the bus, yet they regularly went the extra mile. I became fond of saying, "You can pay people to work, but you can't pay them to care." In spite of difficult circumstances, many of them did care. Such people are solid gold to an employer, and I appreciated them.

I came to love most of the younger people who worked at Gaia's Garden. So many were fighting their way out of deprivation and trauma with courage, optimism, and energy—they touched and inspired me. Somehow, these children of chaos were able to show up every day on time (mostly) and work hard. We met many at their personal crossroads, where some would keep moving toward a quality life and others would slide back down the tubes. Our greatest success as an enterprise was to provide encouragement and a space to learn for those who were ready for it.

Ari didn't see it that way. Frustrated with our power imbalance, my unwillingness to discipline employees to his satisfaction, and his own financial hardships, he became increasingly irate, leaving angry notes for me and the crew detailing our shortcomings. Most of the time, he was right, yet he lacked interest in considering the context or working cooperatively on solutions. Often, while the crew was slammed or recovering from an onslaught, he would appear in the kitchen, read everyone the riot act, then storm out. After one of these "drive-bys," as I called them, Mason broke the tension: "WE'RE ALL GONNA DIE!" The laughter was welcome, but the problems were escalating.

SCHOOLED

In May, near our second anniversary, we were approached to cater lunches at a Montessori preschool. My initial reaction was to decline. I was overwhelmed already, and this seemed like one more huge thing. Too much. Ari argued we should hear the lady out. He was right.

They had about sixty students during the summer and eighty in the winter. Maureen, the director of the school, had worked with Gopal, but there had been problems that went too long unaddressed, so the school had found another supplier. That person had suddenly quit. It was Friday. She needed us to start Monday. The school would supply several hotel pans and a rolling Cambro unit to retain heat during the delivery. She would provide information on serving sizes and suggested menus. Further, she pledged to give us feedback both positive and negative so the relationship could progress smoothly. In other words, we were being offered training, support, and all the extra equipment we would need—and getting paid. Some quick mental math indicated the monthly billings for eighty kids would cover our rent.

Of course, we agreed. The school treated lunch as part of the curriculum—serving it on china, teaching about sharing and nutrition while encouraging conversation. Their values aligned with our menu—everything was to be plant-based. Maureen had done the program herself initially and let us know that for the children, simple and bland were good, and they were highly suspicious of bits of things (like vegetables) in their food. No tree nuts or peanuts were allowed on campus, to ensure against allergic reactions. Sugar overstimulated the kids, so we weren't to use it.

For the first month, I prepared the lunches, which consisted of "entrées" such as mac and cheese, chili, or tofu nuggets with rice, and sides of vegetables and fruit. Daria made a suitably bland salsa (blended, no chunks) for burritos, and we were told one of the children had declared it "good enough to be from a restaurant." High praise indeed.

Maureen gave us the recipe for "shaky shake," which was simply equal portions of brewer's yeast and sesame seeds ground together. The kids loved it and put it on everything. In time, the sesame was eliminated due to allergy concerns, so we just sent brewer's yeast (a source of B vitamins with a slightly cheesy flavor) as needed. I received a desperate call from a mother whose child wouldn't eat anything at home without shaky shake. Would I please, please share the recipe? We both had a laugh when she found out how simple it was.

Some of the parents began coming in as customers. One told Ari that when asked how his day at school had gone, her child would launch into a detailed description of his lunch. As my confidence grew, I decided to hire someone for this project.

The applicants were not impressive, so I picked the one who seemed most interested. Cilla and I worked together for the first two weeks, giving her time to learn all the recipes and get used to the routine. Once on her own, it became evident she was out of her depth, despite having worked for a caterer. After two and a half months, I let her go. We had managed to stay in the school's good graces, but the demands on Daria and me to take up the slack made the situation untenable. I knew Cilla had tried in her own way, though, and I felt some responsibility for putting her into a job she was unprepared for. She left with two weeks' severance, a letter stressing her few good points, and a gift card for the restaurant.

I saw Cilla a few years later. She was working as a magician's assistant and was headed to Canada to audition for Cirque du Soleil. The varied lives of the young people who passed through Gaia's Garden brought me amazement and joy. I love quirky stories, and we had many!

A lovely metalhead girl left our employ suddenly to accompany her favorite band on tour as their manager.

We had two young combat veterans who had chosen different paths for their healing. One had driven around the country in her van for a few years. She was great working in the front of house until her van blew up and she went into full PTSD and disappeared. Another had gone to Peru to take ayahuasca after his discharge. We lost him as a prep cook suddenly when the shaman invited him back as her assistant. I couldn't fault him for that. I would have done the same thing at his age.

BUSINESS AS USUAL

I learned Daria was still seeing Jim when someone reported that her car was parked in the lot next door and her dog was inside, in distress. After a flurry of drama involving police and a broken window, Daria returned to work cursing Jim, who had been entrusted with both car and dog. She vowed this was it; she was done with him for sure. I wanted to believe her, so I did.

Jerome applied to be a cook, telling us he wanted to work in a plant-based kitchen. I was concerned by his shaved head—he had the look of a zealot—but he seemed grounded. After the Jim debacle, I had vowed to check references. Jerome had been cooking at a local Italian restaurant, and their feedback was positive. To my relief, he had skills and worked efficiently on the school lunches and, later, the night cooking shift. He was pleasant, and Paul was back. It seemed we were on track with our employees again.

Jerome self-identified as a drug addict in recovery and shared a tidbit he had picked up in rehab: the Black chef there always put vinegar in the frying oil. The combined credentials of *Black* and *rehab chef* related to deep frying inspired me enough to try it once after Jerome had left our employ. Short on details, I dumped a quarter cup of vinegar into a huge wok of boiling oil. Immediately, a pillar of flame shot up about three feet, then settled into a ring of fire around the small stove. By the time Ari had grabbed the fire extinguisher, the fire was out, leaving me a little shaky with a greasy floor to clean.

On a later occasion, I timidly added a tablespoon of vinegar to the oil before heating it but didn't notice a significant result.

For now, though, Jerome was with us and, having some breathing room, I worked on a vegan Thai green curry sauce. There were good prepared versions, but they contained fish sauce. I loved the scents and tastes of the lemongrass, galangal (blue ginger), and kafir lime leaves. As with our Indian recipes, I felt honored to work with new exotic, fragrant ingredients. It's fortunate I enjoyed the process, since the final recipe was complicated, with extensive prep. Customers said they loved it. Ari was not a fan. A friend came in who traveled extensively in Thailand. I waited for his opinion. "Well, Susan, it's delicious, but it's not Thai." I went with it anyway.

It was with great satisfaction that I began adding my own recipes as we were phasing out the nonvegan ones. Not all were successful, but beet soup, stuffed cabbage, and coconut tofu were among those popular enough to earn a place in the rotation.

Business was increasing, but so were our employee costs. Ari and I both wondered how Gopal had made things seem so easy. Perhaps keeping it small was the key, because we were caught in a vicious cycle of needing more money to cover payroll and supplies, expanding our hours, which necessitated hiring more crew, then needing more money. Our food costs seemed in line with industry standards, but our rent and employee expenses were soaring. Ari was in favor of raising prices more than I was, and

I should have listened to him. We were both afraid of losing customers, and we already heard constant complaints that our prices were too high. Instead of stepping back to do intense analysis and then take appropriate action, I kept my head down and threw money at the business.

I transferred money to our account as needed, running up then paying down then running up again the equity line on Mom's house, which was now mine. I had to liquidate my IRA. When I talked with Richard about the restaurant, he would usually ask, "Are you making any money?"—a question that always made me anxious. We didn't discuss specifics, and our money was separate. I let him know we weren't yet profitable but hoped to be soon. I lacked the words to effectively communicate what I was getting from it—the deep engagement, the creativity, the personal interactions, the sense of community, the chance to do service, and the adrenaline rush. It was my thing, and when Richard and I were together, I focused as much as possible on our things. Richard was always supportive, though, when I had to rush off to the restaurant to cover a shift or deliver supplies—which was often.

I still had the privilege of resources to back this venture and was optimistic enough to believe we would one day get into the black. In the meantime, we made changes where we thought we could.

In September, we raised prices slightly. Keeping lunch the same, at $8.95 for the full buffet, we increased dinner by a dollar, bringing it to $10.95. Hoping to provide a sense of added value, I included a second entrée in the dinner buffet, making sure one was always vegan. We eliminated the student and senior discounts and added the Blue Plate Special, an oval plate smaller than the dinner plate and upon which customers could pile anything from either side of the buffet, one time only, for a cost of $6.95 at lunch, $8.95 at dinner. I was surprised how many people were not familiar with that term.

During the Depression, a working person could get a solid meal—usually meat loaf and mashed potatoes and gravy with canned green beans—for twenty-five cents. Allowing for inflation, ours was also a good deal and became popular. I considered purchasing actual blue plates, but we would have had to sell several hundred specials to cover the cost.

DAYS OF WINE AND SOME BOOZERS

Some people were amazed to learn we had beer and wine. "Sure," I'd tell them. "There's no meat in it." I think they thought vegetarians and vegans were too sanctimonious to imbibe.

The wine and beer weren't big sellers, though, and we dispensed with the port and sake. We sold some wine at night and also had customers who would bring their own and pay a corkage fee of $8. Ari handled these transactions well, but I was not adept at opening wine. Working the front alone one night, I told the first such customer I was not the right person for the job but would provide them with a corkscrew and glasses, waiving the corkage fee. She insisted on taking me through the motions, showing me how to open the bottle and present the cork, insisting on paying corkage anyway. She was gregarious and kind. A few years later, I began seeing her at meetings for recovering alcoholics.

A wealthy real estate agent and his wife would come in for lunch, sharply dressed and with their own expensive bottle. I had gained experience by then, but on one occasion the cork started crumbling. I worked carefully, whimpering softly, trying not to ruin their costly wine, but every turn just made the situation worse. The customer came over to see what was taking so long, then went to his car for his own corkscrew. This didn't work well either. "Oh, just push it through," he said. I associated this solution with drinking under the freeway, not the upscale lifestyle of these customers, but went ahead. He insisted on paying the corkage fee anyway, which was classy. Perhaps he suspected, as I did, that someone had let the cork dry out.

Dr. April Hurley, who worked at the Free Clinic, would buy ten dollar gift certificates to give out to her patients. This was enough at the time for a good lunch. I was touched by one man's shyness. He was homeless and probably felt unwelcome in most places. We didn't have table service, but that day we did. I was honored to serve him, chat with him, and treat him like a valuable human being. I'm sure that's what Dr. Hurley had intended. A couple of old codgers came in another time and asked if they could use their certificates for beer. Figuring it wasn't up to me to force nutrition on them, I served them two rounds each. That probably wasn't what Dr. Hurley had intended, but the guys had a grand time.

We never attracted the clientele that might have demanded to be over-served. Our wholesome, healthy hippie vibe was probably what made blues and comedy nights unsuccessful, despite great talent. There was only one customer who appeared to be a late-stage alcoholic, and she would come in sometimes for her morning drink in such obvious pain that I could only accommodate her need. I looked for an opening to see if I might share some recovery encouragement with her, but she would come, gulp, and go before we had any chance to talk. She was a friend of a friend of the restaurant, and I was assured several of her peers had attempted interventions.

WHY CAN'T WE ALL JUST GET ALONG?

We entered another period of mass dissension in the ranks during the fall. Ari was constantly irritated with Mason, and Butch and Jerome were butting heads. Mason didn't like how Ari talked to him; Ari considered Mason insubordinate; Jerome stood up for Ari, saying Ari treated everyone the same and he, Jerome, had no problem with Ari. Mason thought Jerome was sucking up and undercutting him, and my head hurt.

Butch went on tour again, this time to Europe. When he returned, he told us about performing in Germany for an audience of six thousand and seeing them mouth the words to his original songs! After such a heady experience, I wondered how he could return to a minimum wage dishwashing job. Apparently, he wondered the same, and his work began deteriorating, interrupted by unauthorized breaks and excessive phone time in the bathroom. This prompted a sign that was only moderately effective: "IF YOU NEED TO SPEND MORE THAN 5 MINUTES IN HERE, TAKE ANOTHER 5 AND CALL IT YOUR BREAK. IF YOU NEED TO DO THIS MORE THAN ONCE A SHIFT, CALL YOUR

DOCTOR." To make sure they got the point, I added a graphic of a cell phone in a circle with a line through it. Like Ari's notes, it had some initial impact but quickly became invisible.

Butch was our first employee to be put on probation. It was only for a month, and he improved his habits, but clearly the job was no longer high on his list of "productive activities." He also resented being suspected in a purse theft that had occurred in the office of the Market, since he would walk through there to sneak smoke breaks. We didn't believe he was guilty, but Ari reminded him that since the Jim incident, there had been a sign on the door clearly marking their office out of bounds.

Ian, our rotund customer with autism, was not among my favorites, since he ate huge amounts of food and talked incessantly. My perspective shifted one evening when he informed me he was having a guest in to celebrate her birthday. He had brought flowers for the table, a card, and a gift. Inspecting the buffet tables in advance, he pointed out a few items that needed to be topped up and asked me to make a fresh pan of steamed vegetables. He was right, and I complied.

His guest was the older woman he occasionally dined with; I had seen them together before but had no idea what their relationship might be. After he had paid for their dinners, they seated themselves at the booth next to the register, making it possible for me to hear their conversation. He was telling her what a great year he'd had, listing various highlights, ending with "Last year I didn't have any friends, but now I have good friends like you! And now I have a job and can afford to buy you dinner and a present!"

I was ashamed of my past judgments. Here was a man swimming up-stream, making the best of the difficult hand he had been dealt. He was creative and outgoing and building a satisfying life for himself, including friendships he valued. I had focused so much on how much he ate and how he distracted me from my oh-so-important responsibilities that I had overlooked all that. I vowed to do better.

THE CRUST PUNK

One afternoon, a solidly built young man named Brian came in looking for a dishwashing job. He was dressed completely in black, had a large septum ring (which I would previously have called a nose ring), and his arms were tattooed—although his body art seemed less professionally done than that of my crew members. His résumé was poorly formatted and gave only one reference. Something about him resonated well with me, and he looked strong. I told him I'd let him know.

As soon as he left, Daria and Mason accosted me. "Don't hire him! He's a crust punk!" My education continued. There are subgenres of punk. Mason and Butch were at an upper level, in their opinion, while crust punks were the lowest—homeless, surviving by crime, chronically drunk, drugged, and dirty. I thanked them for their input and, when I got home, called the reference. He seemed puzzled. "Brian, Brian. . . . Uh, I think that's my daughter's boyfriend. He seems OK."

The next morning, Daria and Mason were quick to tell me they had asked around and heard Brian was cleaning up his act. They regretted having said anything and didn't want to hurt his chances of employment. "Don't worry," I assured them, "I already hired him."

The job of dishwashers—or, as we would come to call them, dish lords—is difficult, and their services are vital. They get the least respect and are usually paid the minimum, yet their absence on a shift can be disastrous, especially in a buffet restaurant. The work is physically demanding and repetitive, and there are requirements:

1. Get the dishes clean

2. Break as few as possible

3. Put things back in the right places

4. Work quickly but quietly

5. Keep food out of the grease trap

6. Keep the floor dry for safety and leave it and the sinks clean and dry at end of shift

Brian did all this from the start. He would show up early for his shift so consistently that if he were not there half an hour before his start time, we would become concerned. He was focused and reserved, and he took direction well from Ari. This was a huge relief, since Ari and Mason were bickering constantly. I told Mason he would need to find a way to deal with Ari, since Ari would neither change nor leave.

INTEGRITY

N aomi came to work for us toward the end of 2011. A pretty blonde still in her teens, she had completed a baking program in high school. Unlike most of our employees, she was committed to a career in food service. Her mother, it turned out, was the temporarily lapsed Christian who had returned our dollar. They were both members of the church associated with the plant-based restaurant that had opened north of us, and Naomi had been working there until it closed abruptly. Our competitor had been suffering, in part because some customers didn't like seeing religious tracts and posters; there were also juicy rumors of internal scandals and unpaid bills.

Naomi had some of her own vegan recipes as well as one for a vegan cheesecake that she had learned from the chef at her previous job. I was concerned about the ethics of using someone else's recipe, since I didn't want mine leaving my restaurant. I had a chance to ask Alice, the now former manager of the other restaurant, if she would reach out to the chef and request permission. She was effusive in her praise: "That's wonderful. No one has that kind of integrity anymore. You guys really deserve every one of God's blessings, blah, blah." She promised to check with the chef.

When Naomi felt comfortable with me, she revealed that Alice had given up on getting our almond blend dressing recipe legitimately and had paid Jim to steal it for her. She was planning to use it at a restaurant in a nearby county. By coincidence, I had a friend with access to that restaurant's computer, and she offered to go in and delete the recipe. Fortunately, the other restaurant closed before we had to face such an ethical and legal dilemma.

Alice did come in again, and I confronted her. Her denial was so convincing that I would have believed her if Naomi had not described Jim so accurately and had I not belatedly come to know him so well.

She relayed a message from the chef of her former restaurant requesting we not use his cheesecake recipe, and I told Alice to assure him we would honor his request because "integrity is so important." If she detected the edge in my voice, she gave no indication.

We had a modest holiday party for the staff and celebrated the year's end with another New Year's Eve party for the community. At this one, I put a sectioned pomegranate at each table in observance of the Greek custom of smashing the fruit on New Year's Day to bring good luck. Again, the party was a big success with none of the excessive drinking and drama of my pre-sobriety days.

Richard stopped by and later reported a short conversation he'd had with Brian, our crust punk dishwasher.

"So, how do you like your job?"

"I LOVE my job."

His fervor surprised both of us and warmed my heart.

Daria announced she would soon be moving on. She had worked some shifts at an upscale restaurant and was going through the hiring process. Putting on a professional face, I congratulated her, asking that she keep me informed and give me two weeks' notice. Inside, I was shocked and dismayed. She had been such an integral part of the operation, it hadn't occurred to me she might leave. I depended on her a lot and hated the thought of losing her. Still, I didn't own her and could feel satisfaction in having played a role in her transformation from salad maker/dishwasher to a cook position in a fine kitchen.

A few weeks later, she said the job had fallen through. I had regained my emotional equilibrium and sincerely assured her she could rock it at any venue, encouraging her to try other high-end places, just please give us notice. That was the last we heard of any plans to leave.

In 2011, we had increased our gross from $186,000 to $285,000. We had lost $27,600 in 2010, but our negative at this year's end was *only* $3,600. We were going in the right direction. Surely 2012 would be the year we would break through—that magical third year.

We were voted Best Vegetarian Restaurant in Sonoma County in the *Bohemian Magazine* poll. Our Yelp rating was 4.5 stars out of 5. The new year seemed filled with promise.

SOLIDIFYING

My friend Terry came to work for us as night dining room manager. He was in his sixties and had extensive experience at high-end restaurants in Hawaii and San Diego. Working for us in the evening helped smooth out the financial ups and downs of his real estate business, and his experience and polish were a gift to us. Like me, he was an alcoholic in recovery and seemed reluctant to upsell the alcohol, which irritated Ari and should have bothered me more than it did.

Terry was another person I could trust completely, having known him for years and being sure of his character and loyalty. Unfortunately, he took an almost instant dislike to Ari. Both felt disrespected by the other, although Ari was appreciative of the additional front of house coverage and not always aware of Terry's resentments, which I heard about daily. It was good to have another adult on staff. Ari and I started referring to the "AIC" position–"Adult in Charge."

Brian, our crust punk dishwasher, was showing a lot of interest in our food, so I told Jerome to start giving him prep tasks during slow times. Brian was vegan, and I asked him whether it was for health or compassion.

He responded immediately, "Compassion." Given his tough demeanor and rough background, I found his answer quite touching.

A young woman named Rosie came in with a boyfriend looking for work. We liked her and not him and hired her to be a dishwasher. I learned she had aged out of foster care the previous year and was living and working on a ranch associated with her last placement. Neither of us had any way of knowing she would be a big part of Gaia's Garden—off and on—for the next eight years. She was a dark-haired beauty with an engaging smile. Friendly and hardworking, she was amazingly strong for a slender young woman. One morning, when I asked how she was, she acknowledged being a little tired. "I was loading hay bales all morning." (Hay bales weigh at least forty pounds and some weigh as much as one hundred.)

Happy with our new hires, I was able to relax a little. The food was great, shifts were being covered, the crew seemed congenial, the customers were happy, we were getting great reviews, and Ari had created a lively scene in the front with wonderful music and colorful art. He had even scaled back his critiques, although he was constantly annoyed by Mason's attitude, which he found cocky and disrespectful. I adored Mason, and he was a dependable, capable worker, so I stood up for him, antagonizing Ari even more. I was sure we could come to a workable resolution, and on the whole, it seemed things were going smoothly. Taking some deep breaths and focusing more on marketing, I was blissfully unaware of the maelstrom to come.

PART 3

THE OTHER SHOE DROPS

A GATHERING STORM

I gradually became aware something was off with Daria and thought she might be depressed about losing out on the prestigious job. She was coming in late nearly every day and filling out her time card—which was still done by hand—to her benefit. She got the buffet out in the morning, but her half-hour lunch break would frequently become an hour, and she wasn't getting much else done. For the first time in her life, she had made enough money the previous year to owe taxes, and she was very upset when her refund was much less than expected. Now she was always broke and needing advances.

I was concerned and checked in with her regularly, getting different responses including cramps, stomach trouble, or difficulty sleeping. I asked her to see a doctor, and she said she would. Given how much help she had been in the beginning and how much I had come to care for her, I cut her some slack, confident she would work out whatever it was. Even working at half capacity, she was able to accomplish more than anyone else on the prep side (except for Paul, who was in Bali). There were still days when her work was stellar, so I focused my attention on what I thought were bigger problems, including the growing feud between Ari and Mason.

Ari had lost all patience and was demanding I fire Mason. I refused, and we argued incessantly. I had been trying to institute regular employee evaluations and took the opportunity to sit down with Mason and give him a written summary. After enumerating his good points and accomplishments, I cautioned him about speaking to Ari dismissively or insolently. Ari had talked to him numerous times about staying off his phone while at work and the importance of breaking down boxes to clear the hallway, but Mason had not been responsive. Suggesting some changes that might minimize those interactions, I ended that paragraph with "This is not acceptable if we are to go forward." He seemed receptive, but the friction continued.

These constant arguments between Ari and me about how to deal with Mason were becoming unbearably stressful for both of us. To mediate our disputes, we went back to the counselor who had presided over our romantic breakup. After a few sessions, he told Ari that unless Ari was willing to examine his inner life more closely, there was no point in continuing. Ari flat out refused: This was not about *his* problems. I went a few more times on my own.

Mason and I were to meet again at the end of February to discuss progress in the month since his evaluation, but events over the next week took precedence. Mason, it would turn out, was not our biggest problem. First, our night cook, Jerome, came in on a day he wasn't scheduled to work. It seemed my initial assessment of him as a Hare Krishna–type zealot was not entirely unwarranted. He wandered around the restaurant being gently disruptive—placing flowers, figurines, and notes with uplifting messages on available surfaces in the dining room and the kitchen. We watched him for a while in wonder, then suggested he leave.

The next day, he didn't show up for his 2 p.m. shift. Someone told me he was in the back parking lot, and I found him there, arranging camping equipment in the trunk of his car. "What's going on, Jerome?" His answer was a lengthy description of his inner life, culminating in his decision not to take psych meds anymore but to deal with the mania himself, following the dictates of his own soul. Putting the last bundle in the trunk, he turned to me. "I'm getting married today."

"Really? Congratulations. Do I know her?"

"Of course you do. I'm marrying Daria."

"That's funny, she didn't mention it."

"I'm going to ask her later."

I wished him well, knowing he would never be returning to work. Excusing myself, I headed for the kitchen. Daria seemed surprised when I told her. "What? Of course not! We don't even hang out!" It was the end of her shift, so I made sure she got to her car without encountering her suitor.

That evening, an older couple showed up and introduced themselves as Jerome's parents. He had asked them to drive down from Cloverdale to meet their daughter-in-law to be. I gave them some tea, then expressed my concerns about their son's mental state. Their wearied response let me know I had come late to *that* party.

Jerome finally showed up and greeted his parents. "I want you to meet my bride!"

"Daria? Where is she?" I asked.

"She's in the car."

I immediately pictured Daria's corpse propped up in the passenger seat, wearing a bloody white wedding dress with mascara running down her cheeks. "I'm going to go see her."

I was both relieved and surprised to find her still alive, casually walking her dog. She assured me she wasn't there to meet the parents. She and Jerome were "just driving around." Given our conversation just a few hours before, when she had indicated they were not social friends and expressed bewilderment at his imminent proposal, I was thoroughly confused but didn't have time to follow up. I would soon learn there was a lot I didn't know about Daria.

I needed to cover Jerome's shift, and by the time I came out of the kitchen, everyone had dispersed. He wandered in the next day, and I asked him to leave, as his presence was making the other employees nervous.

Daria was late that morning and worked at about 60 percent capacity. She didn't say much other than that Jim and Jerome had had some kind of angry confrontation the night before, and she hadn't slept much. I was shocked to learn she was still seeing Jim after he had stolen from us, brought drugs into the restaurant, and almost killed her dog, but there was a lot I didn't know. As soon as she left, Mason and Butch cornered me by the dish sink and insisted we talk.

"What are you going to do about Daria?"

"I'm not sure. I'm worried about her; she doesn't seem right."

They stared at me in astonishment, then launched into what I quickly realized was an intervention.

"She's strung out on heroin!"

"She nods out in the booths and has track marks!"

"She's a master manipulator!"

"She shows up looking half dead, like her face is melting!"

"She pulls it together when you're here, then she doesn't do anything and leaves it all for Mason!"

"She didn't get that other job because they wanted a drug test!"

"She was going to take a week off to kick but couldn't afford it because her tax refund was short!"

I knew they were right. Of course they were right. Ari had expressed his suspicions about the job that had fallen through, but we both thought it might have been due to pot, which was not an issue for us. But heroin?

Not Daria! She had been with us from the beginning, almost three years in which we had worked side by side nearly every day—cooking, creating, having deep conversations, overcoming obstacles. We had become so compatible in the kitchen that we navigated its narrow corridor like dancers, anticipating each other's moves in wordless cooperation. We had helped each other push through rough days and had celebrated triumphs both culinary and personal. She had made a vegan Italian wedding soup! She had saved my ass many times. I loved her Goth stoicism, her dry humor, her meticulous work, and her perseverance. She was so smart, so talented! So strong! How could I have missed that she was strung out? I was grateful these two young men had seen what I hadn't and been willing to confront me—but I was embarrassed that they'd had to.

The next day, we got the buffet out, then I requested a sit-down with Daria. I told her she needed a plan, and I would work with her if I could. She didn't deny being addicted, just said she couldn't afford to take time off now and would be talking about her problem with some family members that evening. She would spend the rest of the day, she said, making crackers and croutons. (We made crackers from leftover cornbread and croutons from dry loaf bread.) Instead, she burned a tray of sunflower seeds and spent twenty minutes talking on the phone with Jerome's father.

She called the next morning to say she needed her locks changed at home and would be in later, but she didn't show up until the following morning. Even I knew it was time to take action. Greeting her at the door, I handed her a check for hours worked and for the personal time she had accumulated as well as a letter putting her on unpaid leave until she could provide us with a reasonable plan for recovery. I told her I loved her and that I wouldn't support her downward slide. "Please let me know how I can help." She said only "It's OK" and left.

Jerome called later that day to see how Daria was doing. I told him we could not deal with any more drama and hung up. Despite his gentle and obviously troubled spirit, I had lost all sympathy for Jerome upon being told he had tried to get Naomi and Rosie, our most recent young hires, to come home with him and sample the MDMA (Ecstasy) he had been making there. They were nineteen years old, and he was nearly twenty-six—enough difference in age and development, in my opinion, to be considered predatory. I suspected Rosie could handle most situations, but Naomi seemed fragile. He showed up a couple days later to say goodbye. I told him we had already done that and asked him to leave, which he did.

Reviewing our situation, we had lost our only two cooks and suddenly had an eighty-hour-a-week hole in the schedule, most of which only I could cover. Ari had been too long away from the kitchen to still have his chops, as I discovered when I asked him to prepare spinach for the salad bar. (He used most of the prep space and took twice as long as anyone else.) Paul was gone for a month. Brian was progressing quickly, but only Mason had enough training to help with the cooking. He stepped up, working double and split shifts for several months, cheering me when I was exhausted and discouraged. For me, his extraordinary willingness to do whatever was needed completely overshadowed any issues we may have had in the past.

His heroism was lost on Ari, who continued to order him around and rag on him about what I considered minutiae. Mason was not a "Yes chef!" kind of guy and would get up on his hind legs in a minute. Their dynamic felt incendiary as, indeed, it proved to be. I kept them apart as much as possible. Ari was already delivering the school lunches, which took him away from the restaurant. I asked him to stay out of the kitchen, take over the weekly shopping, and focus on the entertainment. We started meeting once a week off-site so he was still in the loop and could freely vent his complaints about the crew. I would later report on whom I had talked with and what had been the result. Very little ever got resolved.

Still, he and Mason would inevitably come into contact. On one occasion, their tone, tension, and body language seemed so mutually threatening I felt the need to get physically between them and coax Ari out of the kitchen so he could vent to me instead. He wanted Mason fired and I refused, which did nothing to ease his anger with Mason while escalating his resentment toward me and my lack of support.

I couldn't support Ari against Mason, even though Ari was my dear friend and business partner while Mason would eventually be moving on. It seemed unacceptably unfair not to honor the sacrifices Mason had made to keep us afloat, and Ari never seemed satisfied with anything Mason did.

TOXICITY

Paul returned from his travels near the end of March and quickly assessed the troubled dynamics in the kitchen. He, who had never once complained, took me aside to say he would no longer work the same shifts as Ari. Paul was tired of the negativity and resented Ari for shopping on his own schedule, disregarding the actual needs of the kitchen. He felt Ari didn't respect what we did, since he would wander into the kitchen, interrupting the flow with what Paul considered to be irrelevant and ill-timed conversations.

I had said "I'll talk to him" so many times to so many people that it rang hollow. I had no other solution except the obvious—cut Ari loose and try to run the restaurant myself. I couldn't bring myself to do that. We had started together, and under all the bickering and fighting, we had an iron-clad bond. We loved and understood each other. Gaia's Garden was ours, and I had no wish to do it without him. I was also afraid that, despite all the stress he brought, I couldn't do it on my own. I needed someone as committed to this project as I was, and no one else on the planet ever would be.

To a point, our differing positions were useful. We each served as a container for the other—someone to push back against, and that gave me a sense of security, even though the day-to-day skirmishes were exhausting.

I resolved never to tell Ari what Paul had said, relaying the complaints as my own. I knew Ari treasured their friendship and believed those "irrelevant conversations" with Paul to be mutually enjoyable. I wouldn't take that away from him.

We were now operating seven days a week. Ari was working the register on Saturdays so I could have one day off. With Paul having opted out, Mason was the only person available to work in the kitchen that day. There had been a period of calm, and Ari agreed to dial back his critiques. Richard and I had a lovely lunch with friends, and when we arrived home, I was relaxed and happy for the first time in weeks. Once again, it was the calm before the storm.

The phone rang. Ari was yelling. Months of frustration had come to a head. He had sent Mason home for insubordination and was demanding I fire him. I refused and said we would talk the next day. Mason called me shortly after, and I assured him he was not fired and that I would pay him for the hours he had lost. Ari called back: "And make sure you don't pay him for those hours!"

"I already told him I would."

"What! How could you! I want him gone! You need to support me on this! I want him fired! You're castrating me!"

Of course, he felt betrayed: I had betrayed him. I was stuck between loyalty to Ari, whose judgment I no longer trusted, and Mason, who had been my major support for the last difficult months. More importantly, it was a matter of principle. The real struggle for me was between my love for Ari and my values about how to treat employees. That conversation eventually ended with no resolution. In the days that followed, Ari and I argued more bitterly than we had since our romantic breakup. It seemed Mason had indeed been insubordinate, and I should have heard Ari out and been more supportive, but we were beyond that now. I tried to keep it from the crew, but our mutual animosity was evident. Everyone was aware, and everyone was tense. Terry told me Ari was drinking too much and becoming increasingly vicious with the staff as the nights wore on. I kept Ari and Mason separated while striving to find a path to peace, taking the Saturday shift myself. I was feeling a soul sickness I'd experienced before in difficult situations of principle. Usually I would get physically ill, but this time I couldn't afford to.

I requested help from the Sonoma County Organization of Retired Executives (SCORE), which provided free business consultation. They sent us a man who had owned three Panera Bread restaurants. Eying the labels on the buffet tables, he announced, "These need to be more festive."

He told us about his successes, then that our twenty-page employee manual was too thick. "You only need one page."

We finally got him to the subject of Mason and pled our cases, asking what could be done to resolve it. "You two need to get on the same page" was all he said.

Butch, the rock star dishwasher and Mason's friend, gave notice in June and went to work at Whole Foods. He had been working there part-time and decreasing his hours with us for a while. They paid better and offered benefits, and Gaia's Garden was no longer a fun place to be.

One evening during this period, only Ari and I were available to work, and of course we had a full house. The music was great, the customers were happy, but I was overwhelmed alone in the kitchen. Job one was to keep the food coming, and I managed that, but a mound of dishes was accumulating in the sinks, and I couldn't make a dent in it. Ari had been working the register and the soundboard in the front, but now the customer flow had ended, and the sound was dialed in. He was chatting with customers and dancing a bit but otherwise unoccupied. I told him I was desperate for help with the dishes. Telling me he had too much to do, he turned his back and walked away. I was doing what I could with the dishes, gnashing my teeth, when Richard made one of his rare appearances at the restaurant. Seeing my predicament, he untied my plastic apron. "My first job was washing dishes at Denny's." I hadn't known that, but it was welcome news. He hadn't forgotten how, and in no time I was hearing the comforting rhythmic sounds of flowing water and slamming sanitizer doors. Ari wandered in, managing to free up some time to offer Richard a few tips on how things should be done.

"You can get in there better if you use this brush."

"There's water on the floor—the mop's back there in the utility area."

"Be sure not to let food get past the filter."

I was used to containing my rage toward Ari. Though Richard was new at it, he handled his building resentment like a pro, focusing solely on the dishes until the sinks were clear.

NOTHING HAPPENS BY MISTAKE

Heartsick and angry, Ari and I barely spoke for months, but we still had a restaurant to run. He brought in talented and diverse musicians, produced benefits for righteous causes, and oversaw Dining with Authors. On most days, he delivered the school lunches and shopped while I focused on the back of house.

Several employees came and went during this period. The owner of a Thai market sent a relative with blue hair who worked a few weeks, then left us for a server job. A gluten-free baker stayed a short time, then moved to Colorado. One man came in several times seeking a job; when I finally brought him in to clean, he worked one hour—complaining throughout how hard it was—took a phone call, and announced he had to leave for Washington State immediately.

Another applicant, Tony, seemed promising, and Ari was impressed that he had his own knives. We needed prep help, and he claimed skills and experience. I put him to work immediately. When he opened his impressive-looking case, it revealed cheap mismatched kitchen knives, not the professional steel we were expecting. Worse, he didn't know how to use them. He and Mason prepped side by side for a few hours, the silence broken only when Tony announced, "I work out." Mason and I found it both funny and disturbing.

I sat down with Tony the next day. "It appears you have overstated your experience." He looked sheepish and gathered up his things. Mason saw him at the mall later in the week, shoplifting a pair of sunglasses.

One morning, searching for a clean apron, I pulled out one that had been wedged between boxes on a shelf. Reaching in the pocket, I found a business card for a Dr. B., psychologist/business consultant. I couldn't imagine what it was doing there, but it seemed like a sign. When Ari and I showed up for our first appointment, Dr. B. let us know he was running a little late. When his patient emerged, it was Tony. We avoided eye contact as he escaped down the hallway.

Dr. B. was older than we were and from the East Coast. We both felt comfortable with him. I thought he talked too much about his own experiences on our dime, but there was some time for me and Ari to start unraveling our tangled viewpoints. Most of it was already clear, but it needed to be on the table:

1. Ari was in an untenable position. Although we were "partners," the money and the power were mine, and all the employees eventually figured that out. He was expected to manage people he couldn't fire, meaning he had no real authority over them. The stress was unbearable. I didn't have his back. I was too lax and let the employees get away with too much.

2. I was in an untenable position. Having strong principles about

how people should be treated, I could not cosign what I saw as his unfair and ill-timed, ego-driven assaults on people who worked for us. I had helped raise kids; I knew about triangulation and the importance of a united front, but abuse was a deal-breaker, and I saw him as abusive. I didn't trust his judgment enough to have his back.

We were still at an impasse. Frustrated, I blurted out Paul's list of complaints. The blow landed, and I saw the hurt in Ari's eyes. Nothing—not the restaurant, not the money, not my anger and frustration—justified hurting my friend so deeply, but it was done. I told myself he had brought it on himself. I still felt like crap.

We had created a vicious circle. The more abrasive Ari was, the more I tried to compensate the crew by being forgiving of mistakes and lapses. The more I failed to address issues, the more frustrated Ari was and the more abrasive he became. We were polarizing each other. I resolved to take on more of the "bad cop" duties, but this didn't solve our Mason problem.

While our sessions with Dr. B. brought no "aha" moments, they diffused the tension just enough that we could function better at work. Nothing was resolved, though, and flare-ups were frequent.

This feud had gone on for over seven months. The stress was getting to Mason too, of course, and his resentments spread from Ari to me and to our entire operation. He had no idea what I had gone through to protect the job he was coming to detest, and it didn't matter. It had always been about principle. He owed me nothing, and he was right about our toxic dynamics.

I requested a meeting with Ari at his house—where we could yell if need be—and prepared a letter. I agreed to fire Mason, but there would be a price. "This action represents our gross and humiliating failure as partners to manage effectively. . . ." There were paragraphs labeled "Accountability" and "Professionalism" with twelve numbered conditions covering my range of complaints. The last one, "No one drinks alcohol at work," seemed to be the one Ari considered the most unreasonable. Still, he grudgingly agreed. We were finally getting rid of his nemesis. I gave myself adequate time to accomplish this, although Ari would have preferred a more dramatic closure.

The next time Mason complained to me about our dysfunctional management, I agreed with him. "Mason, I've done everything I can, and I don't think it's going to change. You have been loyal to us, but this has become unbearable. I think you should start looking—take all the time you need. I'll give you a stellar reference and do everything I can to help you."

Within a few weeks, armed with a letter that should be in the Letter of Reference Hall of Fame, he joined Butch at Whole Foods.

Mason went on to server positions at some of the better restaurants in the area. Last I heard, he was working his way up the ladder at a successful local beverage company and was still with the same girlfriend. When I see him, we have brief, warm conversations but will never approach the intimacy I so enjoyed when we worked shoulder to shoulder, saving the day every day.

THE CRUST PUNK
EMPLOYMENT AGENCY

With Mason gone, tensions eased considerably, and we were able to focus more on the day-to-day operations. Ari and I were reestablishing our working relationship and again discussed ways to become profitable. We agreed to increase pricing ahead of the fall semester. It had been a year. The lunch buffet went from $8.95 to $9.95. Dinner took a bigger jump—from $10.95 to $12.95. We kept the Blue Plate Special the same, in consideration of students and seniors on budgets. Because our to-go containers were biodegradable, they were expensive. We started adding twenty-five cents for each one, although the implementation of this charge was inconsistent.

Most of the customers seemed OK with the changes. "We just want you to stay here." One customer who came in about once a year complained that every time he came in, we had raised the prices.

An older gent walked in. "How much is lunch?"

"It's $9.95 for all you care to eat, or you can go through one time with the Blue Plate Special for $6.95."

"That's a lot of money for a pile of vegetables!" he said as he headed for the door.

It was disappointing to receive notification that Daria had applied for unemployment insurance. I had been hoping she was in recovery, but her statement to the agency showed otherwise: "Wrongly accused of inappropriate conduct, given unpaid leave." I pushed back, filling out the provided form and saying she was welcome to return at any time after completing a drug program. A worker called and, while sympathetic, told me I had no recourse.

I learned why employers contest these claims. We're not just being dicks—we're supplementing those payments. We had started with a rate of 3.4 percent, meaning we had to pay that amount on every dollar of gross payroll. Because of Lenny's and Daria's claims, we were now at 4.9 percent. As our payroll increased, that extra 1.5 percent became significant. In 2013, it cost $1,650 and considerably more as our staff expanded. It took me a few years to get it back down. Careful documentation and contesting invalid claims eventually brought it to 2.4 percent. I never again granted an unpaid leave in lieu of termination.

Paul and I were the cooks now. Young Naomi was making the school lunches. Brian had come a long way from the dish pit and was progressing rapidly enough to earn a "field promotion" and learn the recipes. When home, he would watch YouTube videos to increase his skills and would return to work to demonstrate fancy garnishes. It wasn't long before he could cook everything and take charge of the kitchen.

Trying to rebuild our crew, I reached out to the culinary program at Santa Rosa Junior College, just down the street. Most of the students were disappointing. One left after one night, stating he needed more structure. We hired another who was strikingly homely. Overriding our initial distaste in the interest of fairness, we found her personality and work habits to be as unpleasant as her appearance. A small woman wasn't physically up to dishwashing, although she did better than a younger, larger male student. A promising prep cook couldn't keep the schedule straight and failed to show up on the fourth day. My fuse was short; I'd had enough bullshit for one year.

Brian reminded me about his friend Rob, who had sent an email back in February when we'd had a full crew. He was the only employee of a Little Caesars franchise in Kmart and was responsible for making the pizzas, selling them, and cleaning up. An introverted vegan, he hated everything about that job and was quite willing to leave it for even a part-time, temporary dishwashing slot.

Rob was another former crust punk moving into the mainstream. His septum ring was even larger than Brian's, and he also dressed entirely in black, his long hair pulled back. Despite his formidable appearance, he seemed shy. Rob worked hard and efficiently, and I soon had him on full time. He was working one night when Ari was presenting a comedy show. As the Mexican comic, Juan Carlos, saw the very Anglo Rob emerge from the kitchen with a tray of dishes, he pointed him out to the crowd. "That's what I'm talking about! They're stealing our jobs!" It brought the house down, but Rob quickly retreated to the kitchen.

A few months later, Brian introduced us to another dishwasher, another septum ring, another man in black. Our kitchen was starting to look like a pirate ship.

I jokingly referred to Brian as "our employment agency." Over the next few years, he brought in several of our best employees, all former crust punks. He had already vetted them, and we trusted him. Brian was a leader, and the guys he brought in were more focused on pleasing him than us, especially in the beginning. Because Brian was loyal to us, this never created a conflict. Only one of his referrals acted badly, leaving without notice. Brian took it personally, so it's probably best the guy had left town.

Brian got along well enough with Ari, and when his proteges bristled at Ari's management style, he'd talk them off the ledge. With Mason and Butch gone and new employees anxious to please us (or Brian), Ari and I began to relax a little. I was able to show him more respect, and he, in turn, was more respectful of the crew. Ari and I were building back our trust. It seemed peace was coming to Gaia's Garden at last.

FINDING THE RIGHT JOB FOR THE PERSON

With the dish pit covered, I tried Rosie on prep. She was willing and worked hard as usual, but the foster care system had left serious gaps in her education. One night, Brian asked her to bring him sixteen cups of water. When he turned around, Rosie presented him with a tray containing sixteen water-filled coffee cups. Not sure whether to laugh or cry, I concluded she might not be ready for kitchen work.

I had noticed she was hypervigilant, as are many victims of trauma. She was keenly observant and quick to detect the smallest patch of dust or disturbance in the force. It seemed good to have such a person watching the front, so I trained her on the register. She was charismatic and openhearted and attracted a stream of young men—most of whom were broke. Ari and I would shoo them away from the cashier's station and require them to buy something for the privilege of gazing at her from a booth. She did not limit her warmth to those boys, though, and was equally gracious to men, women, and children of all ages and social standing.

She was particularly solicitous of a customer who had severe mobility issues, and she would go through the buffet with him, filling his plates as he requested. On one occasion, he had wet himself. I handed Rosie twenty dollars and asked her to go across the street to the secondhand store and buy him a pair of pants. I knew that she, better than anyone, would be able to minimize his embarrassment.

Her main drawback was that she found the register challenging. On one of her days off, a customer asked me, "Where is that lovely young woman who can't make change?" Terry took a paternal interest in Rosie and spent much time bringing her to a reasonable competence.

In December, Cara walked in to apply. She was a vibrant woman in her late twenties who had been traveling in Europe "woofing"—working on organic farms for her keep. I wanted to move Rob to prep, so we had some dish shifts. Ari asked her an oddball question:

"If you're walking through the dining room and you see a napkin on the floor, what would you do?"

She didn't skip a beat: "I'd kick it under a table, out of the way."

Ari and I just stared at her for a moment, dumbfounded. She laughed. "I was joking. Of course, I'd pick it up."

Her chutzpah won us over. Like Ari, she was Italian and from the East Coast, so she did well with his New York attitude most of the time.

Later, she confided to me that before coming in that day, she had been crying in the parking lot next door because no one would even give her an interview. She had pulled herself together and decided to try just one more.

As 2012 came to a close, despite all the drama, we had increased our annual gross income by 70 percent to $407,000, and we were in the black, with a profit of $11,938. I didn't know that at the time. My taxes weren't filed until 2014, and it seemed like I was constantly transferring money into the business account from wherever I could get it.

We were again voted Best Vegetarian Restaurant in the *Bohemian*, kept our 4.5 star rating with Yelp, and gained a 5-star rating with Tripadvisor when a reviewer labeled us "Vegan Paradise with Music."

MOVING RIGHT ALONG

Over the winter break, Ari and some helpers painted the concrete floor in the dining room. It had been an industrial gray and was now yellow with fuchsia swirls, giving it a psychedelic look and providing welcome color. I liked it. I particularly relished an interaction with two of our young customers.

To maximize their appetites, these boys would sit in their car getting as stoned as possible before coming in. They were barely ambulatory on their arrival but were cute and sweet; I had grown fond of them. On this occasion, I saw them staring at the formerly gray floor that now appeared to be a riot of color bobbing and weaving under their feet. They looked panicky.

"What happened to the floor?"

"Nothing. What's going on?"

I savored their paranoid confusion for a minute before admitting that we had, in fact, painted it, and they were, indeed, on solid ground.

Paul gave notice and left at the end of February, having been with us on and off for almost three years. His departure precipitated a flurry of hiring, and we took on four new people—most of whom were part-time. Finn was one of Brian's. He was imposing physically, with a florid complexion and a reddish cast to his dark hair and beard. I could easily picture him wielding a broadsword on an ancient Scottish plain. Instead, he washed dishes. He was fast and meticulous, putting all the others to shame. It was during his tenure that we started using the phrase *dish lord* instead of the usual term that compares that person to an appliance.

I was talking with a customer one day who suddenly tensed up. Following his gaze, I saw he was reacting to Brian and Finn walking toward the kitchen. They looked like a pair from *The Road Warrior*—studded black jackets, black jeans and boots, tattoos, piercings, and attitude. "It's OK. They work for me." He relaxed a little.

Among our new hires, one was a student whose passion was competitive diving. Another was in her late twenties, a photographer, smart, and with a professional appearance. She was hired for the front of house but preferred the kitchen, so we moved her to the back. Sabrina replaced her at the front. She was a natural for the night shift, enjoying the music and events. Ari was happy to see her joining the dancers when she could.

I started monitoring work hours carefully since we had fourteen people now, and employee costs were skyrocketing. Many of our employees were part-time, and scheduling became a puzzle. I enjoyed working on it, but it took a few more hours every week. In addition to adjustments for school schedules and band practices, I had to make sure there were never more than three people on the prep side. Like lab animals, if overcrowded, they turned on each other.

We were now open seven days a week from 11:30 a.m. to 9 p.m. and were making sandwiches to order in addition to the buffet and school lunches. More staff meant more interpersonal conflicts, but at least they weren't all centered on Ari. I started to see cycles: The kitchen crew would be happy and cooperative for a few weeks, then they would be at each other's throats for a few weeks, then back to a lovefest. I became fond of saying, "We have a great crew, but they're not all great on the same day."

Lily, a high school student working prep, left us in May after her graduation, stating she wanted to experience other work situations, ours having been her first. She had performed well and remained cheery for the most part. As part of our closing conversation, she told me I should know Ari had sexually harassed her. I was stunned. It was no secret that everyone felt harassed by Ari at one point or another, but the man I had known well for many years had always shown extreme care and integrity not to cross sexual boundaries. What could have happened?

"He told me, 'I know as a young woman you care about your appearance, but it is absolutely necessary that you wear a hair covering when working with food.' Then, when he was trying to get me to take home one of the gallon glass jars, he suggested I could fill it with the 'severed heads of ex-lovers' or with crayons. I'm not going to report you or anything," she assured me, "but I thought you should know."

Know what? I wondered. I already knew Ari had an odd sense of humor. It was one of the things I liked best about him. "Lily, is there anything else?"

"No, that's it. But he had no right to comment on my appearance."

Ari had had a running conversation with Lily over her unwillingness to cover her hair. This had been but one attempt to elicit her cooperation. I tried to be sensitive to Lily's sense of injury, but it was difficult, having grown up in an era when men could say anything they pleased and literally chase me around my desk without fear of reprisal.

"Lily, I'm sorry you found it uncomfortable, but I've studied the laws against sexual harassment, and this doesn't even come close. The health code is very clear about head coverings, though."

I was pleased to see a generation of women standing up against the type of harassment I had experienced, yet it seemed the pendulum had swung too far in the other direction, at least for this young woman. When I repeated the conversation to Ari, he agreed and denied he had ever said anything about severed heads.

Brian developed sandwiches that were very good and very popular. The Bella Burger was a portobello mushroom cap roasted with garlic and herbs and served on a bun with grilled onions, pesto aioli, lettuce, tomato, and a smidge of garlic butter. The Italiano was vegan sausage on house-made focaccia bread with roasted onions, peppers, and marinara sauce. He had a number of other suggestions for wonderful sandwiches and drinks. I'd ask him to write them down and teach the crew, but he never got to it. Ari kept asking for an avocado sandwich, not an unreasonable request in a vegetarian restaurant, but the only effort to make one came out too mushy, and no one ever followed up. We were all frustrated.

Ari and I were wanting to expand the à la carte items and move away from the buffet model. It had become clear the traditional setup works best with cheap food. We didn't want to sell cheap food, and our customers didn't want to eat it. Many were reluctant, though, to pay for quality. We had come to recognize a buffet mentality. In addition to the element of greed, there was also an expectation that it should be cheap. We would marvel at a couple—both doctors—who told us the only restaurants they enjoyed were Gaia's Garden and Millennium in San Francisco. Ari and I had been able to afford that wonderful restaurant once and had dined fabulously. It was easy for a couple to spend over $150. These same doctors at *our* restaurant, rather than paying $12.95 for a civilized meal, would order the Blue Plate Special for $8.95 (no beverages), piling the plates so high that all the food was mixed together, and they would leave nothing in the tip jar. We were providing fresh, clean food—and lots of it—for the price of a burrito or a fancy coffee. People still complained.

We had a family-friendly policy of charging kids by the year up to five years of age—one dollar for a one-year-old, two dollars for a two-year-old, etc. I would joke that it was primarily a cleaning fee, which the parents completely understood. There were some who tried to take advantage, though. After one woman ordered lunch for her three-year-old and paid the three dollars, she announced she wasn't hungry—then liberally sampled her child's food. After that, we had to make it clear the kids' prices were contingent on the purchase of at least one full adult meal.

In June, we hired Buzz, another of Brian's friends. Unlike anyone we had employed to date (other than Jerome, the zealot), he was an experienced line cook. Buzz didn't take long to reveal he'd had a drinking problem that had derailed his career in construction. He had given up alcohol and had no interest in seeking treatment, preferring to exorcise his demons with physical activity. I could see he was wound tightly, but his skills and excess energy served us well. When it was just the two of us in the kitchen, I would ask him about his music, and he would attempt to educate me by playing clips of psycho punk, hillbilly punk, death metal, horror punk, thrashcore, folk punk, and crust. I was not a good student.

He was very much in love with a young woman who lived in Southern California, and his tenderness touched me. No doubt punk culture includes abusers and bad actors of all kinds, but from what I was able to observe with my crew, they valued their women and were kind, loving, and faithful to them.

Buzz, like Brian, was frustrated by inefficiencies. He was less tactful, but between the two of them, they improved operations and helped bring our crew of amateurs to a higher level, although we all still had a long way to go.

Another price change seemed necessary before school started. We raised the unlimited option at dinner to $14.95, this time adding perceived value by including tea, chai, or coffee. Lunch and the Blue Plate Special stayed the same.

We had been right to hire impudent Cara. She was grateful for the job and was a capable dishwasher but was so enthusiastic about the food we couldn't deny her, so I moved her to prep. It didn't take long for her to take over making the lunch buffet. She and Brian butted heads a lot—he found her gregariousness irritating and disruptive. She accused him of undermining her by not restocking items she needed in the morning. Buzz was working with her in the morning and found her overbearing. Privately, Naomi, our young lunch lady, agreed with Buzz.

Naomi was a delight to work with—talented, easygoing, and funny. She was also troubled and taking a few medications for anxiety and depression. There were a lot of callouts for cramps, headaches, and unspecified disorders for which she would bring in doctors' notes. When I pointed out that she'd had cramps every week for a month, she responded she was "syncing" with a new friend. Her parents were staunchly religious, very sure of what constituted both right and wrong. She was often wrong by their definition and seemed to careen between trying to please them and desperately breaking the constraints.

A relationship, toxic by anyone's standards, nearly broke her. Cara, Rosie, and I counseled her against it at work, and her mother would show up occasionally with a nice Christian boy in whom Naomi had no interest. She took a couple of months off to get herself together and seemed to have succeeded when she returned—happier and more present. Still, there were some serious missteps that nearly cost us our relationship with the school. I put Buzz in charge of the school lunches and let Naomi focus on baking. She created several kinds of cookies that sold well and helped our evening customers meet the minimum purchase. She also developed the recipe for focaccia bread for the Italiano sandwiches.

We had a solid crew now, with Brian, Rob, Finn, and Buzz—the "pirates"– balanced somewhat by the lovely and spunky young women, Rosie, Cara, and Naomi. We needed one more prep person and began another round of interviews.

THE WARRIOR PRINCESS

Jackie was a student at the culinary school. On her résumé, she described herself as "charismatic," which seemed odd and not immediately apparent. She was hard to understand due to her strong southeast Asian accent and rapid speech, but we expected it would be easier to communicate once she overcame interview jitters. She was doing very well in her classes. Ari and I liked and hired her.

Jackie was too much of a challenge for Brian and Rob at night. The guys complained she talked incessantly and that they couldn't understand her. Jackie had preemptively described herself as "a slow learner at first," which proved to be true. I was told she asked the same questions over and over and needed constant supervision. There also seemed to be some kind of disconnect. When directed to monitor the buffet tables, she would keep refilling nearly full containers on the cold salad bar while food on the hot table became depleted, mushy, and dry. If she had a list of cleaning duties, she would do the first but wouldn't move on to the second unless told to. Brian and Rob were kind, and I don't think she had any idea how much they dreaded her appearance on shift each night. Brian let me know they simply couldn't work with her.

I suspected she might be on the autism spectrum and decided to put her on with me in the mornings so I could work with her and observe her more closely. She preferred the day shift anyway. I sought and received counsel from the director of the culinary program, who said she had been unaware of these issues:

"As an employer, all you can do is customize the job to her abilities (within reason), determine your level of patience, and then step back and see if she can perform to your needs. If she can't, then let her go. Honestly, Susan, we have to do that too. Many people who think they can handle the culinary world and all of its multitasking, speed, human interaction, and stress simply cannot. And many of those are folks who don't present half of what you described in Jackie. Thank you for caring."

Surprisingly, Jackie did significantly better with us in the mornings. I asked her to limit the chatter, and she complied, still participating in and initiating conversations but less so. What I most appreciated was that she was teachable and very smart; her initial hesitancy to move forward seemed to have stemmed from a combination of insecurity, strict obedience, and a literal bent rather than any neurological issue. I began to enjoy the mornings as she prepped and Naomi or Buzz prepared the school lunches while I cooked. Jackie had a range of knowledge, interests, and abilities that included martial arts as well as science and literature. She was avidly into Dungeons & Dragons and entertained us with tales of her avatar's exploits. It was satisfying to report to the school that things were now going well, and the director was very appreciative.

Probably as a result, I was invited to lunch and a private tour of the school. As we went from department to department of this state-of-the art facility, I was introduced to each instructor as "She hired Jackie!" The warmth of their responses was heartwarming and a little surprising.

One morning I became distracted using the mandolin—a sharp-bladed instrument for slicing vegetables—and cut off the tip of my finger. What had been softly rounded was now flat and bleeding profusely. I couldn't bandage it one-handed, and, sensing Naomi wasn't up to the job, asked Jackie to help me. She set to work efficiently, telling me that her father, now living in Florida, was a medic in the army. Within a few minutes, the bleeding was contained, and we both went back to work, I with a glove over my bandage.

(The body is an amazing organism. Over the next weeks, my finger not only healed but knew to replace the missing tissue with a perfectly rounded pad. I had a numb spot at first, but that also resolved in time.)

Jackie had settled in and was now accepted as a fill-in on the night shift. One night she cut herself and was bleeding quite a bit. Ari cleaned, sanitized, and bandaged her finger, then called me. I arrived with Richard and offered to take her to the emergency room. "No," she told me, "I just need to get home. My mother-in-law is a nurse."

She directed us to a mobile home park on the other side of town, on the outskirts. Richard announced, "I remember this place!"

"Did you used to live here?" I asked.

Richard sometimes spoke before he thought. "Hell no, I just came here to buy drugs."

Before the ensuing silence could become too awkward, we arrived at a trailer that was small and rundown even by the standards of this sad place. What had been a sitting area was now taken up by a bed upon which Jackie's boyfriend's father lay dying of cancer. We stood in the doorway as nurse Linda examined Jackie's finger. She determined it didn't need stitches. We thanked her and said good night.

I had not given any thought to what it took for this girl to get to work and school each day. Rising literally and figuratively from the squalor in which she lived, she walked to the bus stop at 6:30 every morning—frequently in the dark—and took two busses into town. Santa Rosa did not have a good transit system, and if she missed her connection, she would have to walk or run twenty blocks—many of them long—in order to arrive by 8:30. Yet she would present herself at work with a smile and a willing spirit, ready to start another long day of work and school; at day's end, riding the late busses, she would start her homework. This put things in a whole new light, and I was grateful to have given her the benefit of the doubt—the very least she deserved.

Jackie was sometimes paired with Buzz, and he was not one to hide his frustration. "That's not BACKUP! It's only half full!" Jackie never complained or pushed back—showing a discipline and humility I believe she had acquired through the martial arts. After hearing him criticize her harshly one day, I took her aside. "I know he yells at you. Honestly, since you want to be a professional chef, he is probably like a lot that you'll meet along the way. Don't take it personally, and learn what you can from him. If it gets too hard, come talk to me." She nodded and never complained.

Early one rainy morning, as I headed away from the restaurant to pick up provisions, I saw her standing on the corner, still a block away, waiting for the light to change. Dressed completely in black, standing tall and proud against the storm, she resembled one of the avatars from Dungeons & Dragons—every inch a warrior princess.

ALL IN A DAY'S WORK

Most of our customers were graciously appreciative, but like any service business, we also saw the worst of the public. As we moved away from the "all you care to eat" model, it seemed appropriate to be generous with samples. Often someone couldn't decide between the two soups, for example, or was concerned the curry might be too spicy, so we would give them a cup and a spoon to see for themselves. One woman regularly abused this policy, although it took us a few times to catch on. She would fill two or three cups to their brims, commenting on how good everything was but never buying.

"That was great. I just had lunch, but I'll come back."

"I'm not hungry now, just wanted to check it out. I'll be back soon."

"I left my money at home, but I can't wait to come back for lunch."

Ari and I compared notes and figured out it was the same person. After she had played us once again, he told her she needed to buy something or leave and not to come back except as a customer. She left.

"And if I ever see her fat ass in here again," Ari told me, "I'm kicking her out." I had never heard him speak like that, so the comment stayed with me.

A few weeks later, I was talking with some customers on the patio when—in my peripheral vision—I saw a woman's backside so wide it barely cleared the door. Ari's comment kicked in, and I hurriedly finished the conversation. Coming into the dining room, I saw it was indeed the same woman and that she already had a cup. Rosie hadn't known about her little scam.

"Put that down," I ordered her. "Buy something or leave."

"I was just wanting to see if the soup was too salty—"

"Ari already told you. No more samples."

"But I just wanted to taste it."

Losing patience, I grabbed the cup from her hand. She screamed as though I had assaulted her. As I escorted her out, she yelled at the customers still on the patio, "Never come here! These are terrible people!" Then, to me, "I'm going to tell everybody never to come here!"

It was an empty threat. I had learned by now that, sadly, people so unhinged have few friends.

We kept a one-gallon tip jar near the register. It had no lid in order to facilitate customers dropping bills in. Unfortunately, an elder street denizen found the opening equally convenient for pulling bills out. I came from the kitchen just in time to see him grab the cash and head for the door, and I went after him. Later, Richard was appalled that I had put myself at risk, but, as I tried to explain, the guy wasn't moving that fast and I figured I could take him. Catching up with him on the sidewalk, I ordered him to return our money, or I would call the police. I didn't expect it to be so easy. He reached into his pocket and retrieved a bunch of bills. Handing me most of them, he reserved a stack that were neatly folded. "I already had those," he informed me. I believed him and told him not to come back.

One evening, the crew called me into the kitchen. "Look at Brian's salad!" It looked like any other salad until it began to move. A praying mantis, blending in perfectly with the mixed greens, had somehow found its way in. We never did figure it out. It seemed unlikely it would have survived two wash and spin cycles but also unlikely it had crawled up the table and into the spring mix. Grateful it had been Brian's salad rather than that of a customer, we discreetly removed it to the garden.

SOME DAYS NOBODY'S HAPPY

D espite having a good and dedicated crew, friction in the kitchen seemed to be escalating again. I documented carefully, recording most conversations, never knowing when a seemingly routine complaint might balloon into a lawsuit. In an all too typical kerfuffle, Ari complained to Lisa, a prep cook, about the pasta being overcooked.

"But I just followed procedure."

"Then the procedure needs to be changed, because this pasta is mushy."

"Lily made pasta too. Why are you just talking to me?"

"Lily's leaving in a week. Assuming you're staying, you need to learn to cook pasta."

I received reports on this from both Lisa and Ari and duly noted them in my journal after gently urging Lisa not to argue with an Italian about pasta and to check it occasionally.

The complaints were coming from all directions. Terry, the night manager, thought Ari was drinking too much and singling out Rosie and Lisa. Ari was upset because Terry had interrupted his conversation with a customer. Cara felt disrespected by Brian and the entire night shift for not setting her up properly in the morning. Brian thought Cara was a drama queen and not up to the job. He was not happy with how Lisa monitored the buffet tables and claimed she would slow down if Ari and I weren't present. Our customer with autism, Ian, felt disrespected by Terry and was probably right. Many complained about Ari's delivery of critiques, though they admitted many were fair. Buzz claimed Cara didn't have the right priorities, everyone was frustrated by Naomi's frequent absences, and so it went. Ari found a pad of "employee notice forms" and presented them to me almost daily until he ran out.

Many of the complaints centered on chain of command and job duties, so I created an operations manual and laid these out in detail. Discussing the highlights briefly with everyone, I scheduled half-hour breaks so each employee could read it and give feedback. They all said it was great, but there seemed to be no significant lessening of the collective angst. Brian and Buzz, in particular, wanted more structure. I created checklists for opening and closing and inventory lists for ordering. Brian made an effort to follow these but lost incentive when no one else did. Short of being there all day every day and enforcing compliance, I couldn't see a way to turn the ship around. Instead of being more hands-on, I was overwhelmed with all the other pieces of our project, many of which required me to be off-site, and then would be unrealistically heartened when things seemed to be going well.

Nearly every day, there would be more to scribble in my notebook. I went back and forth, trying to hear all sides and address the real problems. A big part of the real problem was me; there were certainly times when I wanted to tell them all just to shut the fuck up and do their jobs, but I didn't. I was too afraid of losing someone or being sued, too invested in being the cool boss, too worried about making the wrong call. I was still trying to balance what I considered Ari's overly critical approach to management; sadly, I failed to support him on occasions when hindsight would show he'd been right. There was a simmering tension between us most of the time, but we were learning to live with it. Our weekly meetings were held off-site at a Japanese restaurant, and we were able to detach from our usual antagonism and enjoy the food and each other's company. At our own restaurant, we went our separate ways as much as possible.

A lot of my notes centered on Rosie, and we finally put her on sixty days' probation. She had already presented challenges by being on her phone too much, using the laptop by the register for personal projects, and taking breaks without arranging for the register to be covered. Then we noticed she had some sort of Robin Hood complex about giving away food—although we were not rich and she did not always give to the poor. Sometimes at random, but too often to her friends, she would give away cups of tea or soup or make other concessions that were beyond her pay grade.

The compulsion to give seemed hardwired in her, and I theorized it came from her years as a foster child. For some, privation might make them selfish. Rosie, on the other hand, was generous to a fault. At the same time, none of these acts benefited her materially, and I'm confident she never stole money from us. She had integrity in her way; it just conflicted with our way. There were minor shortages in her till but also overages, and they balanced out fairly well over time.

She was upset about the probation, complaining to Terry and Sabrina that we had told her to look for another job or we would fire her after two weeks so she couldn't get unemployment. Nothing even close to this had been said (or considered)! We were learning Rosie's reportage of events was often exaggerated or simply untrue.

These observations of her behavior were revealed over a period of months, which lessened their impact at any given time. Ari and I were both pulling for her, aware of what it had taken for her to reach this level of functionality. Occasionally she would introduce us to her numerous "brothers" and "sisters" from her placements in foster homes. Nearly all appeared ragged, homeless, and addicted. Rosie, on the other hand, worked hard with good energy and self-discipline. She deserved what support we could give her to break through.

EVERYBODY LOVES A LOVER

Ari began seeing a fellow New Yorker, Genevive, who was sparkly and cultured and had a forceful personality. He fell quickly in love, which made life easier for the rest of us since he was in a better mood and taking more time off. She enjoyed playing hostess with Ari during the events at night, and I was grateful I didn't have to be there as much. I wasn't fond of her, and the staff found her overbearing. She would give me permission to attend meetings held at my own restaurant, as though she were throwing me a bone. I didn't need a damn invitation! This riled me, but I tempered my outrage in the interest of peace. On one occasion, a customer corrected me on the date of one of the events.

"The owner's wife told me it was on Saturday." This was too much.

Rather haughtily, I informed him, "*I'm* the owner, I don't have a wife, and it's on Friday."

After a few skirmishes, I realized she might be around a while and that it would be better to extend an olive branch. I apologized for some past rudeness, and she accepted my apology without reciprocating—something Ari was also prone to do. "Oh well," I thought. "If she makes him happy, the rest of us will be a lot happier too."

OUT OF BALANCE

We were keeping our food costs slightly below the suggested industry standard of 30 percent of gross income, but our employee costs at over 40 percent were nearly twice what they should have been; we already knew the rent—which increased by 3 percent per year—was too high. I couldn't do anything about the rent, and it seemed like we needed all our employees. Unlike most restaurants, we couldn't just slap a steak on the grill. Everything had to be hand-prepped, and we were committed to making all our soups and sauces in house. (If the public saw the ingredients in most of the processed foods—especially salad dressings, puddings, soups, and sauces—routinely served in restaurants, they would be, or should be, horrified.) We had expanded our hours and were doing a lot in the kitchen—lunch and dinner buffets, sandwiches to order, school lunches, baked goods, and occasional catering. The best solution again seemed to be to increase our income.

I fell behind on filing our annual tax returns, knowing we had enough accumulated losses that I wouldn't owe the IRS or the state. I had been cashing in investment accounts and pulling money from anywhere I could to make payroll and pay the sales and employment taxes, so I knew our bottom line would show a loss; it was no surprise when I finally saw the numbers in 2015.

By year-end, our gross was up by $81,000 to $488,649. Our taxable "income," though, had careened into the red. The $12,000 profit from last year had disappeared along with an additional $15,000. We ended 2013 $27,000 in the hole.

I was scared but stubborn and so used to living in a constant state of anxiety that even this obvious sign of deep trouble just seemed like one of the daily hurdles. I still had faith we could get it right, it would just take time.

We were again voted Best Vegetarian Restaurant in the *Bohemian* poll, maintained our 4.5-star rating on Yelp, and averaged 5 stars on Tripadvisor.

MEDIATION

O ur New Year's Eve party had been the best so far, so we started the year on a high, which was short-lived.

The employees were still bickering, especially Cara and Buzz. Ari and I, after multiple conversations with them both, came to recognize a pattern. At first look, Buzz seemed like the bad guy, exploding inappropriately ("Get the fuck out of my face!"), but we also saw that Cara resembled the little sister who persistently annoys her brother until he hits her, then goes running in tears to Mom. I told Cara she needed a thicker skin and Buzz that he needed to dial back the angry responses. It was stressful and, at times, ridiculous.

Cara was one of my favorite crew members. She had heart and was smart and adventurous. For some reason, she got into the habit of calling me "Su-ueesan" with an Eastern European accent, and I enjoyed our conversations and banter a lot.

Unlike me, Cara could understand the lyrics of Buzz's music and found them to be sexually inappropriate (they were); Buzz retorted that Cara had been talking about some guy's dick. I told them to play different music and not talk about dicks.

Cara complained that Buzz put up a front when I was around. I responded, "I don't care if he's insincere. He has good skills and is fast and reliable. That's what I care about."

"But he was talking about me to Naomi!"

"I'm not getting involved in that. I try for fair, but I can't promise justice. You can tell Naomi your side if you want to, but the whole thing seems immature."

"What would a mature response be?"

"Just let it slide off your back. Like a duck. Every time he starts getting to you, just tell yourself, 'Quack, quack.'" It had come to this.

I started coming in at 6:30 a.m. to keep a lid on things. When I was there, everything went fine. Naomi was also a buffering presence but was frequently missing work. There was a particularly bad blowup when I wasn't there, and it became clear this tension would only escalate. I told them both we would be sitting down for a mediation.

I had led several mediations as a volunteer before dropping everything to buy a restaurant. This was closer to home, though, and I was anxious. I asked Ari to come and help balance the energies, not fully confident he could fill that role. He was immensely helpful, staying calm and uncharacteristically quiet through much of the proceedings while providing both Buzz and Cara with valuable male support.

I started by affirming their value to Gaia's Garden and their clear commitment to quality work. Cara vented her complaints, followed by Buzz, then we started working toward unity. Their restraint and openness to the process surprised and impressed me; they seemed genuinely wanting to reach peace. I think Buzz appreciated not being thrown under the bus as an abuser and Cara sensed we were in no mood for histrionics. Buzz was willing to acknowledge Cara's passion for the work, that she had improved, and that he could show her more respect. She agreed to honor his personal space and focus more on work than conversation. As he pointed out, these were not just social considerations but were essential in close quarters with people wielding sharp knives.

In the following weeks, it seemed they were working together with more comfort, and that's what they both reported when asked. I wished this process could work as well with Ari and various other employees, but we were still too raw from the Mason saga for me to facilitate, and Ari was more objective about others' conflicts than his own. I could see he was making an effort to compliment good work rather than solely communicating the negatives. Even so, when employees came to me upset, usually all they had heard were the complaints.

NOT ALL WHO WANDER
ARE LOST

I caught Sabrina, our cashier, giving away soup to her boyfriend. She had a mile of excuses including Rosie's bad example. Feeling less sympathetic to Sabrina and reminding her Rosie was now on probation and facing termination herself for the same transgression, I planned to fire her but folded when she apologized and pleaded eloquently for her job. A short time later, she called Ari: She had taken another job and didn't want to give two weeks' notice. Ari agreed—no point having a disgruntled employee on the register, especially one whose honesty was already questionable. She filed for unemployment insurance six months later. This time I pushed back—and prevailed.

Ten days after that, Rosie gave notice, announcing she was going traveling with her new boyfriend. Two rocky weeks followed. All the bad behaviors roared back, and she went into full-on Robin Hood mode. Her boyfriend wanted her to leave before the notice date, and it seemed she was pushing to get fired so she could please him. No dice. We insisted she shape up and complete her two weeks. Having come this far with her, Ari and I were determined Rosie would leave with honor, or at least the illusion of it. I had seen how troubled kids preemptively throw themselves away and knew in my gut that this job, which had lasted eighteen months, needed to count as a success for her, whether she knew it or not. We ended with a small party. Naomi made a cake decorated with yellow flowers and the words "Not All Who Wander Are Lost."

Fortunately, we were able to hire Katie, who had been a customer and already loved the food, especially my beet soup. She was experienced, emotionally mature, and reliable. I was starting to breathe again.

Katie went with Buzz and Ari to set up a booth at the first Sonoma County Veg Fest and sold out quickly. It was our first off-site endeavor; the organization was stressful, but the results were rewarding. The success of the event and its explosive growth over the next years confirmed a significant interest in plant-based food in our county. Despite our best efforts—through radio and print ads, Facebook, networking, Groupon, music, signage, and events—there were still many potential customers who didn't even know we existed. This festival and others like it promised us much-needed exposure.

Naomi, now twenty years old, was having more personal and physical issues. She had been hospitalized the previous fall for a week of psychological evaluation and seemed to have bounced back, becoming a beacon of sanity during the Cara-Buzz conflicts. Now she was reporting fainting spells, bleeding ulcers, cramps, scoliosis, anemia, and conflicts with her parents, her friends, and her lover as well as housing and money problems. I could only suggest she seek medical advice and more counseling. She left us in June to work for a successful bakery.

Buzz found a job with an arborist. The pay was much better, of course, and he could get paid to climb—one of his passions. He filed for unemployment insurance two months later, and I disputed his eligibility to charge our reserve account. Again, the decision was in our favor. Apparently, there were no hard feelings since he returned for a few months at the end of summer.

Cara had been a lot happier with Buzz gone, although she enjoyed reminiscing about the good times they'd had working together. On his return, they seemed to have achieved a level of peace, perhaps because neither was planning to stay much longer.

Despite the incessant drama, we continued to produce for the customers. For St. Patrick's Day, we had a fine dinner featuring Brian's Irish Skillet—corned tempeh and fried potatoes with a mustard sauce. I had developed a good stuffed cabbage recipe, so everyone ate especially well that night—all vegan. Easter and Mother's Day also featured special spreads, with huge chocolate-dipped (organic) strawberries gifted to each customer.

TRANSITIONS

N ow that we had five years in, we were developing history with some of our customers. A young girl was pregnant when we first saw her. She and her sister were lithe and lovely, with multicolored hair and extensive body art. I was particularly envious of the sister's long, autumn-colored hair—shades of orange, yellow, and red. They came in often with the baby, and we were blessed to watch her develop into a toddler and then a stubborn little girl under the loving care of these two sprites.

Another regular customer lost his wife to breast cancer. We saw him worried, then bereaved and lonely, then dating, then remarried.

A Pomo family came in regularly after their patriarch's oncology appointments. We watched him wither away over several months and empathized with the family's growing sadness.

Customers celebrated birthdays and anniversaries with us. Sometimes singles would meet at our long table reserved for "Community," then begin to date. Others would run into old friends and acquaintances with whom they had lost touch. Small groups of vegans would meet up on their way to protests or to decompress afterward. The Very Vegan Book Club would convene at the Community table on Tuesdays. Recovery people would meet with their sponsors, reading and chatting in the privacy of the booths.

Our long-term customer "Poodle lady" asked to speak with me privately. She had remained a chronic complainer although she still came by often. Expecting to hear yet another grievance, I was taken off guard when she announced, "I've come to say goodbye."

Was she moving? Was she gravely ill?

"Oh, I'm sorry. What's going on?"

"I've switched to paleo. I've never felt better, and I've lost seven pounds."

Paleo focuses on protein and minimal carbs. Meat is king; rice, beans, and many vegetables—our stocks in trade—are off the list.

"That's wonderful. I'm glad you've found something that works for you."

I thought that would be the end of it, but it wasn't. She wanted us to change our menu to paleo. I thanked her for her suggestion, explaining we weren't prepared to do that and were committed to our format. (Vegan paleo is a thing but would have required more adjustments than we wished to make.) She launched into a rebuttal that went on for several minutes, until I slowly walked away and sought refuge in the kitchen. We lost customers over the years, but she was the only one to resign formally.

For many existing and potential customers, protein was a big deal. Beans and rice in combination provide a complete protein, and many would be surprised at how much is in vegetables. A cup of broccoli, a portobello mushroom cap, or half a cup of peas have about 4 grams each. I hung a print by Dan Piraro (Bizarro) showing a silverback gorilla (they weigh 400 to 450 pounds, all muscle, no fat, and eat only plants) being queried as to whether he was getting enough protein. Still, for some this was a major concern. Our dinner entrées usually contained tofu or tempeh, which

placated some, but others remained skeptical. We had several vegan ath-
letes among our regular customers—including extreme cage fighters and a
professional ballet dancer—who didn't seem to be lacking any nutrients.

By June 2014, three cashiers, two cooks, and a dishwasher had left. We
needed to replace them with less challenging staff. Fortunately, we had
already acquired a new prep cook, James, who had been working at Panda
Express and wanted a change. Hoping to achieve more staff unity by creating buy-in, I had Brian and Rob join me and Ari for the initial interview.
It went well, and James was invited to join the crew. At the end of the
meeting, he lifted his hat to reveal gauges in his ears. "I was going to ask
if these were OK, but. . . ." He motioned toward our "pirates" with their
septum rings, tattoos, and random piercings. We all had a good laugh, and
I knew he would fit in. James proved to be a stellar employee. He had
acquired good prep skills at Panda Express and was prompt, reliable, and a
hard worker; his manner was easygoing and nonconfrontive. A restaurant
owner's dream.

He gave two weeks' notice to Panda Express, which I regarded with
favor. Even when we were desperate to start a new employee, I had to
support their honorable exit from their last job. I always hoped that when
the time came, we would be given the same consideration.

Rob's friend Marty came in to do dishes. Marty was another man in
black—actually, a perpetual kid—with the requisite septum ring. Brian

made a point of not endorsing him, and even Rob seemed hesitant. We needed someone, though, and decided to take it day by day.

That same month, I brought in a friend who had formal chef training and wanted a temporary job. Sam had crashed and burned and had now successfully completed an alcohol recovery program at the evangelically based Redwood Gospel Mission. He was with us through the end of the year and, with his skills and knowledge of kitchen operations, was a huge help. He humbly did whatever was needed and was a cheerful support to Ari and me as we tried to improve our managerial skills. At the time, none of us anticipated the major role he would play down the road.

Annie came in to work the front of house. She knew all our punk guys, having lived under bridges with some of them; now, she was home with her parents. She had pink hair and was voluptuous, with a large, pleasant personality and a beautiful smile. She got along with everybody, which was a huge relief.

Cara had become a capable cook. Classes at the junior college and Naomi's example had awakened a passion for baking, so I assigned the breads and cookies to her since she seemed happiest when covered with flour. She had been living in her camper for a year to save money so she could go traveling again. An ashram on Kauai hired her sight unseen based on the knowledge of *satvig* cooking she had acquired from us. We signed an agreement as to which of our recipes she could or couldn't use. I was still protective of them since, with the internet, distance alone would not protect our intellectual property. Her plan was to sell her camper and to bicycle several hundred miles down to Los Angeles, then fly to Kauai. I feared for her safety alone on remote sections of the coastal highway, but she laughed off my warnings. It was a relief to receive a postcard and emails from Kauai, but I missed her. After a few years, she came back to the mainland and started a bakery specializing in gluten-free and vegan products and offering a variety of alternatives to sugar.

James took over our baking. He had a talent for it, which surprised us all—even him.

WHERE ARE THE PARENTS?

B uzz called out with a chest cold. He sounded terrible. After three days, I asked him if he had food in the house. "Not very much." This admission from macho Buzz meant the situation was dire. Cara helped me put together a box with dahl, pozole, tapioca, and curry as well as several packages of herbal tea and a container of chai. When I delivered it, he thanked me sincerely. It was the first time I had seen him vulnerable, and I felt bad for him. His mother lived in Rohnert Park, fifteen minutes away. That had me shaking my head, but he was not the only crew member who seemed woefully unsupported.

We had hired Mick, another of Brian's mates, to do dishes so that Finn could prep. Mick was smaller in stature than his buddies but quite strong and capable. He confided in me that in his twenty-two years he had never eaten vegetables other than French fries and the lettuce and tomato on burgers. The string beans he'd had for dinner were his first ever. Could this be true? I interrogated him briefly, and he stuck to that story. His skin looked pasty, which I attributed to a diet of fast food. Who had raised this kid?

I often wondered "where are the parents?" as I got to know my crew. Daria had been abandoned at sixteen, Jim's mother was a drug-addled disaster, Rosie had grown up in foster care, Mick's parents had raised him on fast food, and Naomi's parents were unable to accept her unless she adhered to a strict set of religious principles. Jackie was living in squalor with the boyfriend, although she claimed a good relationship with her mother. I didn't know much about my other employees' family lives, but the crust punk "pirates" didn't seem to have much support either. Learning these backstories increased my respect for their accomplishments and charged up my maternal instincts, which were not always compatible with my position as employer and business owner.

Gentle Rob had been perceived as such a problem by his rigidly "Christian" family that they had sent him to a boarding school for troubled teens. Being abused there, he had run away and hit the road. One day I saw him on break talking with a lovely, sweet-faced young girl. "Who is that?" I asked him later.

"We met hopping trains."

They had seen each other occasionally while separately crisscrossing the country in boxcars—running from their demons, searching for America, and eventually meeting again by chance at Gaia's Garden on a sunny afternoon.

AN ANCIENT STRUGGLE

We met several times with the owners of a faith-based residential program for young women whom a friend referred to as "doves of easy virtue." These ladies, now committed to Christian ideals, were put to work packaging pallets of outdated clothes for sale to overseas markets. The owners had a grand vision of an indoor marketplace and had access to a sixty thousand square foot warehouse. They wanted a variety of vendors, including some to sell food. We were definitely interested. I reached out to them, and they seemed receptive, but first they had questions:

"Why the name Gaia's Garden?"

I explained Gaia was the Greek goddess of the earth, but we were more focused on the Gaia Principle—that we are all connected and our actions affect a living planet.

"Well, you know, a lot of people in the Evangelical community don't come to your place because of the name."

"Why not?" We were stunned.

"It's pagan. We don't support paganism."

I did some research when I got home and discovered a plethora of anti-Gaia sites. For these people, Gaia "worship" is an effort to replace God the Father with Mother Earth, and Al Gore is akin to the Antichrist.

Environmental laws are part of this attempted coup, including those supporting clean air and water, and the Endangered Species Act is seen as particularly heinous. Belief in global climate change is but one supposed heresy arising from what is termed a pagan feminist cult. This, from *The Big Green Lie*, Contender Ministries, October 6, 2002, was typical and often quoted:

Anyone who has studied the global environmental movement has no doubt heard the term "Gaia." Gaia is a revival of Paganism that rejects Christianity, considers Christianity its biggest enemy, and views the Christian faith as its only obstacle to a global religion centered on Gaia worship and the uniting of all life forms around the goddess of "Mother Earth". A cunning mixture of science, paganism, eastern mysticism, and feminism have made this pagan cult a growing threat to the Christian Church. Gaia worship is at the very heart of today's environmental policy. The Endangered Species Act, The United Nations' Biodiversity Treaty and the President's Council on Sustainable Development are all offspring of the Gaia hypothesis of saving "Mother Earth". This religious movement, with cult-like qualities, is being promoted by leading figures and organizations such as former Vice President Albert Gore, broadcaster Ted Turner, and the United Nations and its various NGOs. Al Gore's book Earth in the Balance *is just one of many books that unabashedly proclaims the deity of Earth and blames the falling away from this Pagan God on the environmentally unfriendly followers of Jesus Christ. The United Nations has been extremely successful in infusing the "Green Religion" into an international governmental body that has an increasing effect and control over all of our lives.*

So, what is this new cult of Gaia? It is basically a rehashed, modernized version of the paganism condemned by God in the Bible. Science, evolution theory, and a space age mentality have given it a new face, and made it sound more credible to a modern world, but it is the same paganism in all of its evils. There have been other religious movements that have presented similar revelations about the deity of a living earth, but Gaia has succeeded in uniting the environmental movement, the new age movement, Eastern religions, and even the leaders of many Christian denominations behind a bastardized version of paganism where the others weren't able to.

(Anyone baffled by the anti-environmental and anti-science stance of today's powerful political leaders may find an answer here.)

At a second meeting, still wanting to participate in what seemed like an enterprise with great potential, we agreed to change our booth name to the Garden Shed. We were not proud of the compromise but needed the money. This was agreeable to the organizers, and we made plans to go ahead.

As the project took shape, we received two pieces of news that were of concern. First, we were being placed outside and at the back. Customers, if they even tried to find us, would have to navigate the kids' area—avoiding little maniacs on tricycles and the slip 'n' slide. Another restaurant had a prominent space inside and in front. This didn't bode well for our chances of attracting hungry shoppers.

Probably worse was the theme—"The Good Old Days," meaning the 1890s. It was strongly suggested we have our employees wear red and white striped blazers. Handlebar mustaches would be a plus. What a joke! They hadn't met our pirates! When we talked it over with Sam, he mentioned that chef's coats were also worn in the 1890s and might be an option. That was helpful, but the whole project was now going sour for us. "Good old days" for whom? In addition to the political and social implications of venerating this time period, there was a practical consideration. In my experience, the best customers of markets like this were Latino. Why would that resonate with them?

A final visit to the organization's headquarters reinforced our decision not to participate. While the white dresses worn by my grandmother and great aunt back in the day were well-tailored and ornamented with lace and embroidery—probably uncomfortable but attractive—the young women from the program were decked out in flimsy, loose white shifts designed to hide any feminine attributes they might possess. And they were wearing athletic shoes! It was too much. We thanked them for considering us and dropped out. The market never did gain traction, so it turned out to be a good call on our part.

We got a welcome bump when the annual Harvest Festival invited us to bring samples to hand out to approximately five hundred people. Ari went with Rosie (who had quickly returned from Arizona) and Vicki, an intern from China. Many people there had not heard of us but enjoyed the food and promised to come in. I have a nice picture of Ari and Rosie with their arms around each other; they both look quite drunk.

All in all, we had happy customers with a potential for more, and the staff was capable and seemed to be getting along. I was starting to relax, unprepared for some distressing news.

GATEWAY TO BOUCHON

One prep cook went back to school in August, which was expected. Completely unexpected was Brian's resignation! Brian, our best cook, leader of the crust punks, Ari's even-handed liaison with the kitchen staff, told me he was leaving! It was a gut punch! He had an opportunity to work at Bouchon. Seeing the blank look on my face, he explained Bouchon was an upscale bistro in Yountville, owned by Thomas Keller of the internationally famous French Laundry. The career opportunities were tremendous. Unfortunately, he couldn't give us notice. High rollers like Mr. Keller had no interest in the scheduling concerns of a vegetarian buffet in Santa Rosa.

Typically, he was approaching the opportunity with intelligence and humility. He had been promised a prep job when one came available but would be starting as a dishwasher and taking a pay cut. It was a fifty-four-mile commute each way over the mountains in his old truck. As we talked, I came to share his excitement and was proud to have given him a start. He had done it himself, but we had provided the place and the support for him to shine. I had no doubt he would succeed there. He had been with us nearly three years; of course, it was time for him to spread his wings. He had become disgruntled with Ari's and my dueling management styles and needed a change. I would miss him so much: He had been our rock. It was hard to imagine Gaia's Garden without him, but I needed to accept his imminent departure and cheer him on.

He came in a few more times to help us regroup, and I presented him with a letter along with his last check. In it, I thanked him for all he had done for us, applauding his work and upward trajectory. There was some motherly advice about dealing with coworkers, envious friends, and what I suspected might be a drinking problem. It was also important for me to express these sentiments:

You have many times expressed appreciation that we have provided you with the venue to become who you are today. . . . The last months have been difficult for all of us, and I do feel bad that you are leaving with some resentments and that we have fallen short of how you think we should be managing things. Please keep in mind that, just as we have created a space where people can learn on the job and safely make mistakes, we've never done this before either! I have been way too lax (or checked out) in some areas, and Ari can be a dick at times; our judgment is not always good, but we both are trying to realize a righteous vision, and we are the ones taking all the risk. We have appreciated your caring support, perspective and opinions, and still do.

We were able to pull it together after Brian's exit better than I thought we would. Scheduling became a challenge, but we had a good and temporarily harmonious crew. Rob, Finn, and Sam could all cook. As needed, they would cover prep or jump in on dishes. James and Jackie were coming along and would soon be able to put out the buffet themselves. Terry,

Annie, and Katie could hold down the front, and Marty and Donald were covering the dish shifts.

Things were humming. Ari was bringing in terrific musicians; the art was excellent and diverse. One of Ari's projects was an evolution of the Activists' Lounge concept we had worked on for years—a regular event where political activists could relax, eat, drink, and socialize. Ari, with progressive activist Susan Lamont and a group called 100,000 Poets for Change, produced monthly themed events. Some were taped and shown on our TV's local access channel; all were well attended.

Jackie announced to the crew that she was having a birthday party for herself at her sister's apartment. It was to be a "kid's party"—no alcohol, no drugs, but lots of snacks, games, and "shenanigans." My hardened, street-wise crew was giddy with anticipation. When Rob and Marty asked Jackie what she wanted as a present, she ordered up a tiara. They spent a frantic day shopping, going from store to store. I wonder what the clerks thought, seeing these two black-clad, long-haired, tatted up, septum-ringed tough guys on their quest. I hope their hearts melted as mine did when the two stopped by the restaurant, flushed with triumph, to show off not only the tiara but a wand and a cape as well.

We hired a college student in October as a dishwasher. She had no previous experience, but Ari and I made note that she was a championship swimmer enrolled at the junior college. This meant she was strong and disciplined and liked water! She took to the job like a duck to . . . well, you know. To our delight, she treated Ari as she would a coach—immediately and consistently implementing his suggestions. Years later, his eyes would mist over a little when her name came up. "She was the best."

Katie the cashier left for a server position and didn't come back except as a customer on beet soup days. That same month we hired a blond, good-looking kid who was charming in the front of house. I noticed a significant uptick in patronage by beautiful young women. We agreed vegan women are gorgeous. It's amazing he could concentrate at all as they gathered around the register and buffet tables, radiant young women born to wear yoga pants.

Ari and the crew were getting on better. He even went to see Mick perform with his punk band, and an appreciative Mick bought him a beer. The next day, he asked Ari for feedback.

Ari, a professional musician and teacher, had great respect for anyone called to make music, and he was unfailingly tactful and kind in these instances, telling Mick, "While it's not my style, I thought it was well done and your performance was exciting."

His report to me was a little different: "It was blaring and unintelligible to my brain. Mick's thing was charging back and forth across the stage behind the lead singer while playing the guitar. Honestly, between the stuff that was on the house TVs, the very interestingly costumed audience, and the brewing mosh pit, I felt like I was in a deleted scene from *Idiocracy*."

We both enjoyed having crew members come out of the kitchen to participate in open mics and poetry readings, and Ari encouraged the front of house staff to join the dancers during slow times at the register.

Ari and his significant other, Genevive, had been together a year; she nearly destroyed him in a single day. A series of innocuous events triggered memories of her abusive childhood, which then came crashing down on Ari's head in the form of misplaced vitriol, recriminations, and wild accusations. Further, she made a point of contacting many of his friends, as well as his sons and in-laws, to spread baseless, ugly rumors. She reached out to musicians who played at our restaurant and to some of our customers. Those who knew Ari well gave the accusations no credence, but others may have taken the "where there's smoke, there's fire" approach. There was no way to know. He agonized over whether and how much and to whom to plead his case—wanting to proclaim his innocence but not wanting to protest too much. It was a terrible period; the damage to some of his valued relationships persisted for years. I was outraged by the unfairness of it all and Ari's anguish. This was one of those times when I could put aside our daily struggles and again focus on being his friend.

Meanwhile, my friend Sam from the Mission was having a better time with romance. Having convinced his lady love he was stable in his sobriety, he was preparing to join her in Grass Valley. He brought us another dishwasher from the Mission as a parting gift. The demographics of our kitchen were shifting—most of our crew members were still on the margins of society, but they now included older men pulling out of bad situations. Instead of "second chancers," these were fourth and fifth chancers. I hoped our younger crewmembers would learn from their experiences.

I didn't have our figures at year-end, but I knew I had been cashing in investments and retirement accounts at an alarming rate. In addition to everything else, our old van had blown up, and now we had a $587 monthly payment for a new one and insurance. The 2014 returns weren't filed until 2017, so confident was I that I wouldn't owe taxes. Our gross income had increased again, this time by only $10,000 to $499,000. Our losses had increased to $36,000. Had I been more of a businesswoman and less of a social worker, I would have followed these numbers more closely and seen that this adventure had cost me over $82,000 so far, not including the $105,000 purchase price.

Instead, I kept my head down and pushed forward. I still had some assets—two pieces of farmland I had inherited. While this was reassuring, I was living in a constant state of anxiety, which I did my best to ignore. "Suit up and show up" was my motto.

We were again voted Best Vegetarian Restaurant in the *Bohemian* poll and maintained our high ratings on Yelp, Tripadvisor, and HappyCow, a site for those seeking plant-based dining opportunities.

NO ONE IS A PROPHET IN THEIR OWN COUNTY

In early 2015, we were named by Daily Meal (thedailymeal.com) as one of the fourteen best buffets in the USA! The Bacchanal at Caesars Palace was in first place, followed by the Waldorf Astoria. Several sumptuous, multiroomed emporiums in Las Vegas, the Midwest, and the South—some with ice sculptures—followed; we were number ten (numbers eleven through fourteen were mysteriously absent). A couple who had seen the article came up from San Francisco to check us out and were the first to notify us of the honor. We were pleased but baffled. The listing didn't seem to have been written by a delighted customer; an old picture of the outside and the verbiage had come off Google maps and our website. Only the last sentence was original: "Not only is this one of the best buffets in the country, it also very well might be the healthiest." Perhaps we had been selected for location and diversity, bolstered by our Yelp reviews.

Though gratified, we were concerned it would bring us customers expecting much more than our two buffet tables, and indeed, some walked out disappointed. Still, it seemed like a good opportunity to request a mention in the food section of our local newspaper, which often printed tidbits about restaurants being honored and the comings and goings of chefs. I had not solicited a review before, fearful of the food critic's attitude toward plant-based restaurants, which had not hit the mainstream as they eventually would. Even in our progressive county, vegetarians and vegans were relegated to the fringes, along with old hippies and unhinged radicals—none of whom fit the corporate media demographic.

The press release I sent in was ignored, as were various future attempts to provide suitable content. When I rechecked the Daily Meal listing years later, there was a newer picture of our food on a plate, so perhaps a reporter had ventured in at some point.

We learned too quickly why Brian and Rob had been lukewarm in their endorsements of Marty the dishwasher. He was immature and troubled, frequently coming in late, texting, and taking long breaks. Without Brian as the hammer, he was running amok. Finn, now head cook in charge of the night shift, inherited these problems and was not happy about it. Marty didn't hold up his end on the cleaning, and there were strong suspicions that he was loaded most of the time. Marty complained that Finn demeaned him and had threatened him. The three of us sat down and put everything on the table. Marty promised to improve, as he always did, and then slid back into bad habits, as he always did.

We kept him on longer than his performance warranted due to his seemingly heartfelt efforts to improve and what we knew about his home life. Initially, he lived with his mother, who was a hot mess. She came in one day to visit her boy at work and tried to steal a package of paper towels; Ari retrieved them as tactfully as he could. She was addicted to pills, and one of Marty's unexpected absences had been due to giving her CPR and watching over her all night—she had taken eighty Xanax within two weeks.

He finally moved out of his mom's house, and we were ready to let him go, but then his new home caught fire. Running to alert his two roommates, which saved their lives, he left his beloved pet rat behind, and the sweet creature burned to death. At first, I doubted this bizarre story but found it confirmed in the newspaper. Ari, as critical as he could be, also had a strong compassionate side, and in this instance we couldn't kick Marty when he was down. Trying to keep his behavior contained, we enacted extraordinary measures, making him leave his phone with Terry and having him check in and out when he went on the tens—paid breaks that no one else had to note on their time cards.

Pink-haired Annie and Marty were a couple, but even she was understanding when, at the end of January, we threw in the towel. When I presented Marty with his last check, he acknowledged the action as overdue and cheerfully opined this might be his wake-up call to get his life together. He initiated a goodbye hug and asked if he could come in to pick up his W-2, so his mother wouldn't get it and claim his refund.

Our parting had been a little too soft. Marty became a frequent visitor, usually loaded and with unsavory companions. We banned him from the restaurant, making sure Annie got the message.

We brought Jackie's boyfriend, Ray, in to replace Marty on dishes. I was leery of knowingly hiring a significant other, but he seemed to be a serious and respectful young man. Jackie promised there would be "no domestic drama." I had to tell her later not to lobby for him to get more hours, but otherwise they both acted professionally, taking breaks together when their schedules allowed.

Jackie and James were both being trained to make the lunch buffet. James knew most of it already. Jackie had problems with time management, and some of her dishes had to be remade, but she was coming along. We brought in one of her classmates, Evan, to prep. The school hinted he might have autism but indicated if we could work with Jackie, we would have no problem with Evan. He was shy and somewhat slow on the prep, but Finn and James gave good reports. I had him do time trials to build his speed. Not wanting to pressure anyone to work so quickly they might cut themselves, I advised him to wait for a slow time, tell everyone he was doing a time trial so he wouldn't be interrupted, then note how long it took to cut, say, three gallons of potatoes. In future trials, he could work against his own time, privately and at a safe pace.

Evan was an Evangelical Christian and began complaining about the kitchen culture of profanity and lewd music. I did my best to insulate him, giving him a place to prep that was somewhat private and quiet. The obscenity, both conversational and lyrical, was not lawsuit worthy and was probably typical of most restaurants he might work at in the future. I knew if I read the riot act to the rest of the crew, they would comply only when I was there and would take out their resentment on Evan.

We seemed to be doing OK for the most part, and the staff members were getting along well enough. Little did I know we would soon have an extraordinary opportunity to take it up a notch.

PART 4

THE UNIVERSE
DELIVERS

AN ITAL CHEF

February 20, 2015, marked a turning point for Gaia's Garden. It started out like many other days with Jake, the dishwasher, not showing up. He had been increasingly difficult, loudly complaining about everyone and everything. This day, I called his sober living house and was told he had been evicted—having been caught drunk in his room with a hooker in the closet. Yup, a normal day at Gaia's Garden. With a sigh, I grabbed an apron and started on the dishes. Dishes were hard. I wasn't happy. As I scrubbed and rinsed and stacked plates, I put out a simple but fervent prayer to the Universe: "Please send us who needs to be here."

Within an hour, an energetic young man bounced in looking for work. He was fresh out of rehab and claimed experience washing dishes there and in restaurants. I handed him my apron. As I sat down to rest, two men came in. One was about 6'5" and built like a tank; the other looked to be in his late forties and was small by comparison—but then everyone was. The smaller one was looking for work. Did we have anything at all? I mentioned I had been looking for a dishwasher but may have just hired one. "I can do that," he said. I didn't picture him in that role and nearly sent him away. "Oh, what the hell," I thought. "He made the effort to come in—the least I can do is talk with him." I was also sensitive to the fact that he and his friend were Black, and I didn't want them to feel unfairly dismissed. If that's reverse racism, I have no regrets. The Universe had saved the best for last.

It took only a few minutes before I realized I had already met Abdo. He had come in the year before, scouting locations for a Caribbean restaurant, and had shown me the menu from his restaurant near Sacramento; it contained some wonderful vegan options. While I had said the appropriate words of encouragement, I really hadn't wanted him as a competitor. Now he was here willing to take a dishwashing job? I didn't know what had happened and didn't care.

"I don't need a dishwasher, but I might need a cook."

His face lit up. "I'm a cook!"

"Yes, I know."

A very long conversation ensued. He was from the Caribbean. It was hard to understand him as he expounded at length on Ital (reggae culture) with a thick accent. Eventually I faded and handed him off to Ari; they talked for another forty-five minutes. Abdo came in the next day for a mutual audition. He was awesome—fast, skilled, genial—obviously used to running a kitchen. As he handed a pot to the new dishwasher—who, miraculously, had come back for a second day—I heard him say, "Could you please wash this for me? And I need it right away." I liked this combination of humility and authority.

Abdo came with a book of recipes but focused on learning ours. One night he made his lemon-ginger tempeh, which was both colorful and delicious. Mick, still vegetable-averse, fell in love with it. I liked it too, and I'm not fond of tempeh.

The Universe had come through. I needed to attend to my health but had been afraid to abandon the kitchen, even for a few weeks. I had suffered from back pain for years, and slinging around twenty-five-pound bags of commodities and cases of #10 cans, lifting heavy pots, and being on my feet for ten to twelve hours a day had made it nearly unbearable. The main issue turned out to be my hip, which was no surprise to those who saw me limping around the restaurant. I am blessed with a strong constitution and a high pain threshold, and I treated my body the same way I dealt with the financials at Gaia's Garden: barreling through and not thinking about it much. Ari kept trying to get me to wait for help with all the lifting, but I would become impatient and just do things myself. This was a point of contention dating back to when we had DJ'd together, moving heavy speakers and large cases of CDs. His genuine concern would change to irritation and finally apathy as I ignored his repeated admonitions, behaving—in his opinion—like a martyr.

By now, even I had to admit it was time to step back from the physical demands and the stress of the business and go in for hip joint replacement surgery. I already had cooks, but Abdo was a cut above. He enjoyed coming out of the kitchen and mixing with the customers, offering them tastes of this or that. He'd check in with them to ask how they liked his food. Soon, his good nature and exotic appeal won him a following. Abdo admired Finn and considered him a teacher. He and James also got along well. James, Abdo, and his brother (the big guy) ended up living together on and off for several years. He was less enthusiastic about Jackie and Evan but was sensitive enough to recognize they had some challenges. Ari was glad to have an adult in the kitchen. I enjoyed Abdo's positive energy and how he called me "Auntie" and Ari "Uncle." We felt like one big, happy family.

I was feeling confident about the kitchen when, in April, I presented myself for the hip surgery. It was the first time I had been in a hospital since birth, and I had delayed it as long as possible. I think my epitaph could well be "She hung in until the last dog was dead." Richard and I had attended an orientation for joint replacement candidates; he had pointed out with amusement that while the others limped slightly, I moved like Quasimodo. It was time. The surgery went well, and three days later I was ready to talk to my crew, though not to join them.

Jackie had been taken off school lunches after some serious mistakes and did better working on the buffet, so I had switched their duties and moved James to lunches. When I called to check in, Jackie asked if she could make the sandwiches for the school lunch this time while James made the buffet. I gave permission, then began to hear pieces of a shocking larger story.

DOMESTIC DRAMA AFTER ALL

True to her promise not to bring domestic drama to work, Jackie and Ray had broken up but given no indication of their change in status. Jackie had moved in with an ex-boyfriend, yet she and Ray had continued to speak civilly at work and take their lunches together.

On the night of my surgery, Terry had given Ray a ride home, as he often did. As he recalled, there was nothing remarkable about Ray or the conversation.

The events that followed, though, were beyond remarkable. On arriving home, Ray donned Kevlar armor and packed his favorite knife—a wicked blade with holes for his fingers on one side. His mom drove him to the house where Jackie was now living and waited in the car as Ray knocked on the door. Robert, Jackie's current boyfriend, answered and Ray immediately set on him with the knife, nearly severing his hand. As Jackie grabbed for her phone, Ray knocked it away and dragged her outside, trying to get her into the car. Robert, in a heroic move, regained his footing and came after Ray, only to be slashed again. Fortunately, neighbors heard

Jackie screaming and called the police, who arrived in time to prevent a kidnapping and possibly two murders and a suicide. Ray fled with his mom in her car but was soon apprehended, covered in blood.

Two days later, Ray was in jail, his mother was at home, Jackie's boyfriend was in the hospital, and the remarkably resilient Jackie was making sandwiches.

As I was closing Ray's personnel file, I realized to my distress I had never collected his documents and didn't have his Social Security number. I had to have it, so the only thing to do was to visit him at the jail. He was in a special section, as befitted his charges. I was sent to walk alone down a very long hallway to that visiting area. Still recovering from the surgery, all I heard was the clomp, clomp of my cane as I struggled to make it to the end. After about twenty minutes, Ray was brought up, and we regarded each other through glass. The first thing he said was "How's your hip?"

As I processed that, he continued, "I want to apologize for the timing of all this. I'm sorry it happened while you were in the hospital."

All this? He was facing seven felony charges and possibly life in prison! His concern for my well-being and his bland demeanor touched me but were truly odd. I explained my mission and—since I hadn't been allowed to bring pen or paper—he patiently repeated his Social Security number several times until I had committed it to memory. I knew he hadn't been able to cash his last check and asked if he wanted me to put the money on his books. He asked me to give cash to his mother instead.

Jackie's boyfriend Robert was released from the hospital, grateful they had saved his hand. Jackie soldiered on as if nothing had happened, but as hearings came up, her stoic exterior began to crack. She was very nervous when the day came for her to testify at the preliminary hearing, and Terry and I attended with her since none of her family members was available. I stayed for Robert's testimony; Jackie wasn't allowed in for that part and he had no one else there to support him.

HAIR ON FIRE

Meanwhile, back at the restaurant, May brought an exodus of employees. Mick was moving over to a local pub. Rob interviewed with a top restaurant in Healdsburg and picked up part-time hours there as he gradually eased off our schedule. He had been with us over three years by the time he left, had gone to culinary school, and was well beyond slinging pizzas at Little Caesars—or living in boxcars.

Our handsome young cashier wanted to spend the summer traveling and going to festivals, unencumbered by work obligations. As a parting gift, he sent us three young women to interview for his job. They were all beautiful and intelligent. We chose Chloe. I could see she had strong boundaries, and I cautioned Terry that he needed to maintain a hands-off policy. He had a habit of touching the arms of the young women or putting his arm around their shoulders. Ari referred to him somewhat sarcastically as "Uncle Terry" due to his attentions to the women, although neither of us ascribed to him any predatory intent.

His selective affections were noticed by the male crew members, who would tease the young women after he left. I had mentioned this as a potential problem in his evaluation meetings and asked him to refrain, but he didn't. I had also checked in with the women to make sure they were not uncomfortable with the touching—an uncomfortable conversation in itself. I had assured them that if they wanted me to, I would bring it to a screeching halt without involving them. Most reciprocated his displays of affection, though, so it didn't seem to be an issue, just something I needed to stay on top of and document consistently. Ari noted correctly that if he showed even a fraction of this behavior, we'd be taken to court.

I did receive an email from a member of the Four Agreements study group, which met on Thursdays. The writer stated Terry had made her uncomfortable by sitting too close to her and calling her "dear." I showed him the email, and he seemed properly chastened. The group stopped meeting at the restaurant shortly thereafter. Terry's attentions to the female staff continued, but no one complained.

It was hard to drop the hammer on Terry because he was such a huge help and so loyal to us. He went several years without a raise ("wait until you're making money") and voluntarily took it upon himself to come in before his shift, make our bank deposits, and keep the registers stocked with change.

Despite a new vitality Abdo brought to the restaurant, Ari rapidly became unhappy again, complaining—it seemed to me—about nearly everything. I had proposed various ways for us to work together with some harmony, but none had been helpful. Suggesting he leave notes instead of talking directly to staff as things came up had been one, since Ari's New York edge and insensitive timing put our young California crew on the defensive. As the notes piled up, though, they lost their impact and were usually ignored. We tried setting up meetings—daily, weekly, monthly—with the staff, but it seemed something else would always take precedence. I had already written an operations manual that nobody followed and created checklists that nobody checked. Swept up in the day-to-day operations, I chose to pick my fights. The result was a lack of consistency and structure that would frustrate generations of employees and drive Ari deeper and deeper into a simmering rage.

Finn, the main cook on the dinner shift, and Ari were butting heads constantly. Ari had been calling for both Marty and Finn to be fired since January, when someone had thrown an entire loaf of our house-made bread into the trash instead of making it into croutons. I assumed it was Marty, but the complaints about Finn continued after Marty left. Finn was a solid guy I didn't want to lose, our last crust punk, and Ari's complaints centered less on his work than on his attitude. Ari found him to be disrespectful. When Ari came in with a complaint or a suggestion, Finn wouldn't acknowledge him. I tried to explain to Ari that his attack style of management put Finn into fight or flight mode. He saw his options as either punching Ari in the face or ignoring him, a form of flight. I was grateful he chose that one. I had bumped into Finn accidentally one evening and gotten a bruise—the guy was all muscle. Ari had no patience for my psychobabble, and the situation continued to escalate.

The agonizing months of the Mason-centered feud had made it clear to me and the rest of the staff that I would never cast Ari out, no matter what. Therefore, getting along with him at least superficially had to be a job requirement. I met with Finn in February and presented him with a written evaluation. It detailed his accomplishments and positive attributes, which were significant and many. It also requested he be more responsive to Ari and suggested ways of dealing with him that might lessen the stress, such as asking if the conversation could be held at a more opportune time. Finally, I made it as clear as I could, as tactfully as I could, that unless the situation improved, we would have to part ways.

They had a major blowup in May after a successful evening when the kitchen had been slammed with orders. Everyone was tired and should have been happy—they had done well. Ari took exception to Finn's demeanor. Finn called Ari a drunk and a prick. There had been ongoing complaints about Ari's drinking, and clearly he was not meeting the conditions set forth in the Mason Agreement. I knew he was stressed beyond reason, as was I. Had I not had a program of recovery and a well-earned commitment to sobriety, I probably would have been drunk by 10 a.m. every morning. Whether Ari had a serious drinking problem, was responding inappropriately to the stress, or was being unfairly accused by disgruntled employees was unclear to me. I suspected all these elements might be at play, but in our long association I had never seen evidence he was an alcoholic like me. Once again, I asked him to desist from drinking while on the job. He responded by telling me I should fire Finn.

Fortunately, Ari was going to be gone for four days, and everyone had a chance to cool down a little. I checked in with Finn. It was no secret Ari wanted him gone, and I asked him about his plans. He was working on his résumé, he told me, but wanted to save up money for a car. He was hoping to work for another four to five months. I assured him I would do whatever I could to support this and give him time to move on to a good job.

"Please try to acknowledge Ari when he talks to you. That's his biggest complaint."

"I'll try. It's hard, though, when he bursts in here like Gordon fucking Ramsay with his hair on fire."

Later that night, I wrote optimistically in my journal, "The goal now is to maintain day by day a working environment that is bearable for everyone."

The entry when Ari came back read, "Had meeting with Ari. Most things OK. He wants uniforms and, of course, Finn out. Otherwise, an uneventful day."

I ordered chef coats from the laundry service. Abdo and Jackie had their own, and I charged the rest $1.20 per week, which was what the rentals cost us.

Ari was still wound up over the Finn situation. One of our customers, who had become his friend, confided she had taken Ari for a walk one afternoon trying to cool him down. Fearing a repeat of our battles over Mason, my goal was to keep a lid on things and keep the restaurant running until Finn left voluntarily. This proved to be achievable, but it took a lot of energy, which, since my surgery, had been in short supply.

NOT EVERY DAY IS A DORIS DAY

S weeping dry storage one day, I pulled the chest freezer away from the wall and, to my horror, found a pile of debris that had fallen behind it and a nest of roaches. Lots of roaches. I killed as many as I could, but there were multitudes. The first line of defense was to buy bug spray and "roach motels." The roaches continued to multiply, ignoring the spray and breeding in the "motels." I called an exterminator who came in and sprayed, announcing we would have no further problems. Wrong!

James would come in each morning to see them scattering when he turned on the lights. We had double-checked all the food to make sure it was secure and scheduled a round of deep cleaning to eliminate their food sources—all to no avail.

A customer told me discreetly that she had seen one coming out of a crack in the bathroom floor. We hired a man to replace the floor—it was a $1,000 job due to a relic from when the building had belonged to the phone company: a mysterious box filled with wiring that went nowhere had been sunk in the concrete, which was why the floor had never been quite level.

While talking with some customers, I saw a roach crawl up a wall behind the register. Fortunately, they didn't see it. Finally, I found the right pest control company, and they eliminated them. I signed up for service every two months, ending our roach problem before the health department inspection and adding another fifty dollars per month to our expenses.

Trying to increase revenue, we instituted a Sunday brunch—scrambled tofu, a hash made of corned tempeh, beets, and yams, along with blueberry pancakes, fried potatoes, curry, black bean "sausages" with mushroom gravy, hush puppies, roasted yams with kale, and mango gazpacho. The salad bar and a mimosa were included for $16.95. Another option was a breakfast burrito made with the scrambled tofu, salsa, and fried potatoes for $8.95. All of the items we were adding now were better priced for us and vegan, and most were gluten-free. Veganizing recipes wasn't hard.

A leader in the vegan community emailed us, complaining our brunch prices were exorbitant and comparing us with three restaurants in San Francisco which she said were cheaper. This was a ridiculous claim. She was also upset that we offered house-made fruit syrups instead of real maple, which would have added $2 dollars to <u>our</u> cost. When I responded with item-to-item comparisons, showing we offered far more for less, she backed down, but her begrudging tone showed we had not overcome her perception problem

Abdo took over the brunch on Father's Day. Jackie had forgotten her key, and everyone started a half hour late. Chloe the cashier overslept and came in late too. Abdo was a good multitasker but when he took on too much, disaster followed. He burned the hash and the curry, and the tofu scramble was tasteless. We had a party of seventeen and another of seven and were not well prepared. As I doled out chocolate-covered strawberries, I recited my new mantra, a gift from Terry: "Not every day is a Doris Day."

Abdo was learning our recipes but lacked the broad range of experience needed to understand the dishes. Ari was appalled to find carrots in the eggplant parmesan. I was disappointed when the sauce for the stuffed cabbage tasted like watered-down ketchup rather than having the delicately sweet and sour flavor I expected. We were both tactful, realizing Abdo was a major asset to our operation, and suggested he focus more on the recipes he already knew. He continued valiantly trying to replicate ours—with both successes and failures. The situation was complicated by his being illiterate—something we never discussed but probably should have. He would have his assistants read the recipes to him, claiming he had forgotten his glasses. It was a delicate subject, so we all played along.

It is a mistake to be intimidated by one's chef, but I was not alone. A New York Times article profiled a restaurant owner who was so afraid of losing his cantankerous chef that rather than confront him, he put warnings on the menu labeling certain dishes as subpar. The chef couldn't read English, so he never knew.

An ongoing problem was the naivety of most of our crew to different cuisines. Most could follow recipes, but they had never had an authentic curry, for example, so they didn't know how it should look or taste. The smokers, with dead taste buds, oversalted most things. This created no end of frustration for Ari, who was trying to deal more effectively with them. I tuned out more of his complaints than I should have. We had always been aware we needed more customers in general, but it was clear now our dinner business, specifically, was suffering. The dishes weren't always up to par, and the crew was letting food dry out or get mushy on the buffet table. We both did our best to keep everyone on point, but it was an uphill battle.

Jackie was not doing well at all. Day by day, she had lost much of her spark since the assault. She was coming in late and neglecting prep. Finn complained she would reheat curries and soups from the night before rather than making them fresh, leaving the night shift to make them. James and Abdo had what I referred to as a "come to Jesus" meeting with her, telling her she needed to make the job a priority or quit. Her work and habits began to improve slightly.

Finn gave notice near the end of July. He was joining Mick at the pub. I had mixed feelings, of course. He had been an anchor since Brian had left and was the last of the "pirates." He was a good cook and a hard worker. His absence would give us some breathing room, though, until Ari selected his next target—which I now knew was inevitable.

(Last I heard, Finn was cooking in New Orleans—living the dream.)

We hired an erratic dishwasher with a drinking problem and two more prep cooks—Andy and Dirk. Both were experienced, and both were capable. Ari was particularly impressed by Dirk, whose heritage was Asian Indian. He had been raised in a home that practiced our *satvig* cooking style and seemed an excellent fit for the restaurant. Hopefully, these new staff members would help us get out of the financial ditch.

SKIDDING ALONG THE GUARDRAIL

As we began acquiring experienced crew members, it seemed success might finally be in reach, though for now it was elusive. Money was tight. I dreaded our biweekly payroll and quarterly tax payments as well as Richard's innocent queries about our profitability. I had cashed in all my retirement accounts, the equity line on Mom's house was maxed out, and I failed to qualify for a line on my own house. I tried to sell some gold coins, but the price of gold had tanked to the point of being ridiculous. We used checks for all our purchases in order to gain a few days with the float. Every night I would tally up the outstanding checks against the day's bank balance and the income I hoped to receive from the restaurant and school. This system worked until it didn't. One day, to my horror, I received notice that several paychecks had bounced.

My ongoing anxiety had come to a head. I was frightened and embarrassed but had no choice but to confront the situation head-on. For the first time, I asked Richard for a loan. He immediately provided the $3,000 I requested. Then, I called a meeting of the six affected employees, apologized, and assured them the money was now in the bank (it was), offering either to pay them cash immediately or to wait and see what their banks would do. I knew from experience that some banks would send a check through for a second time before refusing it. I hoped this would be the case for all but didn't know. If there were any fees to be paid, I would pay them, of course, and write letters if need be. It was a humiliating but necessary conversation.

My crew members were very kind. None of them had yet received notices. Rob and some of the others already trusted me. Andy and Dirk, newer hires, were more concerned. They took the cash; the rest were willing to wait.

Andy was able to take the lead cook position at night but was growing increasingly dissatisfied. He wanted more money; I wanted to pay it but couldn't. I received a report he had been cursing and yelling and talking about how working at another restaurant would pay better and that working for us was too stressful. He left without notice within a couple of days. I didn't get to the bookkeeping until much later and found not only had he taken the cash for my bounced check but the check had gone through, and he had pocketed that also. By the time I found this, it was too late to fight it.

I had a more immediate concern: my left shoulder had become unbearably painful. This had been my weak point for decades, since stretched tendons had forced me to give up Tae Kwon Do in my twenties. I attributed the current injury to pulling fully loaded carts behind me at Cash and Carry—a poor ergonomic choice but seemingly necessary to keep the carts from swerving. I found better ways to navigate, but nothing changed—and then my right shoulder, which I didn't use as much, became painful also. I visited my doctor, who ruled out rotator cuff injuries and gave me cortisone shots, which helped but only for a short time. At one appointment, he entered the room triumphantly and declared, "I know what's wrong with you! You'll be better in two to three days. You're going to think I'm a hero!"

The problem, he told me, was polymyalgia rheumatica (PMR), an autoimmune condition causing shoulder pain and primarily affecting women over fifty. My high inflammation numbers had been the clue, and prednisone was the solution. "It's a steroid. You'll be on twenty milligrams, a low dose, for about a year. Then we'll reevaluate."

The prednisone helped the pain, but the side effects were scary; it would eventually take over cortisol production from the adrenal glands and create symptoms of Cushing Syndrome—a moon face, a ring of fat under the neck, high blood pressure, thin skin, a "cortisol belly," soft bones, and high blood sugar. Undiagnosed Cushing's Disease—the full-blown manifestation of the syndrome—had tortured and killed my father. "We're *giving* you Cushing's," said my doctor with a grin when I mentioned that. "But don't worry, all those symptoms will go away."

Trusting him, and willing to do anything to ease the pain, I continued the course of prednisone. It helped. I didn't associate my growing health issues with the stress of the restaurant, nor did I spend much time thinking about it. I had work to do!

A new hire, Reneé, told me there was a "borderline" sexual harassment problem with Dirk, Ari's Asian Indian protégé, and that I should talk with Jackie. When I did, she told me Dirk had told her she was staying with her boyfriend only for "his cock" and then went on to speculate about how much sex she was having. He had also told Reneé, a new mom, that now she had her baby, she could have sex all the time. He had taken the kitchen etiquette of announcing "behind!" when moving into someone's space as a double entendre. This part Jackie felt she needed to write out rather than tell me, which was a surprise since we had privately had many frank "girl talks." The note stated he would air hump behind her and say, "Oh, behind!"

This seemed way past borderline. Ari and I discussed it. He understood the seriousness of the issues, but he really liked Dirk and hoped there might be a reconciliation. I thought the tensions would continue no matter what we did. Also, Dirk wasn't doing that well in the kitchen. I had gotten complaints he was slow and didn't keep the buffet tables stocked when it was his duty. Annie at the register reported he had called her a "kitchen slut" for some reason and wouldn't respond to her requests to refill trays.

We agreed Ari would talk with Dirk to hear his side before we made a final decision to fire him. Ari started the conversation with a mild "These days it's hard to know what's appropriate. . . ." Dirk stood up and shouted, "This always happens to me! I'm done!" Then, he walked out. I took that as quitting and was relieved.

Dirk calmed down later and called Ari. He had his own list of complaints and felt no one cared about the dysfunction in the kitchen. Reneé had carelessly burned him. She climbed up on things without regard to safety. Jackie also talked about sex and wouldn't take his advice on the curry. Meat eaters in the kitchen weren't focused on our mission. He claimed there had been an agenda against him from the beginning. It still seemed best to have him move on. I met him off-site to give him his last check. He was very cordial.

Dirk had told Ari that only he understood our cooking style, having been raised with it, and that the rest didn't really care and were just going through the motions. Ari agreed with this assessment and also saw the need to separate Dirk from the crew but fervently wished there had been a different outcome. I wished Jackie had taken his advice on the curry. Ours were mild by design to accommodate a range of tastes at the buffet, but hers were usually *too* bland.

SUMMER INTO FALL

We had two very successful events that summer. One was a benefit for earthquake victims in Nepal. Abdo, James, and Andy (while he was still with us) were stellar. We even made a small profit after donating as we had promised.

Then, Ari set up a dinner concert with Ancient Future, an internationally known world music ensemble. We sold out at thirty dollars per person. (We should have charged more, but remembering other times we had tried to charge a cover—for Fantuzzi and David Rovics, who should have brought in huge crowds and didn't—we feared another debacle.) Abdo and Rob, who had returned briefly, nailed what was definitely an international dinner buffet: samosas, tomato coconut curry, pozole, peanut ginger tofu, corned tempeh and fried potatoes with mustard sauce, mango gazpacho, and sides of green beans, rice, corn bread, and steamed vegetables along with the salad bar and desserts. The music was superb; the food was abundant, beautiful, and delicious; the packed house was joyfully appreciative; and the musicians were ecstatic. I was filled with a rich satisfaction. This was what it was about. If only every day could be like this!

Abdo took a food booth to a Ziggy Marley concert at Sonoma Mountain. James went with him and reported that all the reggae performers, including Ziggy, had come to the booth—delighted to see Abdo again and hungry for his cooking. He took what would become our standard festival fare—curry, rice, beans, coconut greens, samosas with mango chutney, fried coconut tofu nuggets with sweet and sour sauce, hush puppies, plantains, and chai tapioca. He was in his element at these outdoor events and loved doing them. The venue was impressed, and we were invited back to other concerts that year and in subsequent years. Usually, we were one of only two vendors, so we always did well.

In October, we raised the prices again. The full lunch buffet was now $12.95, and dinner was $16.95.

Fall meant "trimming season" for the marijuana farms north of us. We became used to our employees' scheduling vacations during this time in order to participate. The pay was good, and we benefited from newly wealthy vegans heading south after the work was done. Perhaps that explained the actions of one young couple. Unkempt but polite, they ordered two full buffets. After they ate, the woman went into the bathroom and stayed there. A good twenty minutes went by. We had only the one customer restroom, and seeing a line forming, I knocked on the door and gently called out, "Are you OK?" No answer, so I escorted the customers, including a desperate pregnant woman, through the kitchen to our much less elegant employee bathroom.

When I returned, the other was still occupied. I tried again: still no answer. Trying to be tactful, I asked the woman's male companion if she was alright, expressing concern she might be ill since she hadn't answered or come out. Just then, she reentered the dining room in fresh clothes and with wet hair. Her partner flew into a rage, yelling at me, "YOU WANT A TIP?" as he threw a fifty dollar bill into the jar. "BE NICER TO YOUR CUSTOMERS!" The two stormed out, leaving me scratching my head and the crew well compensated.

On one visit to the bank down the street, I was greeted by an excited teller. "Did you see this?" she asked, showing me her phone. One of Snoop Dogg's sons attending the Emerald Cup—a cannabis-themed event—had visited our restaurant and posted his picture with a thumbs-up on Instagram. This annual event brought us a lot of business, since many attendees were vegetarian or vegan and very hungry.

NO PLACE LIKE HOME

High turnover is common in the restaurant business. Like many, we had our share of problem people while many other employees understandably left for higher pay and more opportunities, or because their school quarters had ended. Several crew members stayed with us for three years or more, which was satisfying and stabilizing. I saw Gaia's Garden as a sort of incubator and was happy for those who left for better jobs. When some of them came back, I could always find hours for them. It was good to have them already trained and for us all to know what to expect. At times, though, there would be flurries of turnovers that were exhausting and very stressful.

Rob, our shy, train-hopping pirate, had been gone only two months when he came in to see if we had hours. His new job had been cutting back and he—as last hired—wasn't getting as much work as he needed. We were glad to have him back, if only temporarily. In keeping with our desire to look more professional, we told him septum rings were no longer acceptable, and chef coats were now mandatory. He agreed to both. We had received feedback from customers who saw septum rings as a sanitation problem. I didn't think they were, but perception is hugely important in the restaurant business. He and pink-haired Annie were now a couple.

Rob stayed with us another three months and was a great help with the Ancient Future concert. While we appreciated his skills, he clearly saw this as a step backward. Run-ins with Abdo and Ari may have expedited his exit, and by the time he left, we were all relieved.

Then, Brian came back! It was for only a short time, but we were happy to see him. He had walked out of Bouchon after exactly a year—having stayed long enough to be sought after by several Michelin-starred restaurants in the San Francisco Bay Area. He wanted to make a thoughtful decision and needed some paid hours in the meantime. He told me that the chef, if not happy with underlings, would throw pots at them. I wore out this anecdote trying to defend Ari's management style: "At least he doesn't throw things." I don't think anyone else considered that a high enough bar to take seriously. After several interviews over a few months, Brian went to a renowned local restaurant where he was able to realize a dream of setting the menu based on what he harvested from the garden.

We hired Preston and Lloyd, both for prep. Preston was a friend of James, an artist and a musician; Lloyd was a long-term friend of Ari whom Ari held in high esteem as a writer, actor, and creative genius. Preston liked Ari and told me he reminded him of the Italian men he had grown up with. He would occasionally complain to me that he tired of hearing other crew members complain about Ari. It was a relief to know Ari had two supporters in the kitchen.

Rosie was doing home health care and occasionally working some hours with us. We were happy to have her rejoin us temporarily, filling in when we needed someone on dishes.

I first learned of the catastrophic Valley Fire when two dear friends from neighboring Lake County appeared at my door. They had lost everything. It did not affect the restaurant directly, but it was a shock to lose whole towns we knew well. Other refugees started showing up at the restaurant. It was easy to spot them: They were still stunned and sometimes dusty. In these situations, we fed them and the first responders, comping meals and beverages. That was one of the few things Ari and I always agreed on.

BLOOD RED BEETS

We hired another prep cook, and dishwashers came and went. One Mission hire was in and out with tenuous sobriety and another was starting to have sudden absences. We brought in Martin, a friend of Jackie, for the dish pit. He was a gentle, depressed soul who trained companion dogs and—unlike most of the others—appeared to be free of substance abuse.

I received a call from Martin one morning that Jackie was having an anxiety attack. When I arrived at the restaurant, he was sitting with her in a booth, trying to calm her. She was trembling and seemed to have trouble focusing. I got her a glass of water, and she managed to drink some. She had already been nervous about an upcoming court hearing, and the anxiety attack had been triggered by beet soup. Our version was a deep red—too reminiscent of that bloody night. Even knowing what she had been through, I was surprised to see my Warrior Princess so shattered. After all, she had soldiered on stoically for months.

Her mother had endured unimaginable horror while escaping from Southeast Asia. Jackie had learned that upsets that seemed like life and death to other young girls—feeling unpopular or losing a boyfriend—were insignificant compared to what her mother had been through. They literally weren't worth talking about in her family. Even her close brush with death had paled in comparison to the family legacy. She had learned to just keep going, but now her stoic front was beginning to fray. It took a while before she could stand up. Martin and I walked her to my car so I could take her home. I repeated my urging that she contact Victim's Services.

We had a staff party at the end of the year, which included a "spring roll-off"—an effort to find a winning recipe for spring rolls. Each of the entries received one point, suggesting everyone had voted for themselves, so the results were inconclusive.

At year-end, our income had increased to $557,230, or by about $50,000. We were doing something right! According to our tax returns, we had come out even, although I wasn't feeling it. I was still moving money around frantically and had run up my credit cards as well as Mom's equity line. Terrified of another payroll crisis, I continued to agonize each night over the expenses of the next day.

Mom had left me a piece of farmland in Nebraska that had been granted to my great-grandfather in the late 1800s by then president Benjamin Harrison. Feeling like a terrible disappointment to my forebears, I put it on the market, desperate to maintain cash flow and finally put the restaurant over the top.

By the end of 2015, we had been named the tenth best buffet in the United States; Best Vegetarian Restaurant by the *Bohemian* for the fifth year; best buffet in Sonoma County by Yelp; and twenty-first out of 420 Sonoma County restaurants by Tripadvisor.

BOUNCING BASKETS IN BONGOLAND

The sale of my farm closed in January, and I was able to pay off all my debts and have some breathing room from the proceeds.

That same month, I was taking school lunches to the van when my cart hit a crack in the sidewalk in front of the restaurant. Trays of sandwiches went flying onto the pavement. It was too late to make new ones, and I noted that most were not actually on the ground. As I desperately retrieved the ones that could be saved, I heard a voice above me: "Can I help you?" It was a male passerby, poorly dressed, possibly homeless. Together we salvaged what we could—fortunately enough to meet the requirements for the school. As I got ready to head out, he asked if we had work. I told him to meet me in an hour.

Dimitri came in on odd shifts for a while to wash dishes and clean, and eventually I was able to put him on payroll. I already liked him and knew a bit about his character. Still, with no résumé or references, I checked into his background online and found that, as I had suspected, he was recently out of prison, having been incarcerated for five years in Georgia on drug charges, which could not have been easy, especially for a Black man.

His behavior was sometimes erratic; Terry reported to me one night that Dimitri had been "bouncing baskets in bongo land."

I asked Dimitri outright if he was on drugs again, and he responded in the negative, assuring me his drug habit was such that if he showed up at all, there would be no question. I believed him; it had the ring of truth. He told me because he was homeless, there were nights when he got no sleep. Sleep deprivation and allergies made him "dingy." Ari set him up with a cot on a protected part of the patio, although I don't think he ever used it. I gave him a letter to present should he be questioned by the police.

As I walked through the kitchen one afternoon, I heard Abdo lecturing Dimitri on how to be Black, which seemed incongruous. The gist was that African Americans had lost their spiritual connection to the motherland and were essentially soulless, whereas those from the Caribbean had maintained their roots. Not sure whether or how to address this as the white lady employer, I asked Dimitri privately if he was OK with Abdo's lectures. He said not to worry—he just tuned them out after a while.

Dimitri sent me an email that was the beginning of an autobiography he had started in rehab. His was an horrific account of abandonment and abuse. I acknowledged that and encouraged him to keep writing; he had a powerful story and wrote well. Some crew members complained I favored him, and they were right. Unfortunately, after a few months, he fell back into his addiction and, as he had predicted, dropped out of sight.

Marie, a relatively new prep cook, complained Ari was sexually harassing her. I found this unbelievable, but the three of us sat down. According to her, on a music night, he had invited her out from the kitchen to "dance for the men." This was so far from Ari's modus operandi that I knew she had misconstrued whatever he had said. He denied having said it, agreeing it would have been highly inappropriate *had* he said it, but that he had only invited her to join the other dancers—both men and women—as he often did when the kitchen was slow. She had also been offended by off-color comments he had made to the entire kitchen and had found it invasive when he mentioned the color of her headband, asking if it was fuchsia or magenta. She acknowledged these latter comments would not have been offensive had they come from a coworker. The power dynamic was what made them harassment, in her opinion.

The meeting seemed to go well. Ari agreed to avoid the jokes and not mention anything about her appearance. In turn, he asked that she acknowledge him when he spoke; she had been ignoring him. Marie thanked me but not him. I had a chance to see them interact subsequently, and they seemed to be relaxed and even congenial.

I continued to document the interactions I witnessed as well as my conversations with Marie. I also spent time studying the statutes on sexual harassment. The following from the Equal Employment Opportunities Commission website was both charming and illuminating: "*Title VII does not serve as a vehicle for vindicating the petty slights suffered by the hypersensitive.*"

When asked, Marie gave positive reports of her interactions with Ari. At one point, though, she said she couldn't work with Abdo because he had been sick for three days and no chef should take that much time off; she had lost all respect for him. She was looking for another job because she wanted to do fine dining and have better support in the kitchen and a faster pace. Later, she told me she really loved this job and was staying after all.

In May, she gave me three days' notice that she was leaving because Ari was drinking again. I asked if there had been any actions or interactions that had upset her, and she replied in the negative. She just didn't want to be around him. I terminated her immediately, preferring not to contend with her any longer.

May was characterized by other odd and intense staff issues. Several staff members wanted May 4 off to attend Mick's wedding. When I asked why anyone would get married on a Wednesday, they informed me May 4 is Star Wars Day (May the 4th be with you. . . .), a holiday of which I had previously been unaware.

On Mother's Day, James was supposed to come in and cook but had fallen out of a tree and was too sore to work.

There was constant bickering between Abdo and Evan, Dimitri (before he left) and Martin, Preston and Jackie, Terry and Ari. Like disgruntled square dancers, they would suddenly change partners and bicker about someone else. Ari talked with Abdo about Evan, explaining Asperger's and asking Abdo not to expect more than Evan could realistically deliver. I was informed separately by Dimitri, Jackie, Martin, and Delores—a prep cook—that things were better. Unbeknownst to me, Abdo's impatience with Evan had been upsetting the entire kitchen for some time.

It was no secret that Abdo would get stoned on his breaks, but it was a battle I chose not to fight, since his work did not appear to suffer, and it seemed to calm him. In hindsight, I should have exercised more authority, but I was afraid of losing him, even though I knew being so dependent on a single employee is a bad practice. I wasn't up to replacing him myself, nor did I think we could find anyone else of his caliber who would work for what we could pay.

Trying to navigate these choppy waters and get along with each other was exhausting to both Ari and me. Then we were suddenly given an offer we couldn't refuse.

PART 5

SHOOTING FOR THE BIG TIME

UPPING OUR GAME

S am, my chef friend who had left for Grass Valley, approached us
with a proposal to take over as executive chef. An executive chef not
only cooks but also oversees the kitchen, handling many of the things I
had been doing—supervising, scheduling, provisioning, menus, budgets,
and training. Sam's culinary career had started in Germany, where he had
apprenticed in fine dining houses. He had a breadth of knowledge far
greater than ours or anyone else who worked for us. We had not thought we
could afford someone of his stature, but his salary request was reasonable,
and this seemed like a win-win. He was restarting a career that had been
derailed by substance abuse, and a recent executive chef credential could
be a big step toward a more lucrative position. Ari and I saw this as the
move we needed to instill professionalism and order in the kitchen, taking
the restaurant to a higher level.

I was thrilled at the chance to turn over the reins to a more experienced
person and to have some breathing room. This would be a chance for me
to focus on administration, marketing, and that belated analysis and for
Ari to expand our entertainment. We were both reenergized. It seemed we
could now realize our grand vision of a successful, eclectic enterprise.

Still, I told Sam the plan would also need to be signed off by Abdo. While Abdo was not an executive chef, he had been loyal and worked hard for us. He was used to running our shop and, as I told them both, "there's no room for two bulls in the kitchen."

Sam went to meet Abdo, who was spending his off day cooking at a food booth, and Abdo immediately put Sam to work. They had fun and both reported looking forward to working together. Gail, now Sam's fiancée, was concerned about job security, so I suggested she write up a year's contract. Fortunately, with the sale of the farm, I now had the funds to guarantee that. Sam would have almost carte blanche. Ari and I were still the final authorities but agreed to exercise restraint. Sam had the right to hire and fire, with the exception of Terry and Abdo. Some of the crew members were excited to have a real chef on board; the others remained silent. Jackie had worked with Sam previously and was one of the excited ones.

The first test of our restraint came when Sam insisted on using onions and garlic. We agreed, excepting the dahl, curries, and salad dressings. This was not a big deal for our customers; there were a few with allium allergies, but even they could still get a meal.

Abdo was freed up to do more off-site vending, starting the season with Day Under the Oaks at the junior college. We signed up for the Wednesday Night Market in Santa Rosa, which lasted the summer. The first few were disorganized, but once a routine was developed, they became easier. I put Juan, Abdo's assistant, in charge of inventory for the events, presenting him with a clipboard and a checklist, and he seemed to enjoy these trappings of authority. Even so, we had to have someone on call, usually Ari, to run forgotten items out to the sites. Abdo's Fourth Street Tacos, made with seasoned baked tofu, were very popular. I would see nonvegan Mexicans return for a second order, which seemed like the ultimate endorsement.

SAVED BY THE BEANS

One morning, I went in early to make chili for the school. The beans had been soaking overnight, and I was distressed to find the pot that contained them on a shelf above the stove. The tall, strong young man who had placed it there hadn't thought twice. For me, it was a major challenge. I had to stretch across the stove and upward even to touch the bottom part of the pot, which weighed at least forty pounds. I would be alone for another hour and needed to get the beans cooking. My plan was to stand on a foot stool, then bring the pot as straight down onto the stove as possible, allowing the cast iron top to absorb the shock. It did not go as planned. The pot dropped with such force that I was thrown off balance and the stool slid out from under me. Most of the impact was taken by my belly, which hit the edge of the stove as the pot came down. It took me several minutes of recovery before I was able to breathe properly, stand, and get the beans started.

I mentioned this to my doctor when I saw him, but the bruise was fading by then, and he was unconcerned. He was upset about the prednisone. "What! That's a high dose! You should never have been on it so long!"—a direct contradiction to what he had told me the year before. He announced he was retiring and referred me to a new doctor to direct my taper. This is a delicate process since the adrenal glands have to be coaxed back into service. I started this with my new doctor, but my inflammation markers kept going up. "Maybe we should up your dose to forty milligrams, "she suggested, "and blow the inflammation out." Sounded good to me. I have since learned that while many doctors prescribe prednisone, few understand it; many are making up protocols as they go along.

A few weeks later, I experienced excruciating belly pain. Richard wanted to take me to the emergency room, but I refused to go. By the next morning, the pain was mostly gone, but I thought it would be wise to poke around my abdomen in case I had appendicitis. I had no rebound pain but noticed a hard lump that I correctly diagnosed as a hernia. Following internet directions to seek medical attention in case it was "incarcerated" by twisted intestines, I finally allowed Richard to drive me to the ER.

The doctor was agitated when he came back with my CT scan results. "YOU HAVE FREE AIR!" He explained that my intestinal wall had been breached, and bacteria could be flooding into what should have been my sterile abdominal cavity, creating sepsis. "When did you eat last? We need to get you into surgery!" He was amazed I wasn't doubled over in agony. "How did you even walk in here?" The prednisone had masked much of the pain. I also had an incarcerated hernia, an unrelated event that needed to be surgically addressed but was the least of their worries. I grabbed my phone and, while being wheeled into surgery, frantically transferred the farm money into the restaurant account for Ari and into a personal account for Richard. When I came to, they had taken out eight inches of colon and attached a colostomy bag to my abdomen. It would be the only way I could poop.

The doctor told us had I not come in, I would have died within forty-eight hours. The hernia, which he had also fixed, had actually saved my life by getting my attention. The colostomy could probably be reversed, and he answered my only question: Yes, we could still have sex. I was on heavy pain meds and in the hospital for twelve days. Sam sent me the best text ever: "Get well, we've got this."

As I came out of a Dilaudid haze one morning, my eyes landed on the white board that named those who would be attending me and had a section for daily goals. That day's was "walk and poop." Picturing myself as a goose, stepping and pooping, stepping and pooping, was amusing enough to make me laugh, which hurt my stitched belly but was welcome relief. Compared to the stress of my everyday life at the restaurant, being in bed on heavy drugs didn't seem that bad.

I never will know whether it was just my time or due to the prednisone or the bean pot incident or stress or having eaten ibuprofen like candy while a mortgage broker. Had the bean pot incident actually saved my life by causing the hernia?

After I was released, Richard moved in full-time for a few months and took care of almost everything I needed. Fortunately, I had nurses to help with the colostomy bag until I became comfortable with it, or we might never have had sex again.

I returned to the restaurant as soon as I could, although I lacked much of the energy and enthusiasm that had propelled me previously. Jackie and Martin had visited me in the hospital and probably reported I looked half dead, which I did. Although everyone was solicitous and appeared glad to see me back, I was not glad to be there. Every morning was like that first leap into a cold swimming pool. I dreaded it, but once in, I would acclimate and be able to finish out the day.

I had initial concerns about working in a restaurant with the colostomy bag, since I now had an exceptionally intimate relationship with poop. The nurses had sent me off with inspiring stories about successful people in my situation—Barbra Streisand for one, but Barbra wasn't working in food service. Fortunately, my fears proved to be unwarranted. I had always washed my hands thoroughly with antibacterial soap, and that was sufficient. I was probably the most hygienic person in the kitchen—and wasn't doing much cooking anyway.

My plans for a comprehensive marketing plan and a thorough analysis of operations were on hold. I could handle only the daily minimum then come home and collapse into Mom's recliner. Still, with Sam and Abdo on board, we seemed so close to success it never occurred to me not to move forward. Looking back now, this would have been the time to sell.

EXIT THE WARRIOR PRINCESS (AND SEVERAL OTHERS)

As Ray's trial approached, Jackie's attendance became more and more sporadic. She had a fainting spell and another anxiety attack. Sam and I agreed she should never be alone in the kitchen. She had difficulties showing up or staying at work and told us people on the bus who knew Ray and his mother were threatening her. At the end of July, she gave two weeks' notice but had trouble fulfilling that promise, and Sam released her early. My Warrior Princess was not broken, but she was suffering. I wrote a letter to accompany her application for disability, stressing the profound differences in her personality and ability to work since the assault. She had been with us for three years and, despite all the drama, had graduated from the culinary school.

Sam brought Peter in from the Mission, a man in his late twenties who had lost his teeth due to methamphetamine addiction but was determined to clean up his act. He was very much in love with his wife, who was also addicted and toothless. Peter recognized they would both go under if something didn't change and that he needed to be the one to change it. He started by washing dishes and cleaning, then Sam taught him to make vegan scones, which started to sell once customers knew they could stop by for fresh ones, breakfast burritos, and coffee in the morning. Our coffee, by the way, was excellent—organic, dark roast, French press, and shade-grown.

Sam's ability to hire stable employees seemed even worse than mine. One dishwasher was fired for coming in drunk the second day; another simply didn't show up. A prep cook left after a month. Several others came and went. There were some good ones, though. Casey, a prep cook, stayed over a year. Heather was hired in September. She was a baker who also worked the front and did prep. In October, Arthur applied for a dishwashing job, and we hired him. Later I learned he had met our ninja dishwasher Ray while they were both in jail, and Ray had informed him of a recent job opening at this quirky but welcoming place called Gaia's Garden.

HONEYMOON'S END

The crew that had so wanted structure wasn't all that happy when they got some. Complaints about Sam replaced complaints about Ari. I kept waiting for someone to yell at Sam, "YOU'RE NOT MY REAL DAD!"

Meanwhile, Sam felt we were tying his hands, and he was right. It was harder than we had anticipated to let go of the illusion of total control. He argued we should get rid of the buffet completely and go to single service. This was a move Ari and I had considered for years and rejected. I was afraid of losing the customers we already had, afraid that our crew wasn't up to making the transition, and afraid of hiring servers, since all tips would go to them, and I would have to pay the kitchen staff two to three dollars more an hour. Ari was no fan of the buffet but shared some of my concerns. We stayed in a holding pattern for several more months.

Freed from some of his duties in the kitchen, Abdo took our booth to Reggae on the River. We made a little money, but I think it was more of a paid vacation for him. He also represented us at Veg Fest, and once again we sold out of food way too early. There were other concerts and the Wednesday Night Market. Everyone loved his food, his personality, and his Caribbean charm. One woman, who had her own Indian food booth, tried to extract his recipe for samosas, an Indian dish. She said they were the best she had ever had. Many of the people who came by didn't know about the restaurant, so Abdo was able to direct them to us.

Sam entered the Harvest Festival on our behalf and won a gold medal for his deconstructed ravioli. It was more food-forward than most of our dishes—two separate four-inch squares of pasta with a kale mushroom filling and basil pumpkin sauce. This brought our first mention in our local newspaper; they had to include us with the winners of other categories. We used the honor to promote ourselves, but his dish didn't sell well as an á la carte entrée and eventually went out of rotation.

Sam's tenure was marked by both successes and failures. He was by far the most knowledgeable person in the kitchen but didn't always deliver. I came in one afternoon to find a train wreck. The curry was burnt, prep hadn't been done, sandwiches weren't available, and the buffet had gone out late—all on Sam's watch.

On another occasion, he insisted on preparing the food for an art reception. I had it down to an easy but colorful spread of fruit, goat cheese with crackers, and brownies, but Sam wanted to make pizza. By the time he had delivered it to the reception table, most of the people had left and the artist—an influential member of the community and a now former supporter—was livid. She left us messages detailing her disappointment and embarrassment and the termination of any further dealings with us.

Over a period of about four months, failures like these began to erode Ari's confidence in Sam, and he could no longer refrain from suggestions, comments, and criticism. On one occasion, when I was away, the buffet came out late again. Ari became upset and, according to Sam, was "rude to everyone." Sam responded by taking the entire crew and Ari outside, telling Ari he was out of line, and asking him to leave, threatening him with a walkout. Ari left. Given my history with Ari, I was initially on Sam's side until I had a chance to talk with the crew—Sam had used them as props! There had been no mutiny brewing in the kitchen; they were as surprised as Ari was. James told me Ari hadn't been that bad, and Rosie had thought they were going out for a fire drill.

This confrontation prompted a meeting with Sam, Ari, and me about their working relationship. I had them come to my house in case tempers flared. It went better than I thought it would: Fortunately, we were all committed to finding a solution. Sam wanted Ari and me to focus on promotion and marketing as we had said we would and to let him run the kitchen. We all agreed this would be best. He noted our concerns with the buffet and promised to address them. I asked Sam to avoid homophobic and sexually oriented jokes—there had been some complaints.

We all tried our best, and there was improvement in the timeliness and quality of the buffet. I hadn't completely recovered from my surgery and had an easier time leaving the kitchen to Sam. Ari tried his best to step back as well. Operations seemed to be on a more even keel other than staff complaints primarily directed at Sam. These were easier for me to field, since I was less emotionally invested in that relationship.

For the holidays, we offered food for pickup. I asked Sam to pack some of the stuffed acorn squash and mushroom gravy for me to take to Thanksgiving dinner with friends. When I unwrapped them, I was horrified to find the filling had been burned and was inedible. I was not only embarrassed but furious, assuming he had also sold these to unwitting customers for their holiday dinners. Maybe I got all the bad ones, because no one complained.

Still, Sam was a good cook most of the time and took over much of the day-to-day staff interactions—which I was finding particularly draining as I recovered. The timing of his tenure couldn't have been better. Without him, we probably wouldn't have been able to run the restaurant as I dealt with bout after bout of abdominal issues. I knew that when he was onsite, things would more or less stay on the rails, and that allowed me a level of comfort I needed. I had hoped Sam would be able to do what I hadn't—establish strict order in the kitchen and get our costs under control. Neither happened.

After another attack of severe belly pain, I was back in the hospital with a colon blockage. This is not simple constipation, as the name would imply; it's caused by scar tissue and adhesions from surgery. Treatment involves a tube uncomfortably inserted through a nostril and into the stomach and requires a three- or four-day hospital stay. I had four of these, about three months apart. Fortunately, Sam, Ari, Terry, and the crew were able to keep things together at the restaurant.

I was doing my own bookkeeping and didn't have exact figures until I filed our tax returns—usually a couple of years late, since I knew we would show losses. I was well aware we were deeply in the red, and Ari knew it too, but I never had concrete numbers to give him. My lack of transparency was due, in part, to ineptitude, but I also feared he would use the numbers to demand changes I wasn't prepared to make.

Ari was pushing for major changes in staffing, décor, format, and pricing. I sensed he was right about many things, but I had become so defensive, I tuned out what just seemed like a barrage of complaints. After all, it was *my* money we were losing! While struggling to be objective, I had become terrified of change, wanting to hold on to the few constants we had, afraid to take any more chances. I agonized over it quite a bit.

One afternoon, I was in my yard ruminating about our differences when Marvin, the neighborhood drunk, came by. Marvin, a veteran marine, had never really come back from Vietnam and was homeless most of the time, supporting himself by mowing lawns. He would frequently lose his mower, but my neighbors and I would secure it until we saw him again. He was beloved by everyone, and most of us had dropped him off at detox multiple times, although he never stayed.

One measure of his charm was that a houseful of Hells Angels let him stay with them for a while, an honor accorded to few Black men. (His drinking had finally been too much even for them, and they had threatened him with a "twelve stomp program.")

On this afternoon, as I was stressing over Ari's demands and trying to sort out how to respond, Marvin steadied himself by holding on to my gate and launched into a drunken monologue that I only pretended to follow. Suddenly he stopped swaying, looked directly at me, and said, "My art teacher, Mrs. Klein, said 'it takes two people to make great art. One to make the art, and one to tell them when to stop.'" He then resumed his ranting, but that one line seemed to have come from God's mouth to my ears.

This perspective helped me understand the roles Ari and I played in the creative process. I had worked successfully in the past with a woman who was a fountain of ideas in desperate need of an editor. At Gaia's Garden there was more at stake, but the dynamics were similar. I came away from Marvin's rant feeling more confident in my need to exercise restraint while appreciating Ari's passion and creativity. We each had our parts to play, and while our collaboration sometimes seemed as awkward as two drunken performers in a pantomime horse, we were both showing up.

TOP OF THE MARK

Abdo and Sam developed rotating menus on Fridays. Abdo finally made his own dishes—an okra stew he called Pepper Pot and Ital Stew, which was coconut-based with purple yam, cassava, sweet potatoes, and other delicious vegetables. Coconut greens, plantains, samosas, hush puppies, rice, and johnnycakes along with dahl and our Caribbean black bean soup rounded out the table. On alternate Fridays, Sam made a Mediterranean feast that included spanakopita, falafel, moussaka, and wonderfully flavored beans and greens—all vegan.

These were amazing spreads that, in a different venue, would have commanded top dollar. We were never able to overcome the perception that ours was a hippie establishment, not suitable for high rollers, and that a buffet should be cheap. Sam and Ari had been right that we needed to eliminate the buffet entirely, but it seemed a bridge too far for me.

I viewed cooking for a buffet as much easier than cooking to order. It required less staff and in many ways was more efficient. Sam and Abdo were the only professionals in the kitchen, and I feared our crew—who could barely manage the buffet and sandwiches—would not easily transition to becoming line cooks. I was also sure we would lose a lot of our existing customers.

Our year-end numbers were alarming. With all this great food, the promotional events, and the gold medal, it seemed surprising we hadn't done better. Our income had dropped by $50,000 to a little over $500,000, and our losses had skyrocketed to $77,000! Of this, $22,000 had been paid to our executive chef for a partial year. Our hopes that Sam's leadership would pay for itself had not yet materialized, but we were hopeful. The other employee costs had gone through the roof, increasing by $38,350 from the year before. Even I had to admit we would have to make significant changes in the new year if we were to survive.

After five years of winning it, we lost the *Bohemian* Best of award to Amy's Drive Thru—a new plant-based concept that had been national news as well as a huge deal in our county. We still had high ratings on Yelp and Tripadvisor.

PART 6

FACING REALITY

EVERYBODY WANTS TO GO TO HEAVEN BUT NOBODY WANTS TO DIE

The huge losses from the previous year evidenced that the buffet model was not compatible with the quality of the food we were providing and, indeed, it was costing us the respect and pricing opportunities more conventional restaurants enjoyed. It was time for me to put my fears aside and get real. In addition to our alarming loss the year before, one incident—too typical—put Ari and me over the edge.

A man had come in with four female companions on a night when we had some fine musicians playing. He had ordered the unlimited buffet for $16.95, and the women had taken some water. We saw him fill dinner plates and large bowls four times. The last round had been too much even for him; he barely touched the huge pile of food he had taken, leaving it for the compost.

Ari, an old-school gentleman in many ways, was irritated by the waste but shocked that this glutton hadn't even bought drinks for the ladies. We had been watching—he hadn't broken the rules by sharing any food with them either. Signs on each table informed customers of a $5 minimum purchase per person during the music: one glass of wine, or a beer, or tea and a cookie would do it. Ari saw one of the women laughingly point to the sign and turn it around. He chose restraint, but when their "host" was making his last trip to the buffet and it looked like they were staying awhile, Ari asked the women what he could bring them. They just wanted water, they replied. Informing them of the minimum, he tried to lighten the mood with a joking, "Hey, help me make some money here," which fell flat. They grudgingly ordered tea, which at $2.95 was below the minimum. It was something, though, and we decided to accept that.

The man left us a scathing one-star review on Yelp, claiming Ari had embarrassed him and his "guests" and was a terrible person, interested only in money. He had thought the restaurant "stood for something," but we were clearly just in it for the profit, and nobody should patronize us. I was infuriated and waited a few days to cool down before countering with a summary of what had actually happened and an anecdote about Ari, whom he had portrayed as a greedy, cold-hearted asshole.

The night before, a toothless, homeless woman had come in, carrying her possessions in several plastic bags. She was rambling incoherently and asking for a hoodie—definitely not a good look for the restaurant. But it was cold out, and she was wearing a thin shirt. I brought her some soup, and Ari went looking for a jacket. He tried our in-house lost-and-found box first without success. The secondhand store across the street was closed, so he walked over to Big Lots and didn't find anything there. Returning, he checked in with the dry cleaners to see if they had any abandoned garments he could purchase. Again, nothing. As he headed back, he saw a clothing bin in front of the Market and there, on top, was a thick jacket that proved to be the perfect size for this petite woman. He brought it to her and helped her put it on, and she accepted this kindness without acknowledgment. She had moved to a table outside by this time and eventually just walked away.

I was keenly aware of Ari's shortcomings but loved him for his deep compassion and generous heart. We were both committed to supporting those who needed it: It brought us joy. It was a big part of our mission. It was not our mission, though, to go broke taking crap from cheapskates, and we needed to find another way.

The buffet was important to many of our customers, especially at lunch. Not only did it provide them with a good, inexpensive meal, it allowed students and workers with limited time to be in and out quickly. It would be hard to eliminate that without losing our base. But then, our base wasn't supporting us.

The options seemed to be:

1. Keep the lunch buffet and make food to order with table service in the evenings. We had attempted versions of this in the past and had not done well at it. Having servers, who would be legally entitled to the tips, would cut the effective wages of our other employees by about three dollars an hour—a discrepancy that would fall on us to remedy.

2. Sell the food by weight. This would require the purchase of expensive scales and present logistical challenges. The cost would be $10,000 to $15,000, which would take a long time to recoup. The format would bring us more money but would be a shock to customers who were used to paying under $13 for a full lunch that also included soup, salad, bread, and dessert. I had recently bought a moderately sized plate of curry, rice, and zucchini at Whole Foods. The potatoes were not organic, and they used canola oil; at $8.95 per pound, it had cost me $16. Still, they were

profitable, and we weren't.

3. Adopt the "Panda Express model"—have servers dish out the food as customers directed, one time through. This would require more staff, and regular customers would resent their lack of autonomy; would our savings compensate?

4. Keep the buffet but focus on single servings rather than "all you care to eat."

We flirted with the first three options but determined the reconfiguration and staffing required, plus dissatisfaction of our customers, would not be cost effective. Nothing we could think of would be a sure win. We had good food but knew we were beloved by many because we were subsidizing their meals.

The simplest step toward profitability seemed to be focusing on portion control by switching to single-service options. This would reduce waste and increase our revenue per customer and might eventually help us cut staff. We drew up new signs with prices for single servings from the buffet in cups, bowls, small plates, oval plates (the Blue Plate Special) and dinner plates. There were some combinations that afforded customers more selection at a discount. It was still possible to get an ample lunch for between $6.95 and $12.95. We renamed the "all you care to eat" option as "The Cornucopia" and priced it at $19.95 for lunch, $24.95 for dinner, expecting not to sell any. I replaced the word *buffet* with *Vegetaria*—a clever term that never really resonated with anyone else.

The only other change we needed to make was to move all the dishware from a side bar to the register area, where we could keep control by doling plates out. We flirted with a promotion like "The food is free, just rent a plate" but had legitimate concerns that the more literal minded would want to bring in their own dishes.

Hoping to minimize the distress to our existing customers, I sent out a letter to our email list of 700 and to 1,200 customers whose information had been captured by our Wi-Fi program. There was an explanation of the new system and our reasons for implementing it. Previously, we hadn't announced price changes, but this new setup was radically different, and most people hate change. We hoped the advance notice would soften them up. I also signed up for another Groupon so that an influx of new customers and temporary discounts for the established ones would ease the pain. We had meetings with our front of house staff, explaining the changes and working through various responses to potential complaints.

We were trying to keep it simple but also to please our customers, so there were other "Secret Garden" options, which we would explain to customers who had trouble deciding. An oval plate without a cup was $8.95, for example.

We also made attractive signs for our growing variety of sandwiches in hopes of leading people away from the buffet. With everything in place for a smooth transition, we optimistically reopened as a Vegetaria.

TAKE ME TO THE TREE FARM

The blowback was intense. Some of our formerly loving regulars stormed out and never came back. Others were so mean to sweet Lorna at the register that she had to take breaks to cry in the restroom. Her partner, Preston, told me she would cry every night when she came home. I assigned Heather, who was more mature and had a thicker skin, to work with her through the lunch hour, but it was too much for Lorna. She gave notice and went to work at a tree farm on the assurance of minimal customer contact. I envied her. Lacey came in to replace Lorna in the front. She was also young but relentlessly cheerful, which blunted the ire of some customers.

New customers, many from Groupon, found the system confusing, but Heather, Lacey, and Terry explained it well, and they went with it—having no previous expectations. We comforted ourselves and our beleaguered front of house staff with the stark fact that the customers who were leaving were the ones we couldn't afford anyway—they were firing themselves. A spate of angry one-star Yelp reviews, calling us greedy and predicting our imminent demise, brought our Yelp rating down from 4.5 to 4. It took several months, but eventually things settled down.

Our food waste decreased by about 60 percent, and our remaining original customers indicated that once they got used to the new system, it was fair, and they were getting plenty to eat. Some of those who had left angry came back, realizing they still couldn't get a better deal anywhere else. As hoped, our sales of sandwiches and tacos, which were priced closer to the standard 30 percent food costs—30 percent labor costs—30 percent overhead costs—10 percent profit rule than was the buffet, increased. We were surprised that some people actually bought the Cornucopia—we often sold several a day. Also surprising was that those who did were usually not the ones who went back to the tables again and again. Most just wanted to be able to take their food in courses in a leisurely manner, keeping their items separated, and didn't find $19.95 for lunch or $24.95 for dinner unreasonable.

The buffet mentality persisted, though. There was a sharp increase in customers trying to return to the "vegetaria" tables with their used plates, so we had to be extra vigilant. We also started finding water glasses that had been used for tapioca. Heather alerted me to one customer who was transgressing in this way, but before I could get to her, she had left—taking the glass with her. I mounted a sign over the glassware, clearly stating they were for water only, and that any other use would incur a $5 charge. Even so, there were customers who claimed not to have seen it as they reluctantly handed over the cash.

Despite careful explanation and signage, there were still those who were either stupid or willfully dense. After dillydallying as to whether they should get the small $6.95 plate or the larger $8.95 plate, they would expect to return for as much food as they wanted. It was a buffet, after all! There was no tactful way to explain that we wouldn't have all these options if everyone could just take the same amount of food—and that every piece of information they'd been given, verbally and in writing, said "one time through." They were in no mood to hear about the "vegeteria" concept, and their outraged bad Yelp reviews were particularly annoying. Others announced on social media that lunch now cost $19.95, completely ignoring the other options we had made available.

It was not all bad, though. One 4-star Yelp review from John I. in Emeryville, someone we didn't even know, said everything we couldn't. I thanked him in a private message, but he'll never know—unless he reads this book—how much his post meant to us.

3/4/2017

We went to Gaia's yesterday for the first time, driving up from Oakland just to try it out. A plant based, organic, non-gmo buffet is probably one of the most challenging things to find these days. All of the food was good and there was a nice selection (2 soups, Ital stew, dahl split pea) samosas, johnny cakes AND cornbread, freshly steamed rainbow veggies, fried plantains, rice and some other goodies. The salad dressings were stocked and varied. There is a spicing counter area to add more variety. AND!... they have very well filtered water which is quite delicious and a rare treat.

While we were enjoying lunch, there was a dad with his 1 year old and mom (dad openly and loudly complaining about his dissatisfaction with the pricing) which led me to read some of the recent reviews from people who are not happy about some recent changes... As an outsider who is regularly searching for this kind of food, I can fairly say that it seems like folks must have had a really good thing going and did not recognize what that really meant. Good luck finding any restaurant anywhere in the continental US that offers what they do at Gaia's Garden at their current prices. If you are writing a negative review about a place that has fed you well all this time and can't name another place that has done so... you are definitely spoiled, disrespectful and not with the times (ever go shopping for organic vegetables yourself in 2017?). Quality food, prepared for you and your dietary prefe rences... If this is not a benefit in your life, you are just looking for ways to express your negativity. You should consider detoxifying your attitude. The food at Gaia's Garden is good medicine. We will be returning.

The blowback continued, but seeing that one objective person understood our situation so clearly was like wind in our sails to continue with what we knew we needed to do.

DOLDREMS

Although we were slowly pulling out of our restructuring crisis, executive chef Sam was losing momentum. Gail, now his wife, was lonely and unhappy with him putting in the hours the job required. The stress of trying to please both her and us was getting to him, and we were obviously in second place. He and Abdo were butting heads constantly. I was grateful he was there, though, since my health was still not 100 percent, and my energy was not what it had been. I could no longer put in the sixteen-hour days I had found so fulfilling, and cooking was beyond my physical ability. My enthusiasm for this venture had been replaced in large part by the stubbornness that had previously fueled my alcoholism and romantic relationships: There had to be a way to make this work.

We considered a breakfast station, which had to be outside while we cleaned, prepped, and cooked for lunch. I had Heather check foot traffic in front of the restaurant in the 6:30 to 8:00 a.m. window, a time when junior college students were heading for class. Between walk-bys and bus passengers, she counted two hundred. We determined that even 10 percent would make the effort worthwhile to start. She put a lot of effort into setting up a nice stand near the sidewalk, and her partner made an attractive pour-over setup for coffee. In addition to excellent coffee and chai, she sold vegan scones and breakfast burritos. Her efforts were rewarded with a few regulars, then chronic health problems surfaced, and she was out quite a bit. I had to take this venture over and had a hard time with it—under the best of circumstances I am not a morning person and now had to be up, out, and cheerful by 6 a.m.

Heather did very good work much of the time, but her health, mood, and production were inconsistent. In addition to other challenges, she had celiac disease. On one end of the spectrum, it is barely noticeable; on the other, exposure to even the smallest amount of gluten can be deadly. To be certified gluten-free, for example, a bakery must have ovens that were never used for wheat baking. No amount of cleaning will render them safe for the most severe cases. We took precautions like having separate cutting boards for wheat products and separate scoops and measuring utensils for flours, which was the best we could do under the circumstances. Heather's sensitivity to gluten was somewhere in the middle, and she was our "canary in the coal mine." Since she could eat the food we labeled as "gluten-free" without incident, we concluded it was acceptable for all but the most sensitive diners—who would have learned not to eat in restaurants anyway. When she made our regular wheat bread, she would wear a mask and gloves, which seemed to provide adequate protection. We used gluten-free tamari instead of soy sauce. A five-gallon container cost us about seventy dollars more.

As we learned, there are a lot of different allergies. Ari's ex-wife was allergic to black pepper. We needed to use it, though, not just for flavor but because it amplifies the anti-inflammatory properties of turmeric. A couple of people were allergic to hing, another to coconut. One woman, covered with hives, asked me if we used latex gloves. Her allergy was so serious that just eating food prepared by cooks wearing latex gloves had caused her present condition. I was able to assure her we used nitrile instead.

About this time, we received our first and only complaint of food poisoning, not surprisingly from Marlene. A regular customer, she was a sourpuss. Unlike many who came in testy and left happy once their blood sugar had stabilized, she always projected victimhood, hypersensitivity, and disappointment. On one occasion, I had given her a tour of the tables, since she had questions.

The polenta was made from corn: "I'm not a corn person."

The curry had potatoes in it: "I'm not a potato person."

We passed the roasted beets: "I'm not a beet person."

I pointed out the house-brined pickles on the salad bar: "I'm not a pickle person."

There was no point asking her, "What kind of person are you, then?" I already knew.

She called to tell me that half an hour after lunch she had become violently ill and couldn't stop vomiting. It was a surprise, since we weren't dealing with meat, fish, or eggs and because we were careful to follow the health department's temperature and storage guidelines. I tried to explain that food poisoning generally takes twenty-four to seventy-two hours to present itself. (The exception, as far as I knew, was staphylococcus aureus, which could show up in about an hour and usually came from meats or creamy dishes—neither of which we served.) As I was suggesting her symptoms may have come from a previous meal but that she should probably consult a doctor, she screamed, "I HAVE TO VOMIT!" and slammed down the phone. That was the last we saw or heard from her. No one else reported any symptoms that day, and we did not agonize over her failure to return.

I was amazed at the high rate of "food poisoning" among our crew over the years, though! Not from *our* food, they would assure me, but from something eaten elsewhere. It was the go-to excuse for calling out sick first thing in the morning, and there wasn't much I could do about it. It was entirely too reckless to insist that someone who claimed to be vomiting and suffering from diarrhea come in to do food prep, even if I were quite sure they were faking it.

RESTOCKING

S am's contract as our executive chef was up. He stayed a few months longer and left in September, much to the relief of his wife. This meant giving more authority to Abdo but also more work for Ari and me. Sam had been there when we needed him the most, but the position hadn't been as successful as any of us hoped, and the downside was becoming more evident. His last official act, catering a wedding, was such a debacle that I had to refund what would have been a tidy profit.

This episode made it easier for me to see Sam go. I was reminded of counsel from a friend: "Some people are just in our lives to walk with us from Point A to Point B. Accept that." Both Sam and the restaurant, I believe, had reached Point B. He had helped us through some tough times, but when he left, so did our hopes of becoming an esteemed Class A restaurant. Now we were just struggling to survive.

I was not physically able to jump in and cook this time and depended primarily on Abdo to keep the kitchen running. Shortly after Sam's departure, Abdo began talking nostalgically about how much Sam had taught him. Still, it seemed Abdo too was becoming weary. Staff complaints about his temper increased, and he and Ari were butting heads about the quality of the food. In hindsight, Ari was right most of the time, but I tended to ignore him since the complaints seemed relentless and I didn't have the energy to confront Abdo or to come in during the evening as well as work during the day.

There were some bright spots. Peter, our recovering addict janitor and scone baker, left in August to work for a homeless outreach agency. They paid better and provided him and his wife, Ruby, with benefits that included living quarters. She took his place as a janitor and dishwasher in the morning. A big sign of their upward mobility was that they both acquired dentures, and now we saw them smiling often. Peter had left us by the time he graduated from Drug Court, but he and Ruby stopped by—dressed to the nines and grinning broadly—to share the accomplishment and have their pictures taken. Ruby was embracing her new, clean life with enthusiasm. Her excitement over going to a sober women's brunch with her Narcotics Anonymous sponsor was such a contrast with the life she was leaving behind, I found it very touching. Preston also left in August, taking his acquired vegan cooking skills and some resentments to a popular burger joint.

Mac came on as a prep cook. He was my age at seventy but seemed in better shape. He had been living and cooking at Sam Jones, the homeless shelter; I learned we had gained a reputation there as an employer who was lax on checking references and didn't require teeth. That didn't seem like a good thing, but Mac was a charmer, knew kitchens, and had prep skills. Once employed, he was able to move into a house with roommates. While not the fastest, he was a steady worker, genial, and one of the very few nobody ever complained about.

Major fires, which had been rare, were now becoming annual occurrences. In October, the Tubbs fire burned thirty-seven thousand acres and leveled homes in northern Santa Rosa, narrowly missing the one occupied by Rob, Annie, and her family. Heather and Mac had to evacuate but were eventually able to return home. Donald, the dishwasher, slept in the dining room with his pet rabbit for a few weeks.

The evacuation area ended one block north of the restaurant. We were not in danger from the flames, but power at the restaurant was out, and we were forced to close. Our neighbor across the street, Steele and Hops, still had electricity and generously allowed us to store some produce there. We lost enough, though, that I filed an insurance claim for business and product loss. We were closed for four days, and the first three counted as a sort of deductible. Still, the check for a little over $1,000 was welcome. Business did not come back right away, as customers grappled with tragedy and conserved their resources. It was the middle of January before we were having days approaching our previous normal. I did not share with anyone except Ari and Richard my dark thoughts that we might have been better off had the restaurant burned down.

As we had in 2015, we comped meals and beverages to victims and first responders. The gratitude of one woman for a calm place to sit and the gift of a pot of tea nearly made me cry.

Heather, our breakfast lady and baker, began reporting problems with Abdo, saying he didn't listen to her or respect her. The kitchen needed a manager, she told me, and she could do it, but nobody recognized her abilities. I knew most people in the kitchen already found her abrasive and would never follow her lead. I paid for her to take the test to be our sanitation officer—a one-day class. She passed it, and while her certificate satisfied the law that we had a sanitation officer, her frustration at not being accorded a higher status just increased. Meanwhile, she was in and out with a variety of ailments, including pneumonia.

A few months later, I presented to the ER again with belly pain. This one felt different, and it was. I had appendicitis but not a rupture. After my previous hospitalizations, that surgery was a walk in the park. Still, it was my third operation in two years, and at seventy-one I was feeling my age, although I was loath to admit it. My close older relatives had been energetic and vital into their nineties. It had never occurred to me I wouldn't follow suit.

Richard and I spent the holidays with our friends Burt and Linda. They had been with me through some of the worst times of my life and had always been lovingly supportive, never giving advice. This time, though, Linda waited until we were alone and told me it was time for me to get out of the restaurant business. She gently reminded me I was old with major health issues, including another surgery scheduled in 2018. Stress was the last thing I needed. I couldn't dispute her wisdom and knew beyond a doubt she had my best interests at heart. I also knew I wasn't ready to give it up yet. There was still so much to be done with Gaia's Garden! There had to be a way we could make this work! At the same time, I was feeling some guilt at having used up so much of my time with Richard by being focused on the restaurant. He had never complained, but we talked about wanting to travel. We weren't getting any younger. When was this going to happen?

By the end of the year, we had reconfigured our pricing and decreased our staff by one executive chef and a prep cook. The fire was one more factor affecting our bottom line; still, even with our rocky start, we had lost $13,000 less than the year before—*only* $65,000. Our gross had dropped by $45,000 to $445,000, in part because we had begun closing at 3:30 on Saturdays and Sundays instead of remaining open for dinner. Saturday nights are usually great for other restaurants, but ours didn't attract that crowd. We had hoped also to cut staffing costs. Our employee costs had decreased, from $261,000 to $224,600, but as a percentage of total sales they were nearly 50 percent—more than double what they should have been. Still, while it looked like we might be turning the battleship, I had once again run out of money. I had one more piece of farmland that my family had preserved for generations. I put it on the market.

Our Yelp rating stayed at 4 stars, and Amy's Drive Thru was once again voted Best Vegetarian Restaurant.

The land sale went through in early 2018, and I was again flush with cash. I was determined that this time it would not all get swallowed up by the restaurant, but for now I could breathe.

HEALTH MATTERS

I t was time for a surgery to reconnect my colon and eliminate the bag. With monthly infusions of a powerful drug that "changes the way your immune system operates" and could cause cancer, according to the disclaimer, I had been able to reduce the prednisone, which interfered with healing. My surgeon and rheumatologist agreed I was ready, and I was anxious to get back to normal. We were all disappointed. The effects of the prednisone had not been sufficiently suppressed. As my surgeon tried to sew my intestines back together, the tissues separated, and the stiches just slipped through them. Surgery went an hour and a half longer than anticipated, outlasting the anesthetic. I came to in excruciating pain as they dropped me onto the gurney. My old bag had been replaced with a new bag in a different place; I had almost died again. It was hardest on Richard, who had spent anxious hours in the waiting room and then seen me emerge from near death. By then, the Dilaudid had kicked in, and I was happily unaware of what everyone, including me, had gone through.

I was well taken care of throughout. Thanks to Medicare and the Cadillac of supplemental plans, I had no medical bills to worry about. Richard and visiting nurses attended to me at home. It was two months before I was able to return to the restaurant, and once I did, Ari and the crew jumped in to stop me anytime I tried to lift something over three pounds. Abdo firmly banned "Auntie" from doing anything in the kitchen. I was grateful, since I had half the energy I was used to. I was now depending completely on Abdo to run the kitchen under Ari's guidance, which most of us undermined out of habit. If there had been problems while I was away, I was spared the details except for a developing feud between Heather and Ari.

They were butting heads, and I received many over the top texts from them both. Heather claimed Ari was disrespectful, unfair, and hungover much of the time. Ari found Heather disrespectful and overly emotional, and he was upset about the uneven quality of her baked goods. I thought they were probably both right and did my best to mediate, but text—all I could handle—is an imperfect medium for emotional conversations. Occasionally I would get a text from Heather saying everything had been resolved, but such interludes were brief. In April, Heather dropped a pan on her toe and was out for several weeks.

Just after the holidays, Arthur the dishwasher had been arrested and put in jail for four months—for drugs and some disturbing but nonviolent public nuisance charges. He had left his backpack at the restaurant, and I went through it carefully, looking for drugs or other paraphernalia that could get us in trouble. It contained only wet clothes, which I took home, washed, and repacked awaiting his release.

I hadn't planned to rehire him, but Ari spoke up for Arthur when he returned, reminding me how hard it was to find good dishwashers. Bringing him back on board turned out to be the right decision. His loyalty seemed to have been cemented by the rehire and a backpack full of clean clothes.

Arthur was reliable and capable and worked hard. He dealt well with dish stress but had some emotional or neurological issue that caused him to talk at length and with great speed, especially when agitated by interpersonal confrontations, which he both instigated and deplored. Once I was back at the restaurant, I spent a lot of time dealing with drama involving him, including a blowup that required a mediation. Still, Ari and I had both come to value a solid dishwasher almost as much as a good chef.

THE CULINARY STUDENT

As I recovered, I took back the weekly shopping at Costco, Cash and Carry, Trader Joe's, and the Asian markets, hiring Rosie to help me. She was still ridiculously strong, slinging fifty-pound bags of flour with ease. She was also beautiful and sexy, and I found it amusing how the male crew at Cash and Carry took a sudden interest in my business. I introduced her to the manager and encouraged her to apply, since they paid well and had benefits, but she was not interested. Nearly every place we went, we ran into someone who knew her—former teachers, social workers, parents of friends, and neighbors of her foster families. They were all delighted to see her and happy she was working, healthy, and clear-eyed. I enjoyed her company.

She was looking for hours, so I gave her some dish shifts. She would catch up quickly and move over to help with prep. This time she seemed to be picking it up, so I scheduled her for prep shifts too. I invited her to lunch one day with an unspoken agenda. We went to the culinary school, which put out lovely meals from a kitchen that was open to the dining room. As we watched the students rushing around, looking very professional in their crisp uniforms, I mentioned to Rosie that she could do that too, if she wanted to. I knew school had not gone well for her in the past but was confident she could learn to handle anything that didn't involve much math. The director of the school joined us briefly, and I introduced them, saying Rosie was considering the program. The director, as usual, was welcoming and positive.

Rosie decided to take on the challenge. Her first required classes were sanitation, knife skills, and an overview of the hospitality industry. I had pictured her as manager of a hotel chain. On more than one occasion, when something went awry in the kitchen—a sudden leak from the sink or an oil spill, for example—Rosie would be the one to take over, barking orders to her coworkers, who would follow her without question. This talent for leadership qualified her for greater things, in my opinion, but she opted for culinary.

Terry was her biggest cheerleader. She would go to his apartment to write and print out her papers, and he would help with the grammar and spelling. At times when the owner of the ranch on which she lived would get drunk and kick her out, Rosie would stay with Terry. He had no kids, she had no father, and their friendship became familial.

We were providing lunches to three schools when Margarita, our school lunch lady, left without notice and owing me money I had advanced to her for dental work. Rosie was not ready to take over school lunches yet, so we hired Betty, one of Mac's housemates, who had prep experience. She was in her early fifties and at her interview volunteered that she had been recently released from prison after serving three years for embezzlement. She was working part-time at a doughnut shop, but no one else would hire her because of her record. She and Abdo got on well, and she worked efficiently, making for a smooth transition. He appreciated her high energy and organizational skills. I was grateful the school lunches were going out well prepared and on time. She seemed grateful to have a job.

Recovering addict Ruby left in June, joining her husband doing homeless outreach services. Both were maintaining their clean and sober lives and were beaming with renewed marital love and optimism.

Bernardo came to work for us that same month. He was working at a pizza restaurant. I had thought he would give them notice, but he never did. He had a daughter and a car to support and needed two jobs. He was good at prep and later took on the brunches. With very few exceptions, he got along well with everyone, worked hard, and was reliable—all qualities I had come to treasure immensely.

HAPPENING/NOT HAPPENING

O ver the years, Ari arranged numerous community-supportive
events. In addition to Dining with Authors, the Redwood Writers
would come monthly and host readings and discussion. For many artists,
ours was their first "gallery" show, and most enjoyed the receptions in their
honor. An acoustic group called Guerilla Acapella held an "open mic" for
anyone to come and sing. (I tried to talk the leader, Jim Paschal, into a
name that might be more descriptive of these sweet events, but he remained
firm.) There was the Activists' Lounge, and we held several benefits for
community organizers and their projects as well as some political candidates. An art teacher would bring her classes in to draw the musicians. A
Sunday jazz jam brought in fine players but a pathetically small audience.
Our ability to host these events and to be in charge of the calendar was
exhilarating.

We continued to host the Veterans for Peace on Veterans Days and had
monthly visits from the Women in Black—six or seven older women who
stood on street corners advocating for peace, rain or shine. In December we

would treat them to lunch, and it was sweet to see how their orders would expand from the usual soup and corn bread to the entire buffet.

It was a happening place, but getting attendees to buy even the five dollar minimum was often like pulling teeth, and some became resentful, posting Yelp reviews about how money-hungry we were.

There were times when I appreciated Ari's bluntness. One night when we had a band in, a woman showed up with her own coffee and parked herself by the sound booth. Ari asked her what she would like to order, and she responded that she wasn't going to buy anything. "I just came to listen to the music. I'm friends with the band."

"Great, then maybe you should attend their rehearsals instead."

Her abrupt exit was no loss. It was baffling to us how the public, including many musicians, didn't seem to care or understand that venues cost money. One band arrived with a group of fans and brought their own wine and snacks to hand out to them, effectively cutting us out of the deal. The leader was offended when Ari tried to collect at least a corkage fee, but eventually the band returned with a better attitude—possibly because *mysteriously*, other venues were closing at an alarming rate.

The music, as wonderful as it was, wasn't paying for itself. Although we paid the performers a pittance if anything, by the time we provided them and their plus-ones with dinner and drinks and paid the licensing agencies $150 per month, we were in the red. Only a few of the bands had significant followings, and ours wasn't the kind of place where people just showed up for music. I was spending a lot of time, money, and energy promoting these events—most of the performers weren't even publicizing their own gigs. Finally, I notified ASCAP, BMI, and SESAC we were discontinuing licensed live performances and switching to Pandora (twenty-nine dollars per month) for background music.

Some of the musicians—notably klezmer, Gypsy jazz, and chamber music players—had enough material in the public domain that we could still have some music nights. Singer-songwriters playing original work were OK but not that popular. Judith Lerner on handpan created a soothing vibe during dinner with collections of sounds that were never the same twice. Even after I canceled, BMI hounded me, questioning whether this or that performer was playing licensed music. They had continued to monitor our website.

KEEPING UP

I became aware the restaurant business was changing, several years after it already had. We still used a cash register and ran orders to the kitchen. Our ancient time clock was so difficult to adjust that I left it the same all year, daylight savings time or not. Most places were moving to POS (point of sale) systems with wireless screens that transmitted orders to printers in the back of the house, kept track of inventory, and also served as time clocks. I explored these and found some attractive deals. They all required three-year contracts, though, and I was not sure we would be in business three years hence. Also, now that I had mastered Facebook and my website, I learned both were passé—young people were using Instagram. James's girlfriend set us up with an Instagram page that I never used to full advantage, even though I took a short class about it.

We got ahead of the curve on the new Impossible Burger, though, and that was a great move. I brought a couple home and pleaded with Richard to try "just one little bite." He was very suspicious of anything made with plants, especially anything he had never had before. Finally placating me by taking the one bite, he quickly devoured the whole thing. Ding! Ding! We had a winner! The first month we offered it, we sold 191—more than all our sandwiches combined. In February, sales went to 282. Impossible

Burger was getting a lot of press, and we were the only restaurant in Sonoma County that had them at the time. They had to be obtained through distributors, and fortunately I had completed the application process early. In March, we finally got a real mention in the local newspaper. The food writer had actually come in and tried the burger. Her write-up was positive and devoid of her usual snark toward plant-based food. She mentioned that our coconut bacon wasn't much like bacon but tasted good—a fair assessment. Sales jumped to 479 in March, then 509 in April before leveling off to an average of about 300 each month.

The Impossible Burger was not without detractors—it was a genetically modified product but not the Frankenfood version where a fish gene was inserted into broccoli. Rather, it employed a process that had been used by breweries for centuries, combining soy roots with yeast. I did enough research to feel good about selling it; some people preferred the Beyond Burger, which was also good and less controversial, so we kept both in stock.

Curiosity about the new products brought in many people who had not previously noticed us. It was also a good choice for the reluctant family member or friend who was afraid of vegan food. At the time, all the cardiovascular doctors at Kaiser were vegan, and plant-based diet classes were very popular there. The main instructor described us as "good but pricey," which I found ludicrous. Still, it was helpful to have that source of referrals. While the doctors didn't necessarily endorse the Impossible Burger, which was not really health food, it was a good transition to a better diet, and it got people in the door. For years we had seen heavy, florid men come in after their first heart attacks. They seemed terrified. I theorized they had envisioned a drum circle surrounding a huge mound of bean sprouts and a banner proclaiming THIS IS YOUR LIFE NOW! It was fun to show them they could eat quite well with us and avoid bean sprouts altogether if they so chose.

ALL I COULD TAKE

Heather returned from her latest medical leave and was baking and working the register. (I had abandoned the breakfast project.) She and ex-con Betty, Abdo's assistant, got into a screaming match over seven dollars in tips that Betty believed had been wrongfully withheld. Heather tried to explain, but Betty refused to hear it. From then on, any time Heather needed to talk with her about work-related issues, Betty would refuse to listen. When Heather explained to me what had happened with the tips, it was clear Heather was in the right and that Betty had misunderstood. Truth no longer mattered. Betty had reverted to a prison mentality, and there was no point trying to reason with her. Heather was understandably unhappy. Clearly, they could not work together. Heather had already suggested that she be laid off, since the bakery items were not selling well. Her difficulties with Betty, Ari, and Abdo, as well as her spotty attendance record, tipped the scale toward that solution. She left with resentments, but the shop was a lot calmer.

Betty was great with the school lunches, and that was one area of our operations that I didn't have to worry about. Perhaps emboldened by her "victory," she became increasingly outspoken and critical of how we were running things. Abdo, who had welcomed her initially, was getting frazzled.

My surgeon was ready to try again, and this time the reconnection was successful. My health events were taking their toll, though. Most days I could barely get out of Mom's La-Z-Boy. Richard cared for me constantly and without complaint. Ari, Terry, and the crew kept the restaurant going. I would do the payroll, menus, and scheduling and have occasional meetings at home with Ari or Abdo. Both insulated me from any crises that may have erupted in my absence. I had become fearful of going into the restaurant and avoided it whenever possible. The stress seemed too great, and my lack of energy was incompatible with the demands of the business. I had little fight left yet saw no viable path for flight.

One issue was that I was having nearly unbearable pain in both shoulders despite the prednisone, and my range of motion was minimal. When he had x-rayed them the year before, my doctor's professional opinion had been, "This is bad."

"Is it bone on bone?" That's what it felt like.

"No. It's worse."

He explained that due to the prednisone softening the bone, it was bone *in* bone. I was not enthusiastic about more surgery. "How old are you?" he had asked.

"Seventy-one."

"You need to get this done! You have a lot of living to do!"

That had won me over. I had told him I needed to complete the abdominal surgeries first. Now, in December of 2018 at seventy-two, I was ready for the first of two joint replacements. Again, compared with the abdominal surgeries, the joint surgery seemed minor, and half the intense, chronic pain I had been living with was gone almost immediately. My energy wasn't returning, though, which was no surprise to anyone except me.

I did not have the numbers right away, but I knew we had lost big in 2018. I had been away from Gaia's Garden more than I had been present and had been shoveling money into the restaurant like an old-time engineer feeding logs into a steam engine. When I did get the bookkeeping done, I saw our income had gone up by $10,000 to $455,000, but we had lost $102,000! I still had money, but another year like that would wipe me out. The only asset I had left, besides my house, was Mom's house, and I knew she had wanted proceeds from that eventually to be shared with my brothers' children. I had finally reached the limit of what I was willing to sacrifice, including my health, which was not what I had expected it would be at seventy-two. The people who knew and loved me the most were unanimous in saying it was time to quit. I didn't want to, but it was finally time to face facts. I thought about a stupid joke. A dog had "made love" to a skunk and was asked about it later.

"I didn't get all I wanted, but I got all I could take."

Our Yelp reviews were back up to 4.5 stars. Amy's Drive Thru won the Best Vegetarian Restaurant in the *Bohemian* for the third year.

PART 7

THE LONG GOODBYE

NOTHING CHANGES IF
NOTHING CHANGES

G etting out was not as simple as just walking away, although I was tempted. A lot of people would be affected—Ari, our employees, the Market, and our community of vegetarians and vegans. I knew I wouldn't recoup anything near what I had invested but hoped for something. Ari agreed it was time to throw in the towel. He was exhausted and demoralized too. For the time being, our exit plans were unformulated as we each tried to process the failure of our dream. Weighing various options, we still needed to run the restaurant, now without hope or optimism.

Betty went to Alaska during the holiday break to see the northern lights. She fell in love with the state and was offered a job training sled dogs. Although she gave us minimal notice and was very rude about it, I couldn't help but feel happy for her. She had a big, rough personality, and Alaska seemed like the perfect place for her. I still enjoy picturing her there.

She left on a Friday, and I needed someone to make school lunches on Monday, so I posted an ad on Facebook. Surprisingly, there was a response from our former lunch lady, Margarita. She was embarrassed about the money she still owed me and said I could take it from her wages. Abdo said he would be not only happy to have her back but delighted. Betty had exhausted him, and he welcomed Margarita's stolid presence. I was grateful to have someone who could immediately step into making the lunches. Training new people was difficult, and mistakes made during their learning curves stressed our relationships with the schools. I couldn't remember how much money she owed me—around one hundred dollars. I told her I would forgive the debt and in return she must promise to give me two weeks' notice should she leave again. We both kept our ends of the bargain.

In perspective, our problems seemed temporarily less dire when our seventy-year-old prep cook, Mac, was diagnosed with mouth and throat cancer and was sent to San Francisco for treatment. On his return, he told me his cancer was terminal, and they could possibly prolong his life with chemotherapy and radiation. He agreed to the latter but confided that rather than suffer through the chemotherapy, he was willing to die. He wanted to keep working, and I assured him we would do everything possible to accommodate his medical appointments and inevitable bad days.

Ari and Rosie were having almost nightly blowups. It looked like we weren't going to exit gracefully. I was working days and spending evenings fielding his angry texts and phone calls. Rosie would call too, asking what to do. Most of the arguments started with Ari complaining about how the food had been prepared or maintained. Rosie was defensive, since she was crushing it in culinary school and had become our sanitation officer. Like Heather, she believed the one-day class conferred more status than we believed it did. Ari was usually right about the food; Rosie still had a lot to learn. His way of presenting the complaints, though, was often harsh, and at times Rosie had not actually been responsible or had been too overwhelmed by lack of support to cover everything. Even when he approached her tactfully, Rosie would push back, driving him into a rage. Terry was protective of Rosie and upset at Ari's drinking.

Then Ari had a blowout with Lacey. She called me in a panic, saying she felt unsafe. I told her to leave, and we'd sort it out the next day. I knew Ari was not a physical threat but also that his rage could be intimidating. I explained that Ari was losing his hearing and had gotten progressively louder even in a friendly conversation. Lacey said she was still afraid of him, and she didn't want to work any shift he was on.

That seemed like the last straw for me. Between the financial pressures, my poor health, and the constant crises centering around Ari, I was done. I told him more forcefully than before that I could not have him managing our crew in the time we had left—it just wasn't his skill set. Once again, I demanded he create a job description to include shopping, events, school deliveries, and anything else that didn't involve the crew. I would work every day except Friday, coming in at noon to oversee lunch and staying until dinner was out and in good shape. Monty, a gentle vegan, would work with Lacey on Fridays since Lacey was afraid to be alone with Ari. Monty was also upset with Ari but not afraid of him. James worked on Fridays, so I knew the food would be good and there would be a moderating influence in the kitchen.

Ari didn't want any part of my plan and decided to leave altogether. He relented the next day and said he could do some of the things I had mentioned. I had now taken on six days a week again, but this time my energy wasn't what it had been, and the restaurant felt like an albatross. Ari was constitutionally unable to avoid reprimanding the crew, and I had little fight left so, as usual, nothing changed.

Adding to the collective angst, Abdo was complaining about both Bernardo and Margarita, two of our best workers. I asked him to lighten up and learn from Ari about what not to do. They were becoming a lot alike. Much of the friction was a common shift problem—both the day and evening shifts felt they were doing all the work while the other shift was unappreciative and lazy. In this case, Abdo *was* doing a tremendous amount in addition to putting out the buffet—baking bread and buns for the burgers and sandwiches as well as prepping all the sauces and condiments and making prepared salads. He did have a bad habit, though, of telling the night shift they had everything they needed. One hour into dinner, they would find there was no rice or curry or whatever. "For God's sake!" I thought but instead said, "Make sure you check the supplies yourself when you start your shift." I made up par lists for each shift to check off what had been done and what was needed. Finn had tried this before, and it didn't work any better this time, although everyone seemed temporarily placated.

I had cut staff as much as I thought I could—mostly by not replacing some who left. While more efficient, there weren't many options when crew members didn't show up as scheduled, so I would usually need to pull myself together and take shifts. This was fairly easy for me in the front of the house but very challenging in the kitchen.

One morning, gentle Monty, a cashier, called to say his brother had attacked him with a broken glass bong. He was out for three days. Margarita was in jail for a traffic violation. That seemed like the perfect ending to a dismal month.

RUBBER MEETS ROAD

Meanwhile, we were struggling over if, how, and when to shut down Gaia's Garden. Even having acknowledged we were done, I still hoped we could find some way to make it work. I wanted to leave, but I wanted to leave on a high note.

Abdo had been pushing for more single service plates, and we were finally ready to implement them. Going with this plan, which would once again change our format, seemed like the next best move—assuming we were staying in. We were torn. I wasn't ready to tell our crew we were trying to get out, expecting they would scatter, and we weren't ready to walk away yet or hire new people. I remembered my friend Paul Beerbohm.

Paul had fought brain cancer successfully for years and had been touted as a medical miracle; then he was told the fight was really over. Nothing more could be done—at best he had weeks. He had heard it before, but this time the doctors were sure. They told him to prepare himself. He agonized over how to approach this development—to keep fighting as he had done successfully for so long or to relax and surrender. I had no wisdom to offer, but his brother—a priest—did. "Say 'yes!' Say 'yes' to life and 'yes' to death." That had worked for Paul, and when he passed, it was peacefully.

Facing a much easier dilemma, I decided to say "yes" to a last-ditch effort to make the restaurant the best it could be and "yes" to finding an appropriate buyer.

Going full speed ahead on two tracks was not easy. I knew I would take care of the crew when the time came, which eased my guilt, but it still didn't feel good not telling them everything that was going on. Up until then, we had been perhaps overly transparent. I worked with Abdo on a new menu while Ari and I spoke with the Market in confidence. They were excited about expanding and gaining frontage on the main street until a contractor's bid for opening up the non-weight-bearing wall between us came in at over $100,000—mostly for permits that were inexplicably required by the city. We considered turning the dining room, which was bigger than we needed, into a sort of food court, subleasing space to a coffee cart, a bakery, possibly a vegan ice creamery or juice concession. I also reached out to a few chefs to see if they might be interested in taking the whole restaurant over. All of this took time and energy, but none of it panned out.

James left in March to work at a fine dining restaurant near the coast. He had been with us for five years, and it was a welcome change for him, a loss for us. I had often said if I had four of him, I could fire everyone else. Lacey also left, wanting to gain experience and more money as a server. She seemed to have resolved her Ari issues, but that may have been a factor as well.

I was wanting to let the staff wither away in anticipation of closing, but we weren't there yet. Anna, a pleasant architectural student, came to work the front, and Mick returned to prep. I felt good when people came back, even for a short time—Rosie, Buzz, Brian, Rob, Margarita, and now Mick. It indicated to me we were doing something right. Several of our crew had left with resentments, yet to many—including some of the resentful ones—we represented home.

The formerly vegetable-averse Mick looked a lot healthier and told me he was now vegan—a 180-degree switch. One night I saw him opening a resistant jar the same way I do—with a series of angular taps to the edge of the lid using the back of a knife, moving in a counterclockwise direction. "Oh," I exclaimed, "I do it the same way!"

"I know. You taught me and Finn."

I was ridiculously pleased to know something I had done had made a lasting impression on these guys. I hoped there was more, but this was concrete. I knew that every time they did it, they would think of me. I was hungry for meaning, for evidence these years and all the money I had lost had been worth something.

We closed for a couple of days at Easter and used one of them to bring the staff in to train on the new vegan dishes Abdo had developed. They were beautiful—sweet and sour tofu, mac and cheese, paprika tofu with a dumpling, pasta primavera, jerk tofu, and samosas. Each plate was colorful and fresh, some garnished with nasturtium flowers from the garden. The taste tests were successful, although the jerk tofu was so spicy most of us couldn't handle it. Abdo said he could easily adjust to mild, medium, or traditional (very hot). We had some discussions on plating, serving sizes, and pricing; I started working on the menus.

The final menu—six pages—was impressive. The first page was for specials, which sometimes included a lovely curried tofu salad plate Margarita developed or Abdo's Caribbean food or fried green tomatoes with corn on the cob and barbecued seitan. Then a page showing the new plates, including curry. There were small plate options for all of these. Burgers and sandwiches filled the centerfold and included a new barbecued jackfruit sandwich with coleslaw—which was better than any pulled pork sandwich I had ever had.

The buffet was relegated to a back page. Ari had been pushing for down-sizing it to a *Diet for a Small Planet* type of layout—basic, tasty nutrition. This was the time. The salad bar remained the same, but the hot table now had brown rice, beans, greens, rainbow steamed vegetables, polenta, three soups—one of which was always the dahl—and three sauces: pesto, marinara, and pumpkin. We kept the lunch prices the same and eliminated the dinner prices and entrées altogether, occasionally bringing them in as special plates.

Because Monday nights were routinely very slow, we decided to close at 3:30, which lined up with our schedule for the weekends.

Unlike our previous reconfiguration, this one went smoothly. Many customers stayed with the buffet, but others, especially new ones, explored the plates and appeared to enjoy them. For $6.95, one could get a bowl from the buffet that provided a nutrition-packed meal or a small plate of the new dishes. Our most expensive items were $14.95, although some people still paid $19.95 for the unlimited buffet.

On weekends, we had the brunch buffet with tofu scramble, potatoes O'Brian, pancakes, yams with kale, bean "sausage patties" with mushroom gravy, hush puppies, or biscuits and tortillas. We had a mango gazpacho on the salad bar along with the regular salad, seasonal fruit, and tapioca.

Some customers still seemed clueless as to what their meals cost to make. One woman, who purchased a small plate for the buffet at $5.95, asked if the coconut milk in the curry and the greens was from fresh coconuts; she seemed disappointed when I told her it came from a can. When I told Ari about it later, he had the perfect rejoinder:

"Yes! We hired three Samoans from the Polynesian Cultural Center. They spend their days in the back with machetes expressing fresh coconut milk for your $5.95 meal."

In April, Food Not Bombs started serving again. We had contributed to them before and had tremendous respect for their work. They provided healthy food without question to anyone who came by. They cooked much of it themselves but avoided the permit issues that plagued chapters in other areas. I'd had a close friend who was homeless with mental issues. While he couldn't handle going to the indoor facilities for food, he was comfortable with these good people. He also told me it was the only time he felt he was getting real nutrition. He and I were no longer in communication, but I remembered his endorsement. After brunch on Sundays, Bernardo would make them burritos out of whatever had been left—scrambled tofu, beans, rice, potatoes, cheese, and sometimes curry.

Ari would also take burritos over to the Joe Rodota Trail, where a homeless encampment eventually swelled to three hundred unfortunate souls. After one such trip, he returned in tears, unable to contain his pain at their privation. This was the side of him I loved and hoped more people would see.

With the new menu and a relatively stable crew, I was more proud of our restaurant than I had ever been. I believed it to be the best we could do, yet we still weren't sustainable. That made it easier for me to let go. I gave a letter to the Market giving them ninety days' notice, contingent on their utmost discretion. If word got out and I lost my crew, I informed them, I would need to revert to the required thirty days. They understood and protected the information. I had been talking with a business broker, Ryn Longmaid, since late 2018. She was a friend and over the years had been generous with information and advice. It was especially helpful that she had owned her own successful restaurant and had entered the brokerage business after having sold hers. I signed a listing agreement in January but tied her hands by not wanting the listing to be public. She reached out to some chefs she knew and made other discreet inquiries. I talked to the Market about taking it over, and they eventually determined it would be more than they wanted to handle.

Because the financials were downright scary, we would need to go with an asset sale—the selling price to be based on the equipment, the location, and customer goodwill. Ryn couldn't justify listing it for more than $59,000. Had I been able to show two years of profit, it would have been over $100,000—approximately what I had paid for it. Her minimum fee was $10,000. She would earn it.

I really wanted to keep the restaurant plant-based. We were the only one in the county besides Amy's—one other competitor had been closed down by the health department. I felt a responsibility to our community and hoped a vegetarian/vegan restaurant would hire my crew.

The ninety days' notice with the Market came and went. They were willing to let us continue month to month, since the prospect of having to cover the rent themselves was terrifying. (It was now over $5,000 per month.) I was meeting with the owner of a vegan restaurant in the East

Bay, and for a time it seemed like a perfect segue. I was perversely heartened when she got a call at 3 p.m. from a panicked crew that had forgotten to order lettuce and had run out four hours after the last produce delivery. It wasn't just us! Her offer, when it came, was ridiculous. I would leave owing her $25,000. She later acknowledged having cold feet.

With people coming and going, it was time for me to talk with the crew. In late June 2019, I sat down with them individually and explained that I was putting the restaurant up for sale. I had put money aside to be able to take care of them. I would do my best to find a buyer who would offer them continued employment, but if that did not materialize, they would all get two weeks' severance pay and one month's notice to find another job. I pledged transparency to the end. Referencing our current wonderful food and service, I told them we needed to maintain our high standard to the very last day. My promise to them of severance pay would depend on that. I had heard a lot of stories about employees coming to work and finding the doors shut with no way to collect their last checks. Perhaps they had too because they agreed to those terms and followed through. Our turnover and the fights in the kitchen were noticeably less than they had ever been.

Now Ryn was free to do her work and publicize the listing properly. It was still a couple of months, though, before she found a buyer. In the meantime, I spent a lot of time talking with enthusiastic vegans and chefs and vegan chefs who would run out of steam when confronted with the need to raise money. Rumors were starting to fly within our community that we were closing imminently or had closed, and business was suffering as a result. I put out some online explanations, and of course we spoke to our customers, but the rumors continued, and they hurt us.

PASSING THE TORCH

Two vegans, Charles and Lisa, heard about the sale from a friend. They had dreamed of having a food truck, but this seemed like the opportunity of a lifetime since I was willing to finance more than half the purchase price. I was concerned for them since—like Ari and me—they had never run a restaurant; I had been well financed, but they didn't have as much cushion. I spoke with them and was as honest as I could be about the demands of the business and the problems we'd had. In August, I accepted their offer.

I think we all expected the transaction to move quickly, like a residential real estate deal—thirty days, maybe sixty days. This was not the case. Ryn shepherded us through the process, and I was wishing I'd had her help when I bought the restaurant. She was representing both sides, educating and reassuring us both. We were also secure knowing the transaction would meet all legal requirements.

There would be code issues, she told us, and these would need to be resolved before we could apply to transfer the beer and wine license—a ninety-day process in itself. Over the years, we had passed all of our health inspections with no problem, but this was a different animal. When restaurants sold, the health department did a completely different and much more thorough inspection requiring restaurants to be brought up to code. Nothing could be grandfathered in.

There were some obvious repairs needed, but we had not expected that much of the flooring would need to be replaced, including my new $1,000 floor in the bathroom—it wasn't coved. Our wood cabinets in the dining room had to go as well as the small refrigerator by the register. The water heater I had paid over $5,000 to install the year before wasn't deemed large enough. There were many other things, including specific wall coverings in food service areas, which were expensive.

Some of the requirements fit in with what Charles and Lisa planned to do anyway, and we negotiated the others. It helped that they wanted in as badly as I wanted out. We also had to negotiate the timing of construction work to minimize the loss of income to the restaurant. Charles enrolled in culinary classes as we waited.

PRIORITIES

In September, Ari let me know he had an urgent need to leave. He had just learned his eldest son, Michael, was very ill with diabetes, and Ari made plans to move to Florida to care for him. It was a happy occasion in some respects because they had been estranged for many years and had recently reconciled.

We had dinner to discuss the exit plan. He needed to leave well before the sale would be concluded, so I would be on my own for the last six or eight months. Ari was my biggest headache, yet the thought of him not being by my side to see this through to the end was deeply painful. I had never wanted to do it without him. I knew I could do it—I had to do it—but he was so much a part of the place I was already feeling lost and alone. For most decisions, we had pushed and pulled at each other, and as frustrating as that process usually was, there was a comfort in having someone to push back on, another point of view, occasional validation.

On the other hand, maybe it was for the best. His bitterness at being relieved of his management role was palpable. No one should have to manage people they can't fire, and I no longer trusted his judgment in that area. I could only hope we could be friends on the other side of our Gaia's Garden experience.

Then, a few weeks later, as he was preparing to leave, Ari received word his son had died. I went to sit with him; there wasn't much to say, but coming together in that way affirmed our priorities. Our friendship, strained as it had been, was what mattered most.

After a few days, Ari returned to the restaurant. Abdo, who had kids, was able to express empathy. The response from most of the other employees could be summed up as "Wow. That's too bad. We need tomato paste."

In the kitchen, I was becoming concerned about Mick. He seemed off, walking around in circles, out of it. Abdo thought he was drunk; I was hoping he might be adjusting to new psych meds. When I went in the back to check on him, he said he was OK and fiddled with a pot lid. I could tell I wasn't going to get any more out of him.

I needed to leave and asked Terry to keep an eye on him and call me if the situation worsened. I found out the next day that as Abdo was leaving, he told Mac to watch Mick and not do any prep. I was paying him just to watch Mick! By around 6 p.m., there was no business, and Mick seemed to be coming around, so Mac left. At 6:30, a crowd showed up, ordering twenty-one short orders within an hour. According to Terry, "Mick tanked." Fortunately, Mac had had the foresight to text Rosie. She came in early and pulled it off.

I was impressed by the teamwork that had saved the night and particularly by how Rosie had stepped up. I didn't have to fire Mick—it was no surprise when he didn't show up the next day. He came in for his check a few days later, and I was appalled at how bad he looked. After ten years, I had become somewhat hardened to the comings and goings of employees with substance abuse problems, but when Mick came in for his check, he was shaking, bloated, and pasty, so sick and so miserable, I felt my heart break. I was familiar with alcoholism's many forms and knew from personal experience there was a way out for many. I was furious that it had taken Mick, a good young man with such a hard life already. We exchanged texts for a while, and he said he was sober and working.

Rosie was one of the few bright spots that month. She received a special jacket from the culinary school for having a 3.4 grade point average, and I think I was even more stoked than she was.

I hired a new dishwasher, Chui, who was charismatic and a good worker. After a few weeks, the crew in the kitchen informed me he had worked for us for half a day a couple of years before and walked out midshift. There had been a leak by the dish sink that we were getting fixed, but in the meantime, it had been necessary to mop constantly. That had been too much for him. By the time I learned this was the same guy, I had already been impressed by his demeanor and skills, so I ignored that bit of information, assuming Chui had matured. After Mick left, I moved Chui over to prep and also started training him on the register. I had been honest with him about our situation, offering training and a reference as incentive; he was excited about learning front of the house and had been studying how to make change by watching YouTube videos. Impressed, I gave him a crash course that included most of what I had learned about customer service. It seemed like he could do well as one of the utility guys I had come to treasure.

We again needed a dishwasher. Steve, a previous employee, was available, clean and sober again, living at the Mission, so we invited him back. He worked for a couple of days, then told us the Mission wouldn't let him work. He sent Tommy, who worked about a week, then told us he couldn't stay either, and he sent Robby.

On Robby's first day, I found that a cashbox we kept in a cabinet behind the register was missing. It had contained $700 from one of Abdo's events. I didn't think Robby would have taken it on his very first day. He was mopping and hadn't even reached the register area yet, nor would he know about the cashbox. I asked him if he had seen anyone near the register, and he reluctantly identified Chui. Chui was very familiar with the setup and had no business in that area at that time of day. When I talked with Abdo, Ari, and Margarita, they all thought Chui was the most likely culprit—they weren't as fond of him as I was.

There were other details that pointed to Chui, so the next day, I sat down with him and told him he was being laid off. He looked shocked. I told him the loss of $700 had been such a blow that I couldn't support his position and would have to do it myself. There was nothing to be gained by directly accusing him, but I hoped he would get the point.

On his second day, Robby informed me, "You've lost control of your kitchen."

I wondered, "Did I ever have control?"

Richard and Robby encountered each other on the patio with immediate recognition. Twenty-five years before, they had known each other from jail and from drinking and drugging on the streets. Richard told me Robby had probably stolen the money. "Addicts will steal your wallet then help you look for it." I thought Robby was clean now and perhaps had changed. Richard was not so charitable. Robby left a few weeks later, and I hired Margarita's husband, Manuel, at which point our stressful turnover finally stopped.

I had already been impressed by Manuel. When Margarita was in jail, he had called me at her request in search of bail money. We both wanted her out: They had a young son who needed his mom, and I needed her for lunches. The bail money was $700, and I expected I would be asked to pay it all, which I was reluctantly willing to do. Instead, Manuel, whom I had never met, told me he had $500 of it, they just needed the other $200. As it turned out, she was released on her own recognizance and didn't need any of the money, but I had learned quite a bit about Manuel's character and devotion to his family.

I was having less and less tolerance for high-maintenance customers at this point, but there was one frail older lady who was a total pain in the butt yet so sincerely fragile that I found myself catering to her as one would to a wounded bird. She couldn't eat much and was concerned about food being too salty or spicy, so I would give her several cups to use for sampling. She was always careful to let me know she wasn't abusing the courtesy, just taking small amounts. Once she had made her selection, I'd sell her a clean cup ($3.95) and throw in a piece of corn bread, which didn't usually come with it. One of the cashiers had mistakenly included it with her order in the past, and she never could accept that it wasn't protocol. The corn bread had to be from the center of the pan, since she didn't like any crispiness on the edges.

When I told her we would be closing, she panicked. We both knew there was no other place she could go that would be so accommodating. Recovering somewhat, she asked if she could buy a package of our napkins. Everyone else's, she told me, irritated her; she thought theirs might have been stored next to detergent or some other item to which she was allergic, but ours had never caused her a problem. Unfortunately, the package I gave her had a vague scent that bothered her. We tried three or four others, and none was acceptable. Finally, I opened one and had her check out the napkins in the middle of a package, and they seemed to be OK, so we pulled the center ones from several packages, and she went home with those as a parting gift.

GOD'S GRACE OR DUMB LUCK

In October, the Kinkade fire broke out north of us. We were not directly threatened, but 250,000 people were preemptively evacuated. My crew, as well as customers, were scattered all over the Bay Area, and our power was out, forcing us to close for ten days.

Business suffered considerably during this fire season, but I didn't care. I just wanted out. There had been a development that had completely changed my situation. I had expected to live on Social Security and the rent from Mom's house, taking out a reverse mortgage on my home if things got desperate. That would cover my basic needs without much else. Then, an investment I had thought was worthless paid off big time. There was enough to cover my total investment in the restaurant and quite a bit more.

Richard was convinced God had rewarded me. "I knew He would take care of you, but I thought it would come from the restaurant!" I didn't see it that way. Probably millions of people have worked as hard as I have and with intentions at least as good as mine, yet they don't win lotteries or their equivalent. I had prayed every day that the Divine's love and healing would manifest in everything we did at the restaurant. I had given it and the people involved my best. I had been confident that if I stayed on this path, I would be taken care of, not knowing what form that care would take or whether I would like it. Yet I could not say God had singled me out for reward based on my merit, although I was beyond grateful.

I had been relieved of financial worry at a very good time in the scheme of things—my ability to work had become limited. I had benefited from privilege but now also had the means not only to live comfortably but to share that privilege with others in a concrete way.

We needed a prep guy in December, and since it seemed we were close to closing the sale, I brought Charles and Lisa in on the process so they might continue his employment. Both Charles and Rosie had been impressed by a fellow student at the culinary school. They raved about his skills and great attitude. After a week or so, both of those qualities were dissipating. Ari dubbed him Pebbles due to his topknot, which resembled a hairdo from *The Flintstones*, and was not a fan. I came in one day as he and Ari were butting heads. Pebbles was using too much water when wiping down the dining tables, leaving them wet and streaked. The kid didn't like Ari's tone (which was mild in comparison to his capabilities) and announced he was leaving. "If you leave, don't come back," I told him. He left. It had taken this long, but finally Ari and I had fired someone together, side by side, as a team! After Charles took over the restaurant, he rehired him; Pebbles's tenure was short-lived. Whatever problems he had were not limited to Ari.

The costs of achieving code compliance, the rumors of our closure, the fire season, and our ongoing systemic problems resulted in an especially disastrous year financially. By the end of 2019, we had taken in $409,078 and showed a loss of $143,079. At least it helped offset my non-restaurant income in what had otherwise been a very good year.

The restaurant had been set up as a C corporation with the expectation of profits that would be retained in the corporation and not be taxable until withdrawn. In the absence of profit, the losses accumulated instead. I had tried to find a way to capitalize them and sell them to someone needing a write-off, but that's not how it works. Then, surprisingly, I was the one in need of a write-off and was able to convert to an S corp, which allowed most of the accumulated losses to benefit me by being written off against my personal income.

(Had I known about it sooner, I would have investigated becoming a B corp, or a benefit corporation, since I believe we met the requirements for community, worker, and environmental responsibility and might have been able to receive grants.)

We still had a 4.5-star rating on Yelp, and Amy's was once again recognized as the Best Vegetarian Restaurant in Sonoma County.

2020: THE END OF THIS

For the most part, I focused on moving into an easier future, but there were moments when grief nearly overwhelmed me. One evening, walking toward the restaurant from the side, it looked so beautiful to me, so elegant and inviting, that I didn't want to let it go. Why had more people not seen what we had? Why had we not been successful? Why had so many of the crew left with resentments?

There were high points, of course. I had always said I wanted our employees to leave better off than when they had arrived, and most had. We had been an excellent launching pad. Brian, formerly a homeless aspiring dishwasher, could choose among Michelin-starred suitors; Cara had her own bakery; Jackie and Rob were sought after by high-end restaurants. Rosie was in school, doing well. Most of our employees with culinary aspirations had gone on to restaurants that probably wouldn't have hired them before, and others were living their best lives. We had nurtured artists and contributed to our community. We had made a slight dent in the suffering of animals and shown others they could do the same. By eschewing animal agriculture, we had probably saved a billion gallons of water and millions of trees.

Still, I was plagued by feelings of guilt and failure. A big part of my motivation had been a desire to help Ari, to give him a stake in something meaningful and profitable. What we had in Gaia's Garden seemed like neither—especially for him. At least for me, the successes of some of our employees was on the plus side, but not so much for him. So there he was, ten years older, still with nothing. Maybe if I hadn't ridden in on my white horse, his different path would have led him in a more rewarding direction.

I considered that had I just gifted him $100,000, perhaps we'd have both been better off. Of course, there had been no way to know that, and he owned some of our failure, but most of the decisions had ultimately been mine. I had been driving the bus, and now it had gone off the cliff. I was able to balance these dark thoughts by knowing they were hindsight, and my motives had been good. And, of course, Ari was an adult making his own decisions and had a big part in both our successes and failures.

The escrow was dragging on. We had all been sure it would have closed by January 20, when Richard and I were scheduled to depart for Kauai—a ten-day trip we had been planning for a year. That was not the case.

We needed to reopen after the holidays, after all. Charles and Lisa had been hard at work bringing the space to code, and the dining room and kitchen had been rearranged; it was stressful. We couldn't find things, and some items we relied on had been thrown out. Dust from construction projects was a constant challenge. We decided to close for the evenings in January, since our customer count had become dismal, and to shut down operations completely as of February 3, just servicing the schools until escrow closed.

Although Donald was no longer employed as our dishwasher, he was hanging around quite a bit, and we'd give him leftovers. I was already on my last nerve when I saw some lines he had written on the whiteboard in the employee restroom:

"Boss makes a dollar, I make a dime
That's why I poop on the company time."

For the first time since I'd walked through the front door of Gaia's Garden, as a new owner full of hope, I lost it.

"GET THE HELL OUT OF HERE! HOW DARE YOU! WE'RE DONE! FUCK YOU! DON'T COME BACK!"

He seemed baffled and started to make some "just a joke" kind of excuse. I'd had it. Ten years of working my ass off, never taking a penny out of the business, giving it all my time and my energy, losing hundreds of thousands of dollars, ruining my health, putting up with his lazy ass—and he dared to imply I was exploiting the staff? It all came to a head at that moment.

"OUT!"

Later, Ari made a mild attempt to speak on Donald's behalf but quickly backed down.

A year later, I learned this couplet was circulating on the internet and part of a song. That would have done nothing to change my mind. I wish I had told him and a few others off sooner.

Before I left for Hawaii, I gave the thirty days' notice to the crew. They took it in stride except for Rosie. She had been with us—on and off, mostly on—for eight years, from the ages of nineteen to twenty-seven. We had been one of the few stable "homes" in her young life. As I sat across from her, I saw tears rolling down her cheeks. I tried to reassure her. "You'll be OK, honey. I love you, and we'll still be family."

"I know. But it's the end of *this*."

Then, I was fighting back tears myself.

I had hoped Charles and Lisa would hire all or most of our crew, and they had initially thought they would. As they got to know this quirky bunch, though, they began having second thoughts. I was disappointed, but of course it was their right to have their own people. They knew they wanted to retain Margarita and Manuel, Anna, and possibly Rosie. Charles talked with a friend who offered Arthur a job detailing cars, but he declined.

I drew up letters of reference for everyone. This was not hard. They had stuck with what they knew was a sinking ship for seven months, based on my word and the feelings they had for the place and each other. Throughout, they had done their best and kept the quality up. Most of my crew didn't have résumés, so I was able to help create them. In the process, I learned more about Mac. He had been in a car accident and had amnesia for many years. A worker at the homeless shelter had made it a project to find out who he was, and as a result of her care and her vigorous online research, he gradually began to recover his memory. He had recently reconciled with his son, a story he told me as he shed tears of joy.

I had given most of the employees significant raises for the last couple of months to help their negotiating positions in the future. The business couldn't afford it, but I no longer cared.

Kauai was lovely, but I spent many hours in paradise obsessing over a jigsaw puzzle, barely able to appreciate the island's many attractions or to be present with Richard and our friends, although as usual I put up a fairly good front. I craved oblivion, but that option was not compatible with sobriety.

When I returned, there was one weekend left of our public service. On our last day, Sunday, we had a full house. "Where were all these people when we needed them?" I wondered. Then, looking around, I saw that these were the people who had been our support the entire time, now assembled to say goodbye. Resentment turned to gratitude, and we had a lovely brunch. Later, Bernardo wrapped up everything he could into burritos for the homeless.

Margarita and Manuel were our only employees now, carrying on in what felt like a vacuum, putting out the school lunches. We finally closed escrow on March 5, 2020. As Charles and I were returning from Ryn's office, I mentioned to him in casual conversation, "This Covid virus looks like it may be serious."

I had thought Ari and I would go through the restaurant, having a sort of ceremony to say goodbye, but neither of us had the taste for it. It hadn't felt like ours for a while. It had a completely different look now—minimalist, industrial. On March 5, when I signed the last documents and officially turned the restaurant over, I left quickly with a lump in my throat, not wanting to feel more sadness or dampen the joy of the new owners.

GOOD TIMING (FOR US)

Two weeks later, Sonoma County put a ban on indoor dining and closed the schools due to the pandemic. Charles and Lisa had been dealt a huge blow, but they were better prepared for it than we would have been. They were younger and energetic, with new ideas for both the menu and the organization. They had a far more impressive network of support than we'd had, plus our customers would at least give them a try. Charles had been involved in many activities, and it seemed that everyone he had ever met liked him a lot. I did. He had a way of making whomever he was with feel like the most important and wisest person ever. Lisa and I had butted heads during the escrow, but she was smart and focused, with extensive contacts in her field of education. It seemed they would avoid the partnership problems Ari and I had had.

They were committed to being 100 percent vegan. Ari and I had noted over the years that vegans who wouldn't patronize us because we weren't pure enough would lose their minds when a meat-serving restaurant introduced a cauliflower steak or a small vegan menu, urging everyone to go there and show support. But that was behind us now.

Lisa and Charles eliminated the buffet and served complicated dishes for higher prices. When they tried simpler fare, which I preferred, it didn't sell well and was taken off the menu. They were making it work, which was quite an accomplishment in that environment. To-go service mandated by the ban on indoor dining allowed them to keep a lean staff, and they were staying on top of the analytics—very conscious of costs. I hoped they learned from our mistakes. Lisa was a master of spreadsheets. Charles had a real knack for negotiating and finding good deals on equipment. Sadly, that had become even easier as so many restaurants and catering companies went out of business due to the pandemic. It may have been helpful that they didn't have the privilege I'd had of throwing money at a failing business. They couldn't afford to fail, and it showed.

They had many of the same issues to deal with as we had, though, and Charles and I enjoyed occasional long chats about the restaurant business. There was clearly a balance to be struck between caring about individual employees and making the hardheaded decisions necessary to maintain a business. They seemed to be walking that line better than either Ari or I had.

Due to lost revenue during the remodel and transition and my share of the costs to bring the restaurant up to code, I managed to lose $53,959 in those last two and a quarter months. A significant part of that was severance pay and some bonuses, and I was proud to have done right by the crew. I also left with all bills paid—an unusual scenario for a failing restaurant—and 4.5 stars on Yelp.

The new restaurant, Cozy Plum, was later named the best vegan restaurant in Sonoma County. (East West Café was voted best vegetarian in the first year the categories were separated.)

PART 8

EPILOGUE

THE FAMILY AFTERWARDS

Ari had planned to take an extended road trip, but the pandemic and inertia put his travel plans on hold. We both needed more downtime for healing than we had anticipated. At home, he set about organizing and disposing of a lifetime's accumulation of art, DVDs, and household goods. Happily, our friendship has survived our years in business. Having come through the fire and now relieved of our mutual stressors, that bond is even stronger than before. We text each other often and share meals every other week or so. The axes have all been ground: There is no longer any reason not to accept each other unconditionally — no deal breakers.

Richard and I have weathered the pandemic and are still in love — mostly due to his good nature. We were married in September 2022. I am beyond grateful for his support over the previous ten years and for his unstinting care when I was at my worst. As my health seems to be returning by increments, we have taken some wonderful trips and plan more.

Recently we've embarked on a small project that includes Ari—shares in a converted camper van. We burst out laughing when I asked rhetorically, "What could go wrong?"

I check my crew's Facebook pages from time to time and am gratified to see how many have friended each other and that they have an enduring network. Sadly, there have been a disproportionate number of tragedies among my former staff, highlighting the fragility of life—particularly among the at-risk people we hired and came to love.

Mick succumbed to alcoholism and committed suicide in 2021. He was thirty-one years old. I heard about it from Annie. She and Rob had moved to Arkansas with her parents. "I thought you'd want to know," she texted, "we're a family." Mick was very loved by his friends, but that's not always enough. It didn't save Ari's talented friend, Lloyd, either. He died from chronic alcoholism in 2023 at age sixty-four.

Manuel and Margarita moved to a coastal town up north, where Manuel and his son could fish and kayak to their hearts' content as the family awaited the birth of their second son. Manuel was living his dream when, on January 2, 2022, he was killed in a vehicular accident. Of all the deaths I've known of in my long life, this may have hit me the hardest.

Terry, Anna, Rosie, Lacey, and I had a lovely, luxurious brunch just before restaurants closed for indoor dining. Jackie had to work that day, so we were looking forward to another one. Shortly after, Terry was diagnosed with prostate cancer that had metastasized to his bones, and he was given about a year to live. Rosie helped get his apartment set up for his return from the hospital and visited him often, using her caregiving experience to help with his feeding tube.

I visited Terry every Wednesday until he passed in January 2022. He chose to suffer most of the pain in order to be cognitively aware during his last year. Early on, he told me, "I thought I'd have more time," a sentiment that has stayed with me as a reminder to live my own life as fully as possible. That was the closest he got to a complaint, and he was always gracious. After some conversation, I would read a draft of this book to him. We enjoyed reminiscing about our Gaia's Garden experience and discussing how a venture, so soulful and excellent in its intentions, could have become unsustainable.

Jackie has regained her warrior spirit and seems more like her real self. She has remained employed at good restaurants and continues to live with Robert. In 2017, Ray, then twenty-seven years old, was sentenced to eleven years in prison. I ran into him unexpectedly in 2024, so he must have been well behaved while incarcerated. We had a short, cordial exchange, and once again I saw no evidence of his dark side.

Arthur got a job at a local grocery store with a large selection of prepared foods. He had once told me, "I'd be homeless without this job at Gaia's Garden." I was so happy my assurances to the contrary had been correct—at least for a while. The last report I got, though, was that he is homeless again.

Rosie told me Mac was in a county-run RV shelter for medically fragile people near the Fairgrounds. I was able to find him there to deliver his W-2 in January 2021, and we had a pleasant visit. Though alarmingly thin, he still had his upbeat personality as well as the cancer. Neither Rosie nor I have heard from him in the last year, and we believe he has passed away.

Happily, some have moved forward in what seem to be positive trajectories. Peter and Ruby have stayed clean and sober for over seven years now and are still employed in homeless services.

Evangelical Evan came out recently as transgender, which probably surprised his fundamentalist congregation, but he seems quite at ease.

The pandemic derailed Rosie's studies, and she went to work as a security guard and home health worker. She is the only member of our crew with whom I'm in close contact. We text back and forth and occasionally have lunch. Together, we located Jerry's grave, which, thanks to Rosie, is now consistently adorned with an abundance of flowers. She also decorates his parents' markers, even though she never met them. She is back in culinary school, getting straight As.

Abdo and Bernardo went to work at the branch of the Market that had a buffet and food to go, improving their offerings significantly. Bernardo recently texted Ari to announce he has moved on to a Michelin-starred restaurant, thanking Ari for his guidance. I suspect many of our employees—even those who disliked him—will hear his voice in their heads over the years and come to appreciate the knowledge and standards he was trying to impart.

I was hoping one day to hear from Daria, our very first employee, but it hasn't happened. I check her Facebook page occasionally, although we're not "friends." She joined her mother in the Midwest and is into death metal. She looks healthy and, perhaps, more open.

I haven't received a 7 a.m. crisis call since March 5, 2020, and for that I am very grateful. I sank into my chair for the first few months, lacking the energy to deal with my worldly possessions and deferred housekeeping. Between my poor health, the state of the nation, and the pandemic, as well as having time to fully grieve the loss of Gaia's Garden and our dreams for it, I was feeling a deep sadness. Fortunately, a friend invited me to join a writing class on Zoom, and I became obsessed with finishing this book, which has been a therapeutic, illuminating, and humbling experience.

People who write and teach about memoir stress the necessity of showing what the subject has learned. How have they changed? They want the culmination of "the hero's journey." I think they're looking for moves like "Delia frees herself from the toxic relationship" or "Cheryl finds God." I'm not sure if "Susan throws in the towel" rises to that level, but that's what happened. Besides learning — belatedly — when to fold 'em, what *did* I learn? That's a question I can only begin to answer now that I have some distance from Gaia's Garden.

There are a few obvious takeaways regarding restaurant operations, which the reader has probably seen by now. First, stay on top of your income and expenses! Second, don't rush to expand unless you are sure you can benefit thereby. And third, try for fewer employees: paying more for two good ones is probably better than having four who are less professional.

On a broader scale, the recovery program that saved my life emphasizes taking things one day at a time, staying in the present, and doing the next right thing. As Queen Elizabeth advised, "Stay calm and carry on." This practice kept me moving forward without freaking out but with self-imposed blinders. Focusing on what was in front of me, I was able to face crisis after crisis with a certain equanimity but didn't stop to look around enough. There are other parts of the program I might have focused on more. We're encouraged to identify and accept the reality of situations whether we like them or not. Decisions made from illusion or fear will be flawed, as many of mine were.

Several new restaurants have opened in our area, and many of these are vegan or have significant vegan offerings. They seem popular and may be successful since all are charging quite a bit. This seems to be true around the country, with some famous chefs reengineering their menus to be substantially or entirely vegan. Still, it's not easy to find a plant-based meal on a budget, and I get occasional messages from former customers bewailing our demise.

Ari has complained for years that in his ventures he was always a little too far ahead of the curve, and that may have been true this time too. On the other hand, we had minimal competition and still couldn't make it happen. One new local enterprise has been discovered recently by our hometown press as a venue for food, art, music, and community events, as though it were a new concept. That was literally our motto and mission for ten years!

I read of a restaurant in the Midwest that serves meals based on doshas (body/energy types). I had pitched this idea (Café Ayurveda) to a local practitioner, but her response was lukewarm, and it never happened. Sour grapes are probably not good for any body type, though, and I must acknowledge we made serious mistakes.

Ari and I have enough distance from it to miss things about the restaurant. Having our own venue was a joy and came with the opportunity to support worthy causes in a meaningful way. I still don't enjoy home cooking much, so having to deal with dinner myself seems like a hardship now.

Given the major changes to the industry that the pandemic has dictated, much of our experience might already be outdated. Still, I hope it has been entertaining for you and that it has been useful to other would-be or novice restaurateurs. Technology changes, but people don't. I also hope it has helped customers understand some of what goes into making their meals besides the obvious cooking and serving. Perhaps some will have more understanding of what it takes to provide "a pile of vegetables."

RECIPES

INTRODUCTION TO THE RECIPES

We got used to people nervously announcing, "I've never had vegan food." Ari's rejoinder would be, "You've never had a vegetable?" These recipes are all vegan *and* gluten-free, quite delicious and not weird at all. They are either ones we developed or ones I purchased from Gopal. His were vegetarian but not necessarily vegan. It is fairly easy to veganize anything. Vegan mayonnaise, butter, and cheeses are readily available and increasingly good in quality. Soy or coconut milk are good substitutes for dairy. Textured vegetable protein (TVP) has the mouthfeel of hamburger; just make sure it's saturated with a tasty sauce, otherwise it tastes mousey—or what I think mousey tastes like. Tofu, beans and tempeh provide protein. More and more plant-based "meats" are coming on the market if you prefer to use them.

If you've read my memoir, you know I'm not a chef. I've spent many, many hours adjusting these recipes for the home cook. It's not just math! These are as close as I can come to the dishes we served in the restaurant.

I haven't included the dinner entrées but, instead, refer you to the internet, which is awash with excellent vegan recipes. That's where I got many for the restaurant.

Equipment:

You're already cooking and can probably make do with what you have. Here are some helpful items you'll find in most commercial kitchens that will make your cooking easier and more fun.

A set of metal bowls, small to large

Small bowls for spices

Good sharp knives

A thick plastic cutting board

A nutribullet or food processor

A blender

A wok for curry; a large frying pan will work, but it should have at least 3" sides.

Two sets of measuring cups and spoons—one for dry, one for wet ingredients. Professional spoon sets will include ½ Tbsp, which can be helpful. I love my one-quart measuring cup, which I had never had prior to owning a restaurant.

Tongs

A set of whisks

Parchment paper. This goes under anything you're baking or roasting. It minimizes stickage and makes cleanup much easier. You can buy enough to last a lifetime at restaurant supply stores much more cheaply than at a regular grocery store.

A seed grinder

A note about restaurant supply stores. Their equipment will be certified NSF, which stands for National Sanitation Foundation. It will be more expensive than you might find elsewhere but will also be more durable. The prices are ridiculously high at some outlets, but in our area most restaurateurs shop at US Foods Chef'Store (formerly Cash and Carry), which is reasonable. It's worth a field trip for a home cook. Some items, like spices, are significantly less expensive than in regular grocery stores, and case prices on frequently used items can save you a bundle.

Ingredients::

For South Indian cooking—and most of these recipes are based on that—the following are good to have in stock. All of them have health benefits. The seeds will keep, but get the powders in small amounts, as fresh as possible.

Asafoetida (hing). This is a lifesaver for people with allium allergies or following *satvig*, as it provides pungency. If you don't have or want it, substitute an equal amount of onion powder. Hing is sometimes cut with turmeric or wheat flour. We preferred the pure stuff and wanted it to be gluten-free. In one Indian market, the owner grabbed a container out of my hand, offering another one. "You no want that! Take this, this white people's hing!" I assured her I knew what I was doing, so she sold me the unadulterated powder, shaking her head, making it quite clear she was not responsible for the outcome. She was right to be concerned. If you overdo it, your result will taste nasty.

Baking soda helps neutralize the acidity of tomatoes.

Black pepper (in addition to flavor, it enhances the anti-inflammatory properties of turmeric)

Coconut milk. Gopal used Chakoah brand, so we did too. I only recently learned the cans may have BHA in the lining. Is anything safe anymore? Still, it's creamy and works well. I've seen recommendations for Traeder Joe's brand if you want to avoid the possibility of contamination.

Coriander powder, coriander seed

Curry powder

Cumin seed

Fennel seed

Fenugreek seed (I use this only for kale or spinach curry)

Garam masala powder

Mustard seed (black from the Indian markets, brown if you don't have an Indian market available)

Salt. Everybody knows salt. What I've learned from cutting down these recipes is that it offsets sweetness. So, if a dish tastes too sweet, and you scanted the salt, try a little more.

Sambar masala powder (again, from the Indian markets) This is a mix of coriander, chili, cumin powder, tumeric, fenugreek seeds, mustard, black pepper, fennel, cassia, cloves, curry leaves, nutmeg, cardamon, asafoetida and mace. It will amp up all the curries. Worth acquiring.

Quality counts. Beans over a year old will resist softening no matter what you do. Tomato products vary in acidity and sweetness, so more baking soda or sugar may be called for.

There are two more things very handy to have available:

Ginger Chili Relish

This is an easy and delightful condiment for use in or on curries and soups. We had customers who put it on tapioca, but I never have.

I make a lot for freezing, forming balls with a small ice cream scoop or using an ice cube tray. The formula by weight is two parts ginger to one part serrano peppers. For a small amount, rough cut a one-inch piece of ginger and one or two sliced serrano peppers (leave seeds in if you like heat, seed them if you don't). Grind them together. The color should be bright green, the texture a very fine mince. I use a Nutribullet (1-2 pulses), or you can use a food processor. If you have neither, mince everything as finely as possible, then grind in a *molcajete* or other mortar and pestle setup. If you have extra, it is a nice garnish for those who like heat and a good addition to all kinds of food. It will keep for a week or more refrigerated.

Roasted Chili

I love having roasted chilis in the freezer for use in green chili sauce or a pot of chili. I buy half a case of poblano peppers, wash them, lay them out on parchment paper, and roast at 400 degrees for about 20 minutes, turning once. The skins should be significantly blackened—use the broiler if that's not happening.

Immediately put them in a paper bag or airtight container so the steam can loosen the skins.

When they're cool enough to work with, remove the seed bulb and the skins. You probably won't get all the skins off, and the peppers will come apart, which is OK (unless you plan to make *chili rellenos*, in which case you'll have to be more careful). Working with batches of six, immerse the chilis in a bowl of water. Most of the remaining seeds will rise to the top. You don't have to get them all, but the more left in the chilis, the spicier they'll be. Squeeze the chilis dry, put them in sandwich bags, and freeze them.

Pro tip: You'll be getting the hot (picante) residue on your hands, so either use thin gloves or just make sure not to touch your eyes or anyone's private parts for about twenty-four hours.

Process:

Professional chefs use a process called *mise en place*. This simply means having all the ingredients available, prepped, and measured before beginning to cook. You've seen that on cooking shows, but it works just as well at home. If you have an item that requires a long prep (such as yellow split peas for the dahl), you can get that started and assemble everything else in the meantime. You'll be glad you did.

NOW FOR THE RECIPES

PLEASE READ THE INTRODUCTION FIRST

CURRIES

(All make 6-8 cups)

Like abstract art or jazz, the masters understand the basics. Curry has a form with plenty of room to improvise. Our recipes are a South Indian style, using asafoetida (hing) instead of onions and garlic for pungency. You can substitute equal amounts of onion powder or ¼ diced onion if you prefer. These recipes are mild; add more ginger/chili relish or whatever you want if you like it spicier.

Start with a chhonk — spices cooked in oil — then vegetables, then liquids, then more spices and a finish. (Traditionally, the chhonk would just be the oil and seeds, but I've lumped a few steps together because they're the same for each recipe.) Serve as is or over rice.

Here's the basic form for six servings:

Mise en place is highly recommended (you'll have three spice mixes)

1. Make the chhonk

Heat 1/3 cup of neutral oil with a high smoke point (rice bran, grapeseed, or [ugh] canola) in a wok or frying pan with at least 3" sides – medium heat

Add the spices for the chhonk:

 1 Tbsp cumin seed

 1 tsp brown or black mustard seed

 1 tsp fennel seed

Cook for about a minute at medium high heat until the mustard seeds pop. If the spices burn, start over.

Add 1-2 Tbsp of ginger-chili relish (see recipe in previous chapter). Cook for a minute or two.

Add spices:

 ⅛ tsp asafoetida or onion powder

 1 tsp black pepper

 2 tsp turmeric powder

2. Add vegetables (2+ quarts) — see variations below – high heat

3. Add liquids —see variations below — simmer

4, Add Secondary Spices:

 1 Tbsp of coriander powder

 1 tsp Sambar Masala (optional, but worth having)

2 tsp salt

Spices specific to your kind of curry – see variations below

5. Finish

Let it simmer for 10 minutes or until all vegetables are tender; thin it if you want to. Coconut water is usually best, although a little plain water is OK and unsweetened chai works nicely.

Garnish with chopped cilantro.

The following are some of our recipes to start you off. The garbanzo bean curry is shown step-by-step, followed by variations.

Garbanzo Bean Curry

Ingredients:

1. Chhonk:

1/3 cup of neutral oil with a high smoke point (rice bran, grapeseed, or canola)

1 Tbsp cumin seed

1 heaping tsp brown or black mustard seed (black is more authentic but harder to find)

1 heaping tsp fennel seed

1-2 Tbsp of ginger-chili relish (see recipe in previous chapter)

⅛ tsp asafoetida (hing) or onion powder

1 tsp black pepper

2 tsp turmeric powder

2. Vegetables:

1 qt. cauliflower—bite-size florets

3 cups zucchini sliced into "coins"—⅜" thick

3. Liquids:

3/4 cup tomato puree + ¼ tsp baking soda

3/4 cup water

4. Spices:

1 Tbsp coriander powder

1 tsp garam masala

1 tsp ground fennel seed

1 tsp Sambar Masala

2 tsp salt

5. Finish: 1-2 cans garbanzo beans (15 oz each), drained

1/4 cup chopped cilantro

Process:

1. Chhonk:

Heat oil in a wok or frying pan with at least 3" sides – medium heat.

Add cumin seed, mustard seed, and fennel seed.

Cook for about a minute until the mustard seeds pop. If the spices burn, start over.

Add ginger-chili relish. Cook for a minute or two.

Add hing, black pepper, and turmeric.

2. Vegetables:

Add cauliflower, coat with spiced oil, turn, and sauté over medium high heat for 5 minutes.

Add zucchini, turn, and sauté for 5 minutes more.

3. Liquids:

Add tomato puree, baking soda and water.

4. Secondary spices:

Add coriander powder, garam masala, ground fennel seed, and salt and Sambar Masala if you have it.

5: Finish:

Add garbanzo beans.

Simmer for about 10 minutes. Make sure cauliflower is tender.

Sprinkle with cilantro prior to serving.

Cabbage Curry

Ingredients:

Oil, spices and relish for chhonk (see above)

1 quart yellow potatoes cut in 1" cubes

1 quart chopped green cabbage (about ½ head)

1 can (28 oz) diced tomatoes plus ¼ tsp baking soda

½ cup water

2 tsp salt

½ Tbsp coriander powder

½ tsp ground fennel seeds

½ tsp garam masala

2 cups frozen peas

2 Tbsp minced cilantro

Process

Add potatoes to enough boiling water to cover. Return to a boil for 10 minutes or until potatoes are just tender, drain and let them cool.

Make the chhonk (see above).

Add cabbage to chhonk and sauté well on high heat. Some burned fringes will enhance the flavor.

Add potatoes.

Add diced tomatoes, baking soda and water. Keep heat at a simmer.

Add 2 tsp salt; ½ Tbsp coriander powder; ½ tsp ground fennel seeds; ½ tsp garam masala. Simmer for five minutes.

Add frozen peas and simmer for another five minutes. Top with chopped cilantro just prior to serving.

.

Yam Curry

Yams? Sweet potatoes? Who knows? Grocers I talk to don't seem clear on the concept; even produce master Joe Imwalle isn't sure. He calls the ones you want yams, but I think they're technically sweet potatoes. They have reddish skin and orange flesh. These are the best for color and aren't too sweet.

Ingredients:
Spices, relish and herbs for chhonk (see above)

1 quart of yams, peeled and cut into 1-inch cubes

2 cups yellow potatoes cut into 1-inch cubes

Oil for deep frying. Use one with a high smoking point: Rice bran is my favorite, but sunflower, soy, or canola are among those you could use. Amount will vary according to your container. My wok takes about 2 quarts. You want enough to cover your yams.

2 cups zucchini cut into 3/8" rounds. Cut these in half if your zuch is thick

3/4 cup tomato puree + ¼ tsp baking soda

3/4 cup water

2 tsp salt

1 Tbsp coriander powder

1 tsp ground fennel seed

1 tsp garam masala

1 tsp Sambar Masala

2 cups frozen peas

2 Tbsp minced cilantro

Process:

These are the basics for deep frying, but if you're not familiar, you may wish to consult the internet. Safety first!

Heat oil and test temperature by dropping in a piece of yam. When bubbles form around it and it starts getting a light crust, add the rest slowly to avoid splatter. If you have a deep fry thermometer, you want about 350 degrees. Fry until tender, then remove yams, drain well and set aside.

Do the same with the potatoes.

When it's safe, reserve 1/3 cup oil for the chhonk.

Make chhonk (see above).

Add zucchini rounds to the chhonk; sauté until they start to brown.

Add tomato puree, baking soda and water.

Add yams and potatoes.

Add salt, coriander powder, ground fennel seeds and garam masala.

Simmer for ten minutes.

Add 2 cups of frozen peas and simmer for another 5 minutes.

Top with minced cilantro just prior to serving.

This also works well with the addition of kale and 1 tsp ground fenugreek (no cilantro) or chopped cabbage and 1 cup of diced tomatoes instead of puree.

Coconut Cauliflower Curry

Ingredients:

Oil, spices, relish and herbs for chhonk (see above)

1 quart of yellow potatoes cut into 1" cubes

1 quart (about half a head) of cauliflower cut into pieces about 1" (slice between "branches.")

1 can (13.5 oz) coconut milk

2 tsp salt

1 Tbsp coriander powder

1 tsp ground fennel seeds

1 tsp curry powder

1 tsp sambar masala (optional)

1 Tbsp tamarind paste (optional)

2 cups frozen peas

2 Tbsp minced cilantro

Process:

Place potatoes in enough boiling water to cover. Return to a boil, then after 10 minutes or until potatoes are just tender, drain and let them cool.

Add cauliflower to chhonk and sauté over high heat until cauliflower is tender.

Add potatoes.

Add coconut milk and let it boil for a few minutes.

Add salt, coriander powder, ground fennel seeds, curry powder. Add sambar masala and tamarind paste if you have them.

Add peas. Simmer for five minutes more.

Add minced cilantro just prior to serving.

The curry should be a lovely yellow color. Sometimes the peas and cilantro will give it a greenish cast, especially the next day. Consider adding a little tomato puree—just enough to make it orange—if the color is not appealing.

Kale Curry

Ingredients:

Oil, spices, relish and herbs for chhonk (see above)

2 quarts (2-3 bunches) fresh kale, large ribs removed, coarsely chopped. You can also use frozen spinach or chard or a combination.

1 quart (2–3) Yukon gold potatoes (reds are OK; russets can get mushy), cut in 1" cubes

1 can (24 oz) diced tomatoes + ¼ tsp baking soda

1 can (13.5 oz) coconut milk

2 tsp salt

1 Tbsp fenugreek seed powder

1 Tbsp sambar masala (optional in other recipes, it really amps this one up)

Process:

Add potatoes to enough boiling water to cover. Return to a boil and cook for about 10 minutes, until just tender. Drain and set aside.

Make chhonk (see above).

Add greens. Oil should be hot but not enough to fry the greens—just cook them until tender. If mixing greens, kale will take the longest, so add it first.

Add the potatoes.

Add the tomatoes and coconut milk.

Add salt, fenugreek and sambar spice.

Simmer for 10 minutes.

Add salt to taste.

Brussels Sprouts Curry

Even people who don't like Brussels sprouts will probably like this.

Ingredients:

Oil, spices, relish and herbs for chhonk (see above)

1 quart yellow or red potatoes cut in 1" cubes

1 quart Brussels sprouts trimmed and halved

1 can (13.5 oz) coconut milk

Half that amount (6.75 oz) tomato puree

2 tsp salt

1 Tbsp coriander powder

1 Tbsp curry powder

1 tsp ground rosemary

1 cup frozen peas

2 Tbsp minced cilantro

Process:

Boil potatoes and Brussels sprouts separately until almost tender. Set aside,

Make chhonk (see above).

Add potatoes and Brussels sprouts.

Add coconut milk and tomato puree.

Simmer for 5 minutes.

Add salt, coriander powder, curry powder, ground rosemary.

Simmer for about 15 minutes.

Add peas long enough to thaw and heat (about 5 minutes).

Thin if needed with coconut water or plain water.

Sprinkle cilantro on top before serving.

Soups

(All make 6-8 cups)

Dahl

This was definitely our signature soup. It was our one product that cooks weren't allowed to "improve." We had many requests for the recipe but wouldn't give it out—until now.

3 quarts water

2 cups yellow split peas

⅓ cup tomato puree

¼ bunch cilantro roughly chopped—stems OK

2 tsp salt

2 Tbsp (vegan) sugar

2 Tbsp flavorless oil (rice bran, grapeseed, or [ugh] canola)

1 tsp cumin seeds

1 tsp black mustard seeds

½ tsp fennel seeds

1 tsp ginger chili relish (see recipe in the introduction)

pinch of asafoeteda or 1/8 tsp onion powder

½ tsp turmeric

2 tsp coriander powder

Process:

Pour water into a stock pot and bring to a boil.

Turn down the heat (to avoid boiling over) and add the split peas.

Simmer the peas until they are completely broken down—about 2 hours.
Blend cilantro and tomato puree, then add to the peas with the salt and
sugar.

Whisk well and let it simmer, stirring occasionally, while you prepare the
chhonk.

If you haven't done mise en place, this would be a good time. You'll be
working quickly.

Make a chhonk. In a small sauté pan, heat the oil.

Add cumin, black mustard, and fennel seeds.

Sauté for a minute or two until the seeds start to pop.

(If it burns, start this part over.)

Add ginger chili relish, simmer for a minute.

Add turmeric powder, hing and coriander powder.

Simmer for another minute, stirring constantly.

Add this to the stock pot.

That's it!

If refrigerated, it will solidify. You can reheat with added water and it will
still be good. It will keep for a few days but may lose some flavor. You can
make it ahead up to the chhonk, then finish it before serving.

Creamy Beet Soup

This is a lovely, tasty soup. A customer who said it was great gave me her family's very complicated method for keeping the soup red. Apparently, she didn't notice the soup she was sipping was a beautiful crimson. It's not that hard to retain the color. I peel the beets for that reason and boil instead of roast them. The soup would still taste good if the peels were left on, and the roasting process caramelizes the sugars, but I like it my way.

Ingredients:

1 quart stock if you have it, or water

4 medium beets (5–6 cups) peeled and cut in 1" chunks (be careful)

1 can (13.5 oz) coconut milk

½ cup chai tea*

⅛ tsp onion powder or a pinch of hing

½ tsp tarragon

¼ tsp thyme

Pinch of nutmeg

½ tsp cinnamon

¼ tsp oregano

¼ tsp basil

⅛ tsp cumin powder

½ Tbsp salt

3 drops orange extract

Process:

Bring water or stock to a boil and add beets. Keep them on a low boil until tender enough to be blended—about 25 minutes. Drain the beets, retaining the liquid, and set aside.

In a small pan, bring the coconut milk to a boil and let it simmer for 5–15 minutes. (A Thai elder told me always to boil coconut milk, so I do.)

Assemble the spices.

Put half the liquid in a saucepan and add chai, spices, and salt. Bring to a boil and simmer for 10 minutes.

Put the beets in a blender with the rest of the cooking liquid and puree until smooth.

Add beet puree and coconut milk to the spiced stock, stir, bring to a boil, and simmer for 10 minutes.

Add orange extract and stir.

Serve as is, or garnish with a dollop of coconut cream, sour cream, or chopped fresh parsley.

* Chai tea: We always had a good supply made up and added it to curries, soups, and barbecue sauce. You probably don't. You can use a Yogi Tea bag or other chai mix to get a strong half cup for this purpose. Our chai was actually Cinnamon Spice Tea that we bought in bulk from Ancient Healing Ways. If you enjoy experimenting with spices, that one contains cinnamon bark, ginger root, cardamom seed, clove, and black pepper. In any case, no sweetener, milk or black tea.

Caribbean Black Bean Soup (Spicy)

Ingredients:

6 cups vegetable stock or water (8 cups for brothier)

1 6 oz can tomato paste

2 cups black beans soaked overnight and drained

1 cup diced carrots

½ cup diced green or red bell peppers

½ cup diced celery

1 bay leaf

Pinch of hing or ⅛ tsp onion powder

½ tsp thyme

½ Tbsp parsley flakes

½ tsp black pepper

½ Tbsp ground coriander

1 Tbsp ginger chili relish (see recipe in previous chapter)

1 Tbsp salt

3 shakes of Tabasco or Cholula sauce

Process:

Whisk vegetable stock or water with tomato paste until smooth.

Add the drained black beans and bring to a boil. Turn down the heat and simmer, covered, at least an hour or until the beans are very tender.

Add the carrots, pepper, and celery and simmer for 10 more minutes. Add spices and relish and simmer for another 10 minutes.

Shake in the hot sauce. This is more for depth of flavor than heat. Garnish with cilantro or parsley if you want to.

Mung Bean Soup

This is a quick soup that doesn't require soaking or prep, so it was a go-to when we ran out of another type. It's hard to mess up unless you use mung bean sprouts instead of mung beans, which one of our cooks did. In her honor thereafter, we began including some sprouts, and they do make a nice addition.

2 quarts vegetable stock or water

¾ cup tomato paste

2 cups mung beans

1 tsp ginger chili relish (see recipe in previous chapter)

1 Tbsp salt

½ tsp turmeric powder

1 tsp ground cumin

½ tsp garam masala

½ tsp black pepper

2 tsp ground coriander

1 bay leaf

⅛ bunch cilantro

½ cup water

3 shakes Tabasco sauce

¼ cup dried seaweed (optional)

Small handful of mung bean sprouts, rough chopped (optional)

Process:

Whisk water and tomato paste together until smooth.

Add mung beans.

Bring to a boil, then simmer, covered, for 45 minutes or until tender.

Add ginger-chili relish, salt, and spices.

Blend the cilantro with the water and add to the soup.

Shake in the Tabasco sauce.

If using seaweed, soak it in water until soft, then mince and add to the soup.

Throw in some mung bean sprouts at the end if you have some.

Add water if needed, then bring to a boil and turn off the heat.

Tomato Coconut Soup

This was a favorite at the restaurant, since it's very tasty, a little fancy, and easy to make. Ari gave it a porn name, Tommy CoCo, which we used affectionately from then on. This will make 4-6 servings, and it keeps well.

Ingredients:

1 can (6 oz) tomato paste

1 quart water or vegetable stock

1 cup diced potatoes

½ cup diced celery

1 cup diced zucchini

½ tsp turmeric powder

½ tsp black pepper

1 tsp dried basil

2 tsp dried parsley flakes

1 Tbsp coriander powder

2 tsp salt

2 tsp (organic) sugar

1 can (13.5 oz) coconut milk

1 Tbsp neutral oil

¼ cup dried shredded coconut

Process:

Whisk the tomato paste with stock or water and turn on the heat. Add the potatoes, celery, and zucchini; bring to a boil, then reduce to a simmer. Add the spices, sugar, and salt, then cover and continue to simmer. Add the coconut milk.

In a small sauté pan, toast the oil and coconut, stirring frequently, until the coconut is golden brown. If it burns, start over. Then add it to the soup. Bring the soup back to a boil for a few minutes.

Check that the potatoes are done.

It's also good without the vegetables if you're in a hurry or don't have them. You can even leave out the sauteed coconut. Lots of ways to go.

Ari left notes everywhere.

Sadly, most were ignored.

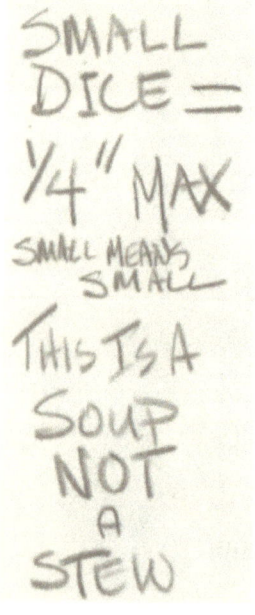

"Pozole"

Why the quote marks? This vegan version of a classic Mexican soup substitutes yams for ham and white beans for hominy, so it's tasty but not traditional. You could use hominy—I chose the beans because I couldn't find affordable non-GMO hominy.

Ingredients:

2 cups of dry white beans prepped the night before. Put dried beans in 6 cups of water and bring to a boil. Leave overnight, then drain.

2 quarts water or stock

1 can (28 oz) diced tomatoes + ¼ tsp baking soda

3 cups peeled and diced yams (½–¾" dice)*

3/4 cup small-diced red bell pepper (¼" dice)

1 tsp cumin powder

1 tsp dried oregano

2 tsp salt

1 cup chopped, roasted, seeded green poblano chilis (about 3)**

1-½ cup chopped cabbage

1 tsp lime juice

Process:

Put beans and the vegetable stock in a saucepan. Strain juice from the tomatoes and add just the tomatoes. Bring to a boil, then turn down heat to a simmer. (Make yourself a Bloody or Virgin Mary with the juice.) If you're using dry beans, cook until they're really soft. You don't want mush, but beans can be treacherous little bastards, seeming soft then hardening up when they cool if not cooked enough, especially if they're old, Or just dump in canned beans and simmer for ten minutes.

Then add yams, bell peppers, spices, and salt, and simmer until the yams are tender. You can trust the yams.
Add chili, cabbage, and lime juice. Simmer for another 10 minutes.

* Yams? Sweet potatoes? Who knows? Grocers I talk to don't seem clear on the concept; even produce master Joe Imwalle calls the ones you want yams, but I think they're technically sweet potatoes. They have maroon skin and orange flesh. These are the best for color and aren't too sweet.

** See instructions in the introduction for preparing chilis in bulk. If you don't want to do that, you could roast two or three over a flame on your gas stove, then follow the bulk instructions for peeling and seeding. Yes, you can use canned chili, but it won't be as *authentico*, and we're already pushing the limits on that.

Corn Chowder

This only makes about four servings in our house,

Ingredients:

1 pound frozen corn

2½ cups warm water

1 cup finely chopped cabbage

1 cup diced potatoes, ½" dice

¼ cup diced celery—small dice

1 cup chopped cauliflower (approximately ⅜" pieces)

½ tsp dried dill

½ tsp dried basil

¼ tsp turmeric powder

1½ tsp salt

Pinch of black pepper

½ can (6.75 oz) coconut milk

Process:

Blend half the corn with enough warm water to just cover. Place it in a saucepan with the rest of the corn. Add the cabbage, potatoes, celery, and cauliflower.

When the soup begins to boil, turn the heat to low and add the spices, salt, and pepper. Cover and cook for 10 minutes.

Add the coconut milk and bring the soup back to a gentle boil for a few minutes. Make sure potatoes are done. You now have a great corn soup.

For more of a chowder, whisk ¼ cup of water with 2 Tbsp of cornstarch. then whisk it into the soup and let it boil gently until soup thickens.

Yam Soup

I yam what I yam, but am I a yam? Gopal and Joe Imwalle called them that, but I think they're really sweet potatoes. You want the ones that are maroon on the outside and orange on the inside,

Another easy one.

Ingredients:

1 qt water

1 qt yams, peeled and cut into 2" cubes

1 13.5-oz can coconut milk

Pinch of hing or ⅛ tsp onion powder

¼ tsp black pepper

1 Tbsp dried dill

½ Tbsp cinnamon powder

1 Tbsp salt

Process:

In a medium saucepan, boil the water and add the yams; cook until soft (about 15 minutes).

Heat the coconut milk in a separate pot and boil it gently for 5 minutes.

Blend the yams with the water and return the puree to the saucepan.

Add the coconut milk and turn on the heat to medium.

Add the spices and salt.

When the soup begins to boil, turn off the heat.

Corn Bread

This version is dark, moist and a little heavy. It's vegan *and* gluten-free.

Ingredients:

1 cup gluten-free pancake mix (Bob's Red Mill)

½ cup corn meal

1 Tbsp sesame seeds

½ Tbsp baking powder

⅛ tsp baking soda

1 scant tsp salt

1 cup plain soy milk

¼ cup water

3 Tbsp neutral oil (rice bran, grapeseed, or canola)

3 Tbsp molasses (unsulfured)

Process:

Preheat the oven to 300°.

Mix the dry ingredients in a large mixing bowl.

Form a well in the middle.

Mix liquid ingredients together and pour into the well.

Whisk thoroughly, then pour the batter into a greased 8 × 8" pan.

Bake for 45 minutes.

Turn off heat and leave the pan in the oven for 10 minutes.

Let cool at least 15 minutes before cutting.

Note: This baking time is perfect for *my* oven. Took me several tries, though, so if your oven is different, consider adjusting baking times.

SALAD DRESSINGS

Here are the three we had that were vegan. Almond Blend was a huge favorite. Gopal sold it to me, but I later learned it was a gift to him from a nice lady who lived in rural Mendocino County. Should she come forward, I'll gladly give her credit.

Almond Blend Dressing

Ingredients:

1½ cups neutral oil (rice bran, grapeseed, or canola)

1½ cups water

1½ cups finely ground almonds*

¼ cup soy sauce

¼ cup lemon juice

1 Tbsp celery salt

A pinch of Hing or 1/8 tsp onion powder

1 tsp black pepper

¼ cup parsley flakes

2 Tbsp nutritional yeast

Process:

Blend all ingredients together.

Makes a bit over a quart.

* We used a food processor to grind the almonds. You want them ground fine but not enough to make almond butter!

Tofu Dill Dressing

Ingredients:

2 cups neutral oil (rice bran, grapeseed, or canola)

½ cup lemon juice

½ cup soy sauce

1 tsp salt

2 Tbsp molasses

¼ cup dried dill

1 tsp black pepper

1 box firm silken tofu

Process:

Blend all ingredients together.

Makes about a quart.

Oil-Free Dressing, aka Sun-Dried Grape Balsamic

Ingredients:

2¼ cups raisins (sun-dried or not!)

1 cup lemon juice

3 cups balsamic vinegar

Process:

Blend all ingredients together.

Makes about a quart and one-half. Will keep for a long time refrigerated.

DESSERTS

Coconut Tapioca

This was my first effort at a vegan desert that couldn't be stuffed in a pocket. I thought it was a failure at first, but by the next morning, it was perfect. Take the stirring instructions very seriously. If the pudding sticks, it will be welded to the bottom of the pot. Our harried cooks would often neglect to give the tapioca the attention it needed, and the dish lords were getting surly. I instituted a rule that whoever was responsible for the stickage had to clean the pot, which helped for a while. If you are casual about the stirring and are not a tatted up 22-year-old on your third Rockstar, you might just have to throw the pot away.

Ingredients:
1 quart water
½ cup tapioca pearls
½ cup (organic) sugar—this will be quite sweet; I prefer a little less myself
Pinch salt
1 can (13.5 oz) coconut milk

Process:
Bring the water to a boil.
Add the tapioca pearls to the water and simmer for 20 minutes.
Stir frequently, especially for the last 10 minutes. <u>Use a metal spoon and scrape the bottom of the pot as you stir.</u>

Whisk the sugar, salt, and coconut milk together and add to the simmering tapioca.

When the mixture returns to a simmer, stir <u>constantly</u> and cook for a full 5 minutes.

Pour into a container. Let it cool, then refrigerate overnight. It will set up nicely. The next day you can thin with one cup of water (or coconut water if you have it). I like it thick with cinnamon powder on top.

Makes a little more than a quart. It will keep for a few days in the refrigerator. If it starts to taste like yogurt—toss it.

Variations:

Piña Colada Tapioca: Use 1 cup of pineapple juice and 3 cups of water; cut the sugar to ⅓ cup. Add pineapple chunks toward the end. Be <u>very careful</u> to prevent burning. Thin the next day with more pineapple juice.

Chocolate Tapioca: Follow the basic recipe but blend ½ cup of unsweetened cocoa powder in with the sugar, salt, and coconut milk.

Chai Tapioca: Use a quart of strong, unsweetened chai* instead of water. Amplify the spices after adding the sugar, salt, and coconut milk with 1 tsp each o cinnamon, ground cardamom, ginger powder, and chai masala powder or T-masala powder and ¼ tsp of black pepper.

* Chai tea: We always had a good supply made up and added it to curries, soups, and barbecue sauce. You probably don't. You can use Yogi Tea bags or other chai mix for this purpose. Our chai was actually Cinnamon Spice Tea that we bought in bulk from Ancient Healing Ways. If you enjoy experimenting with spices, that one contains cinnamon bark, ginger root, cardamom seed, clove, and black pepper. In any case, no sweetener or milk. Ours had no caffeine, but it probably doesn't matter if yours does.

Chocolate Pudding

Ingredients:

1 quart plain soy milk, divided

Scant 1 cup of unsweetened cocoa powder (alkali-free is healthier; cruelty-free is kinder)

¾ cup (organic) sugar

1 tsp vanilla

Scant ½ tsp salt

¼ cup cornstarch

2–3 drops lemon extract (optional)

Process:

Blend 3 cups of the soy milk and the cocoa in a blender until smooth.

Pour into a pot and turn the heat to medium.

Stir in the sugar, vanilla, and salt.

As the mixture comes to a simmer, blend the last cup of soy milk with the cornstarch and add it to the pot.

Stir repeatedly and bring the mixture to a low boil. A metal spoon is best, to prevent stickage.

Add the lemon extract and let the pudding bubble for about 5 minutes until thick, stirring constantly.

Pour into four 8-oz containers; it will thicken more as it cools.

* Variations: Also add 1 tsp of orange <u>or</u> mint extract.

You can make parfaits when it's cool by layering with (dairy-free) whipped cream.

Coconut Macaroons

These are quite elegant, but I assure you they are very easy and are vegan (if you use vegan sugar) and gluten-free. This recipe makes about 16.

Ingredients:

1 cup (organic) sugar (I prefer to scant it)

¾ cup almond milk

3 cups shredded coconut

1 tsp vanilla

1 tsp salt

1 cup almond flour

8 oz (vegan) chocolate chips (optional)

Process:

Heat the sugar and almond milk until the sugar has dissolved.

Transfer to a bowl and stir in the coconut, vanilla, and salt.

Stir in the almond flour.

Parchment paper on a cookie sheet is all you need, or oil a cookie sheet. Use an ice cream scoop (2" in diameter) to create mounds. If you don't have a scoop, make 16 mounds as neatly as you can. Bake at 350° until the coconut starts to brown (about 20 minutes).

An optional but fabulous finish is to melt 8 oz (vegan) chocolate chips in a double boiler (or make a facsimile with two pots), making sure the chocolate doesn't burn. Also make sure water doesn't get into the chocolate. After the macaroons have cooled, dip them in the chocolate to coat just the bottoms, then place them on their sides and let them cool. Once the chocolate has hardened, put the cookies upright, then rewarm the remaining chocolate and drizzle it over the top.

Keep the macaroons cool until serving, so the chocolate doesn't melt.

PS: Chocolate melted this way works well on jumbo strawberries too. Again, parchment paper is your friend.

Cinnamon Apples

These make a quick and simple sugar-free dessert. It was popular with the schoolkids and with the teachers, who didn't want to deal with a bunch of hyped-up youngsters.

Slice at least one apple per person. Gala or other sweet apples are best, since you won't add sugar (or use Gravensteins and add sugar). Sauté them until just soft in some (vegan) butter with cinnamon or pumpkin pie seasoning to taste. That's it.

ABOUT THE AUTHOR

At 16 years old, Susan Church-Downer was told by a cynical college professor that she had no ability to write and nothing to write about. Accepting his critique, she abandoned her dream until retirement. Fifty-five years later, she reclaimed her passion, writing memoir, poetry and one short story – so far.

Now in her late 70s, she looks back on a patchwork of experiences and can't stop writing about them. A second memoir, "Drunk Luck – Sex, Drugs and Healing in the 1970s" is scheduled to be published in 2025. A third, as yet untitled, is the story of an unlikely family coming together during a criminal trial. That's probably enough memoirs so, after that, she plans to write fiction.

Susan lives in Northern California with her husband, Richard, whose kindness and support of her writing projects cannot be overstated.

A blog about the creation of this memoir, along with more recipes and some poetry, is available at www.susanchurchdowner.com.

www.ingramcontent.com/pod-product-compliance
Lightning Source LLC
Chambersburg PA
CBHW030907120626
46554CB00001B/39